On the Firing Line

Essays in the Defense of Liberty

Larry D. Pratt

Table of Contents

Foreword

The gun control debate rages without any likelihood of coming to an end. Some of the leading figures change and organizations change names from time to time, but the debate remains unchanged.

The debate over guns is fundamentally not about guns. The debate is really about control. Who is to control the lives of private citizens—will it be each person or will it be the government?

I hope that the essays in this book will help to equip those eager to preserve individual liberty. While the focus of these essays is firearms, they touch on a wide range of other freedom-related issues.

It is also hoped that the essays in this book will be of interest to those individuals who are interested in individual freedom but have not completely made up their mind on the issue of gun control. Seeing guns in the larger context of freedom may be persuasive to them.

Lastly, as one who believes in miracles, I hope that some who strongly support controlling the firearms owned by private citizens will re-examine their position.

Section One

Section One

FIREARMS AND
FREEDOM

Firearms: The People's Liberty Teeth

Now that the Brady Bill has become the law of the land, does that mean it has to be obeyed? Certainly, federally licensed firearms dealers obey it because they operate under federal government authority. But what about sheriffs and police chiefs?

Many sheriffs in several states have refused to do the background check mandated by the Brady Law. One such sheriff is Ray Nixon of Lincoln County, Montana. He addressed a meeting of the unorganized militia in February of 1994 at a crowded meeting in Eureka.

The concern of the militia was to lawfully reinforce the sheriff in case the federal government might contemplate another Waco or Weaver type massacre in Lincoln County. Citing the Militia Act in Title 10 of U.S. Code and the Montana Posse Law, the members of the unorganized militia offered themselves to be deputized by the sheriff. Military service and NRA firearms certification was considered an adequate qualification for membership in the sheriff's posse.

The Lincoln County unorganized militia that evening began the process of forming a lawful force to resist any tyrannical act on the part of the federal government. This was not a bunch of vigilantes or a mob that night. This was the militia of the Second Amendment and of the posse law of Montana.

The Lincoln County militia had reached the point that the colonial militias had in 1774 when they began to form and to drill. In 1774, as in 1994, there was still hope of reconciliation with the growing tyranny of the central government. But after years of encroachments on their liberties, the colonists of 1774 and the militiamen of 1994 decided to be prepared.

The Meaning of Well-Regulated Militia

This helps us understand the now greatly misunderstood words of the Second Amendment which reads, "A well-regulated militia being necessary for the defense of a free state, the right of the people to keep and bear arms shall not be infringed." Opponents of the individual right to keep and bear arms have greatly misunderstood the initial clause of the Second Amendment.

For many in our time, it is inconceivable to think of anything being well-regulated without a law mandating the regulation and a bureaucracy to conduct the regulation. In the 18th century, the word "regulation" did not at all require government involvement. The actions of the American colonists make it plain that a well-regulated militia was well-rehearsed and well-drilled without the control of the government. Indeed, the colonial well-regulated militias shot at the King's policemen (the King's soldiers were acting in the capacity we now consider a police function, but there were no police departments then).

When the Reverend Josiah Clark met the British forces at Lexington on April 19, 1775, he was serving as the elected commander of his well-regulated militia. He had regulated his men many a Sunday afternoon following church services. The British had made the importation of powder (semi-automatic) rifles? illegal and General Gage had sent his men to confiscate colonial stockpiles, along with other war material such as muskets and food stores.

It is interesting to note that then, as today, the city people were disarmed first. General Gage had earlier registered firearms in Boston, and then shortly thereafter, he confiscated what he had just registered. He did it in the name of crime control. Throughout history the names of tyrants change, but their methods do not.

The Effectiveness of the Militia

The militias of the communities outside of Boston had been alerted by messengers from Boston the night of April 18. Paul Revere was one of these messengers, although he was captured before he got very far. The British were defeated rather soundly by the militia at Lexington and the other companies that came from surrounding areas answering the call.

The day following the battle of Lexington, Lord Dunmore of Virginia ordered the looting of the colonial powder magazine in Williamsburg. He should not have been surprised at Patrick Henry's response, since the patriot orator had only a month before delivered his stirring call to arms at St. John's Church in Richmond before the Second Virginia Convention.

Some cautioned against using force in response to Lord Dunmore's theft, and the matter seemed to pass without colonial response. By the end of April, however, news of the British attack in Lexington reached Virginia. By May 2, 1775, Patrick Henry was on the move. Stirring the Hanover Volunteers to action with a fiery speech, they elected Henry their captain and rode off to Williamsburg. So popular was Henry's action that by the time the Hanover volunteers got to Williamsburg, their ranks had swollen to 5,000 from the cheering crowds that lined their way. The powder was compensated twice over, and shortly afterwards, Governor Dunmore, fearing for his safety, ended up onboard a ship in the York River.

Well-regulated these militia were, but controlled or sanctioned by the established government they were not. The actions of the colonists indicated that they viewed militia as something that free men had an unalienable right to organize among themselves.

Revolution or War?

Was the formation of colonial militias the action of revolutionaries? Revolutionaries are not concerned about the legitimacy of government. They appoint themselves and strike out using force. The American colonists had remonstrated for a decade before the War for Independence, asking the English king to stop the violations of the colonial charters, to which the kings of England had agreed to submit themselves. The colonists had complained through their own elected governments. When hostilities broke out, it was a war between a government supported by the people and a foreign government that had become illegitimate.

We should consider some of the complaints the colonists enumerated in their Declaration of Independence. It sounds so very contemporary. For example, "He [King George] has refused his Assent to Laws, the most wholesome and necessary for the public good." Does that not apply to the refusal of many urban jurisdictions to make it easier for people to legally arm and protect themselves from the criminal element? In addition, our government virtually refuses to execute murderers and often sets them free to kill again.

Another complaint was that "He has called together legislative bodies at places unusual, uncomfortable, and distant...." The Senate provided another example with the midnight deals cooked up by Senators Dole and Mitchell, followed by passage of the Brady Bill with only three Senators present and voting.

This complaint rings true still: "He has obstructed the Administration of Justice, by refusing his assent to Laws for establishing Judiciary Powers." Juries are prohibited from hearing whatever case a defendant wishes to make. Also, the jury's power to refuse to convict someone who has broken a law if that would be an injustice has been hidden from jurors. This has made a mockery of justice.

And finally, this one could be found in almost any daily paper: "He has erected a multitude of New Offices, and sent hither swarms of Officers to harass our people, and eat out their substance."

Government, Not the People, to Be Held Suspect

The words of the founding fathers reflected the actions they took during the War for Independence. Their view of government was one of deep suspicion. The task they set for themselves in establishing a government once they had thrown off the British tyranny was to limit and restrain their own creation.

A couple of Jefferson quotes are illustrative: "When governments fear the people there is liberty. When the people fear the government there is tyranny." And, "The strongest reason for the people to retain the right to keep and bear arms is, as a last resort, to protect themselves against tyranny in government."

Patrick Henry warned during the Virginia Ratifying Convention debates over the adoption of the present Constitution: "Guard with jealous attention the public liberty. Suspect every one who approaches that jewel. Unfortunately, nothing will preserve it but downright force. Whenever you give up that force, you are inevitably ruined." What exactly was Henry warning of? He foresaw that the new government would dangerously centralize power unto itself. In Henry's words, it would "oppress and ruin the people."

Even a defender of the new Constitution, James Madison (author of the Second Amendment) shared in *Federalist Papers*, Number 46, the same suspicion of government: "Besides, the advantage of being armed forms a barrier against the enterprises of ambition, more insurmountable than any which a simple government of any form can admit of. The governments of Europe are afraid to trust the people with arms. If they did, the people would certainly shake off the yoke of tyranny, as America did."

George Mason, an ally of James Madison and George Washington, articulated his suspicion of government this way: "To disarm the people is the best and most effectual way to enslave them." Mason defines the militia as "the whole people, except for a few public officials." Noah Webster, a patriot and scholar, defined the militia similarly as "the effective part of the people at large."

Webster wrote that: "Before a standing army can rule, the people must be disarmed as they are in almost every kingdom in Europe. The supreme power in America cannot enforce unjust laws by the sword because the whole body of the people are armed, and constitute a force superior to any band of regular troops that can be, on any pretense, raised in the United States."

The Militia Act of 1792

The first Congress of the United States under the new Constitution adopted the Bill of Rights. Five months later, that same Congress enacted the Militia Act of 1792. That Act has two important lessons for understanding the meaning of the militia. First, the law required everyone covered by the act to have a military rifle and the ammunition for it. Second, military firearms were to be in people's homes, not in armories as in the case of a National Guard—that did not exist at the time.

The Militia Act of 1792 helped put feet to the suspicions the founders had of government. The militia was seen as a practical way of containing the dangerous potential of government.

Anti-gunners often ask regarding an AR-15 or an AK-47, "Why would anyone want a gun like that? You cannot hunt with it." Even if that were true, the answer constitutionally is, "So what?" Truly, the Second Amendment is not about hunting or target shooting as a recreation. Arguably, those pastimes are protected by the Ninth Amendment, which says, "The enumeration in the Constitution of certain rights shall not be construed to deny or disparage others retained by the people."

AR-15's and other semi-automatic rifles should be in the hands of as many Americans as want them precisely because they make anti-gunners in general and many politicians in particular nervous. That was the express purpose the founders had in mind for the Second Amendment.

Government Needs to Fear the People Again

When a government no longer fears the people, atrocities, such as the murder of members of Randy Weaver's family by U.S. Marshals and FBI agents, become possible. Emboldened by the lack of resistance when murdering women and children in Idaho, the Feds moved to Waco, Texas, and slaughtered nearly 100 people, including four of their own agents.

Following on the heels of these acts, the government now has the audacity to insist that the militia be disarmed by the illegalization of semi-automatic rifles and shotguns. Why should they not be so bold? After all, where was the outcry when they first restricted, then outlawed new machine guns? The politicians of this century have been able to accomplish a more effective disarmament of the American militia than George III and his minions such as General Gage, Governor Dunmore, and others.

The events in Lincoln County, Montana, and many similar activations of the militia in counties across America is one of the most hopeful signs for the preservation of liberty in our time. One can only speculate about what would have happened had there been an effective militia in Naples, Idaho, which could have been mobilized after the U.S. Marshal murdered Sammy Weaver by shooting him in the back. It is entirely possible that Vicki Weaver would not have been murdered later on by an FBI trained assassin while she was holding a baby in her hands.

Had the Feds feared a militia as active as the one in Lexington on April 19, 1775, it is entirely possible that the massacre of Branch Davidians in Waco, Texas, on April 19, 1993, would never have occurred.

Long live the militia! Long live freedom! Long live a government that fears the people!

"Militia" Is Not a Four-Letter Word

Following the tragedy in Oklahoma City, a campaign of political opportunism was generated. An effort was made, which is ongoing, to vilify the political opposition credited with throwing the anti-gun leadership of the Democratic party out of their long-held power in the U.S. Congress.

President Clinton publicly attributed the loss of 21 seats in the House of Representatives to the pro-Second Amendment vote in the 1994 elections. While the President's number is low, it was sufficient to turn over control of the House to the Republicans for the first time in 40 years.

Nothing is fair in warfare or politics, it seems. The President, along with many in the media, cranked up a campaign to neutralize a crucial part of his opposition. Critics of the government in general were accused of having created a climate of hate that somehow provoked those who committed the bombing atrocity in Oklahoma City.

Soon the opposition frenzy focused on the militia. When the key suspect, Timothy McVeigh, was found to have attended a militia meeting or two in Michigan, the case was closed. For the President and his supporters, the militia had been found guilty. Inadmissible as evidence was the fact that McVeigh's rhetoric was unacceptable to the militia members he met with and they disinvited him from future meetings.

Also inadmissible in the "conviction" of the militia was the fact that virtually all militias are lawful. It is not against the law to put on camouflage clothing, to own more than one gun, or to run around in the woods. Peaceful assembly is protected by the First Amendment, even as the right to keep and bear arms is protected by the Second.

America does not need laws against militias, nor even a congressional investigation. We will not be made safer by expanding unconstitutional powers of Federal agencies to intimidate political opponents of the party in power. Violating the Bill of Rights will not make us safer; it will only endanger our freedoms.

Let's hope the politicians decide to restore capital punishment in America rather than conduct a witch-hunt against the constitutionally protected liberties of the people. Punishing the guilty seems more valuable than persecuting the innocent.

The People Are Part of the Answer

Anti-gun politicians and many police administrators have the idea that defending oneself is the same as being a vigilante. The push to enable more people to carry concealed firearms has often been met with disbelief by the elite—"We can't have a bunch of shooters walking around out there!"

There seems to be no amount of facts that will convince such critics that the American people are not the irresponsible children they assume them to be. Many states which have made it easier for people to carry concealed weapons have found little change in their murder rates, but then their homicide rates were below the national average in the first place.

Florida's experience, however, was quite dramatic. In the first seven years following the passage of the Concealed Carry Law, the murder rate, which had been above the national average, fell 22 percent even while the national rate was rising 15 percent. Kennesaw, Georgia, took a slightly different approach over a decade ago. The town required that every household have a gun and ammunition unless the homeowner was legally disqualified from gun ownership or had moral objections against using firearms. The armed burglary rate in Kennesaw over the next decade dropped over 75 percent from its previous level.

As a general matter, it is those areas of our country where firearms ownership is the highest that the murder rates are the lowest. We have ten states with murder rates below most European countries. Our lowest ten are all high firearms ownership states such as Montana, South Dakota, and Vermont. The European countries (with the seldom mentioned exception of Switzerland) are the models of low crime and onerous gun control which Handgun Control, Inc. would like us to emulate. Switzerland is one of those "troublesome" places where gun ownership is nearly universal and the murder rate is about the lowest in all of Europe.

Where the U.S. has high murder rates are precisely those jurisdictions in which the effort to disarm the civilian population has been most successful—Washington, D.C., New York City, Chicago, Los Angeles, etc.

About a decade ago, I had the opportunity to travel in Guatemala and the Philippines. I found their successes in fighting guerrillas mirrored our own experience—showing the benefits of an armed citizenry.

Both countries in the early eighties faced overthrow by well-entrenched guerrilla movements. In Guatemala, according to Jews for the Preservation of Firearms Ownership, genocide was being practiced. My own observations there led me to conclude that the Guatemalan military's response to the guerrillas had been genocidal up until a radical change in fighting the guerrillas was adopted under the government of Efrain Rios Montt.

The military had no way to identify the enemy. Many Guatemalan officers pointed out to me that they saw the U.S. suffered from a similar problem in Vietnam. The guerrillas rooted themselves so deeply into the community while possessing a monopoly of firearms that they were even levying taxes. The people in those controlled areas had two choices—cooperate with the guerrillas or die.

General Rios Montt changed three hundred years of policy in Guatemala. He decided that the government had to trust the people. He armed the farmers and taught them how to use their guns. The people all of a sudden could function as the eyes and ears of the military because they could fight back when the guerrillas retaliated. Within months, the military was able to track the guerrillas so well that they were able to force them into an untenable location and wipe them out in a pitched battle.

Even genocide had not been able to end the strife for years and years, but cooperation with an armed people brought peace within months.

Would it not be worth trying the same thing in our violence-torn cities? The criminal element operates nearly as effectively as did the guerrillas. They penetrate deeply into the community and make it impossible for a disarmed inner-city resident to cooperate with the police.

Someone may object that Guatemala's success worked in the countryside but would not work in the city. While I fail to see the logic of that response, the fact of the matter is that, in rather similar circumstances, armed militias put the guerrillas to rout in the Philippines—in the cities.

When Maurice Turner was Chief of Police in Washington, D.C., he tried to do something that is still found in many counties around the U.S. He prepared people who lived in the most violent neighborhoods by sending them through the police academy so they could supplement the paid police force as volunteers. When the City Council realized that these auxiliaries would be armed, they prohibited them from carrying guns, thus killing the program and insuring that the murder rate in Washington would continue to climb.

We need to urge our politicians to stop treating us as the problem. We, the People, in addition to being their boss, are a necessary part of the answer to the crime problem.

The Patriot —A Great Movie

The Patriot, starring Mel Gibson, is a great movie which I highly recommend.

It demonstrates, among other things, the effectiveness of a well-regulated militia where private individuals—including very young men—have firearms and know how to use them. Our freedom and independence was not won by men using slingshots. There are lots of guns and shooting in this film.

We see two of Gibson's young sons carrying rifles, coming in from the field where they have been hunting by themselves. We see King George III being burned in effigy while a group of citizens are firing rifles and pistols into the air. One militiaman gives his young son a wooden model of a pistol. We even see a preacher picking up a rifle and going off to war for America.

There are also other things in this movie which are wonderfully "politically incorrect" in many quarters. The film opens with a home schooling scene wherein one of Gibson's daughters is teaching a younger son his alphabet with flash cards.

And (gasp!) Gibson even seems to believe in God. At one point, before firing on some British troops, Gibson says, softly: "Lord make me fast and accurate." And, as Gibson holds one of his sons who has been killed, he says. "God help me. God help me."

Not surprisingly, *The Patriot* has drawn fire from all the usual suspects, individuals such as the gun-hating moviemaker Spike Lee who says: "I despise the film." This is the same Spike Lee who has said: "The problem is guns. The reason the United States is the most violent country in the history of civilization is the proliferation of guns." And, yes, this is the same Spike Lee who said, as a joke, about Charlton Heston: "Shoot him with a .44 Bulldog." Pretty funny, huh?

The American Ambassador to Britain, Philip Lader, has told one of the biggest of the Big Lies being told about this excellent movie. According to the London newspaper *The Independent* (15 July 2000), Lader accused this film of "damaging Anglo-American relations by falsely portraying British soldiers as evil and vicious." Lader says citizens on both sides of the Atlantic should "look more clearly at what the real facts were."

Well, does the Ambassador think America went to war against King George III over irregular mail delivery?

Even the most superficial research shows that the real facts are that some British soldiers *were* evil and vicious! For example, there was British cavalry Colonel Banastre Tarleton.

In her book, *The First Salute* (Alfred Knopf, 1988), the highly respected historian Barbara Tuchman says that Tarleton was "hated and dreaded" and known as "no quarter Tarleton" because of his "violation of surrender rules in the Waxhaw massacre, where he had caught a body of American troops that held its fire too long before firing at 50 yards, too late to stop the charging cavalry. After surrender, they were cut down when Tarleton's men, let loose to wield their knife-edged sabers, killed a total of 113 and wounded 150 more, of whom half died of their wounds."

In addition, Tuchman quotes from the eye-witness memoirs of a Swedish Lieutenant, Karl Gustaf Tornquist, who described what he saw when he passed through the Williamsburg (Virginia) countryside which had been ravaged by the British: "On a beautiful estate a pregnant woman was found murdered in her bed through several bayonet stabs; the barbarians had opened both of her breasts and written above the bed canopy: 'Thou shalt never give birth to a rebel.'

"In another room, was just as horrible a sight—five cut-off heads arranged on a cupboard in place of plaster-cast figures which lay broken in pieces on the floor. Dumb animals were no less spared .... We did not find a single trace of inhabitants, for those who had been unable to flee lay on the ground as a token of the Godless behavior of their enemies."

Tuchman adds: "According to another account, which Tornquist evidently could not bring himself to mention, the unborn baby had been torn from the womb and hung from a tree." She notes that, after his previous observations, Tornquist said that the British troops under Cornwallis, on their way to York, destroyed "everything which lay in his way, not sparing defenseless women and children."

So, Mr. Ambassador, *The Patriot* was actually kind to the British butchers, because Cornwallis was not depicted in this light.

We might add that America is not the only place to have experienced the lash of British imperialist tyranny. The British Army, under orders from London, carried out genocide against the Boers of South Africa at the turn of the last century. Men, women, and children were slaughtered, starved, and killed with the pestilence of concentration camps.

In another government-directed policy, the British army slaughtered a whole generation of leaders in Kenya in order to make the Africans compliant subjects of the Empire. The only thing good about the British Empire, Mr. Ambassador, is that it is finally over.

I suspect that Ambassador Lader is also upset that America was the one place where the evil British Empire got beat by farmers. The militia— another name for an armed populace—played a key role, whether in the defeat of General Burgoyne in the North or General Cornwallis in the South, or containing General Gates in New York.

The Patriot is not evil or vicious. See it and take the whole family. It's basically an accurate film that will bring a lump to your throat and a tear to your eye. And you'll thank God that we're free and independent, in part, because we had private citizens who had firearms and knew how to use them.

Section Two

THE SECOND AMENDMENT UNDER ATTACK

Taking Back Stolen Ground

Fear ruled the day as lawmakers enacted two oppressive gun control laws on the final day of last year's Congressional session. Regrettably, the Republican legislators on the Hill feared the establishment inside the Beltway more than they feared their constituents—enough to negate their oath to uphold and defend the Constitution.

Legislators snuck two restrictive amendments into a 2,000-page omnibus appropriations bill which was still being debated, but not yet printed. Senator Inhofe (R-OK) said that two or three hours was not enough time to read such a lengthy bill, so he wisely voted against it. Unhappily, only 14 of his colleagues in the Senate voted with him.

GOA cautioned House members about the gun control provisions in the bill. Meanwhile, representatives were being told that Gun Owners of America was misinformed and that there were no gun control amendments in the Omnibus Appropriations Bill. GOA had been right all along, however, and it seems that Republican leaders will say anything to keep their troops in line.

The country is still finding out just how far-reaching these two gun bans are. Republicans were willing to stomach more gun control in order to get back home at the end of September and campaign to save their jobs.

Senator Lautenberg's Gun Grab

One of the gun control measures was authored by the anti-gun zealot, Senator Frank Lautenberg (D-NJ), who found a way to hide gun control behind the skirts of women in need of protection. For the first time, the federal government is expanding its intrusion into the criminal justice arena by prohibiting Americans from owning guns if they were convicted of a mere misdemeanor. In other words, Lautenberg federalizes state laws dealing with husband and wife relationships and even those of parent and child—that's all covered under the term "domestic."

We should keep in mind that as late as 1934, President Franklin Roosevelt's assistant attorney general, Joseph Keenan, testified before Congress that "the Federal Government has no police powers." The Constitution has not been changed to authorize police powers. The only thing that has happened is what our forefathers called "usurpation." In today's terminology, it is an illegitimate power grab by the federal government.

Lautenberg's measure means that if one were convicted of any kind of domestic violence misdemeanor (a slap, a foul mouth, spanking a child), one is forever prohibited from owning a gun. This prohibition will be imposed no matter how long ago the infraction may have occurred. Keep in mind that battery—that is, serious violence—is not the subject of misdemeanor domestic violence. Such serious violence is, and has been for a long time, a felony.

Who is affected by the Lautenberg gun ban? An increasingly large number of women are being kept from owning their best means of self-defense. This is because police are more and more arresting both partners in a domestic dispute and getting misdemeanor convictions against both the man and the woman.

Moreover, there is an ever-growing number of jurisdictions that are hostile to spanking—this does not mean beating—children. Parents can be and have been arrested and convicted for disciplining their children. This is a domestic violence misdemeanor and has resulted in the loss of gun rights.

One candidate in a police academy recently realized that he can never become a policeman and can never own a gun. Ten years ago, this Ohio resident said some really nasty things to his father who had him locked up overnight to "teach him a lesson." The authorities insisted, in spite of the father's objection, on convicting the lad of a very mild misdemeanor—a mere $25 fine. But because it was a domestic violence misdemeanor, there will be one less policeman in our country thanks to Sen. Lautenberg. Police departments across the country have begun laying off sworn officers because of convictions twenty and even thirty years ago.

Senator Kohl's Gun Ban Zones

Senator Herb Kohl (D-WI) pulled off the other sneak attack against the Constitution, enabling Congress to re-enact a bill the Supreme Court had correctly declared unconstitutional. The Court ruled that Congress has no authority to pass legislation affecting possession of firearms in so-called school zones. The Court went into detail to point out that the Commerce Clause (in Article I, Section 8), which has been used to justify anything the federal government wants to do, is not a blanket authorization of power after all. Justice Thomas stated that this totalitarian view represented a wrong turn for the Court for the last 50 years.

Kohl's measure prohibits possession of a gun within a thousand feet of the outer perimeter of a school's property—typically a gun-ban zone is of a diameter of about one-half mile. The limited exceptions include on-duty policemen, people with concealed carry permits if the permit was obtained through a background check system (some states have no such permission slips), guns transported when they are locked and unloaded and with the school authority's permission, and private homes (although it will be illegal to take the gun from the private premises to public property without a principal's permission).

Senator Kohl got the Congress to make it virtually impossible to legally pass through most cities and towns in the U.S. with a firearm.

Until members of Congress fear their constituents more than they do now, we can expect the Congress to continue to knuckle under to the frenetic cries of "we must protect women and children" as the excuse for passing more restrictions.

Feeling the Heat

Everett Dirksen, the late Republican Senate Minority Leader, was fond of saying, "When I feel the heat, I see the light." At present, the Congress is unable to see the light. They need to feel the heat. Those who wish to live under the Constitution and enjoy the freedom and liberty it is supposed to protect must regain the zeal for liberty that filled the breasts of the founders of our Republic.

The founders were right. Eternal vigilance is the price of liberty. The fight will never end. Let's take back stolen ground so the enemy has to fight on our terms, not us on his.

Repeal of Semi-Auto Ban Is Only the First Step

In March of 1996, the House of Representatives voted to repeal the ban on semi-automatic firearms and large magazines. While the vote was certainly a good first step, the bill clearly did not go far enough.

The repeal bill which passed on Friday does nothing to protect gun dealers from the BATF, which has used provisions in the crime bill to drive thousands of gun dealers out of business since 1994. If Congress is going to heed the wishes of the electorate, they need to pass a full repeal of the Clinton gun control package.

The American people sent a strong message in the 1994 elections regarding gun control. Even President Clinton had to admit that the gun ban "cost the Democrats an estimated 21 seats in the House and therefore handed control of the chamber to the Republicans."

Having said that, the House's actions represented a good first step, and the Senate should follow suit. The gun ban is completely unconstitutional and prevents decent citizens from owning good self-defense firearms.

As for its unconstitutionality, even the Supreme Court had to admit last year (in *U.S. v. Lopez*) that there was no authority in the Constitution to pass gun control laws like the one banning possession of a firearm near a school. Moreover, several prominent law journals and criminologists have done excellent work recently in stating the case for the individual right to keep and bear arms.

Despite all this scholarship, some pundits feel the founders would never have intended the Second Amendment to cover the modern type of firearms in existence today. Of course, to argue this would be like saying the First Amendment was never meant to cover modern forms of the press such as radio and T.V.

In fact, the Second Amendment was specifically intended to protect an individual's right to own the type of firearms in "common use." Consider the statement by the Supreme Court in *U.S. v. Miller* (1939): "The Militia comprised all males physically capable of acting in concert for the common defense...[and that] when called for service, these men were expected to appear bearing arms supplied by themselves and of the kind in common use at the time."

So what is one to conclude from all this? First, the Constitution gives Congress no authority to enact gun control legislation. Second, and perhaps even more surprising for modern-day pundits, the Constitution allows the Congress to *require* gun ownership (see Article I, Section 8).

This should not strike fear into one's heart. Law-abiding citizens use guns to defend themselves against criminals over 2.4 million times every year—or 6,575 times a day. A substantial number of these self-defense firearms are semi-automatics and are internally indistinguishable from the firearms banned in the 1994 crime bill.

The 1994 crime bill banned many of the very guns with which the Korean merchants defended themselves during the 1992 Los Angeles riots. Those firearms proved to be extremely useful to the Koreans. They were facing mob violence, and the police were nowhere to be found. Truly, they needed firearms that would shoot more than just six bullets. When it was all over, their stores were left standing while other stores around them were burned to the ground.

The Sarah Brady crowd would like people to think that these guns have become the criminals' "weapons of choice." Not true.

The Bureau of Justice Statistics reported in 1993 that violent criminals only carry or use a "military-type gun" in about one percent of the crimes nationwide. And according to the FBI, people have a much greater chance of being killed by a knife or a blunt object than by any kind of rifle, including an "assault rifle." In Chicago alone, a person is 67 times more likely to be stabbed or beaten to death than to be murdered by an "assault rifle."

One can't have it both ways. If one wants to ban truly dangerous weapons, then one should start by banning knives and baseball bats. Of course, such an option would be as ineffective in stopping crime as banning firearms. Hopefully, the current Congress will restore some sense to our criminal code and take steps to uphold the Second Amendment.

Gun Control: Unconstitutional and Harmful

The Founding Fathers enacted the Second Amendment as part of a larger Bill of Rights because they wanted to spell out individual rights that would be free from any governmental jurisdiction. They clearly stated that the right of the people to keep and bear arms "shall not be infringed"—a right so important that they also spoke in terms of the whole population being the militia. Just months after ratifying the Bill of Rights, they passed the Militia Act of 1792 requiring virtually all able-bodied males to keep military rifles and the ammunition for them in their homes.

The Founders were explicitly seeking to establish a national government that would do only those things that were specifically delegated to it. The Tenth Amendment drove this point home by stating that "the powers not delegated to the United States by the Constitution, nor prohibited by it to the States, are reserved to the States respectively, or to the people." James Madison, in *Federalist Papers*, Number 45, said that "The powers delegated by the proposed Constitution to the federal government are few and defined. Those which are to remain in the State governments are numerous and indefinite."

The historical fact that gun control was not considered to be a legitimate power for government officials was recognized even years later. The Fourteenth Amendment was justified by its sponsors in the Congress as, among other things, a way of overriding state (Jim Crow) gun laws intended to keep blacks in de facto slavery. The Fourteenth Amendment was explicitly a vehicle to incorporate the Second Amendment to apply to the states.

In our time, there has been a tendency for courts to ignore the plain intent of the framers—both of the Constitution and of the Fourteenth Amendment. However, the courts are not the last word on what the law of the land is. Clearly, Abraham Lincoln was not of the opinion that the Supreme Court was the supreme law. The Dred Scott decision meant that fugitive slaves would have to be returned. Instead, Lincoln directly defied the Court and ultimately issued the Emancipation Proclamation. That is the way our system is supposed to work. All federal officials take an oath to uphold the Constitution, not just judges.

Recently, there has been some sign of backing away from judicial tyranny by the courts. In the Verdugo-Urquidez case, the Supreme Court did acknowledge that the Second Amendment protects an individual's right. In the *U.S. v. Lopez* decision, the Court held that the Congress had no jurisdiction to legislate a gun ban in school zones. Generally, the Court held that the Commerce Clause (which has been used to justify so much federal gun control) could not be used to pass that gun ban.

Furthermore, scholars are increasingly taking the pro-gun view. Dr. Jim Wright and Dr. Gary Kleck have each backed away from their earlier support for gun control after doing massive studies on the subject. Dr. Kleck's research has uncovered the fact that as many as 2.5 million people use a firearm to defend themselves every year. This means that firearms are used more than 60 times more often to protect the lives of honest citizens than to take lives.

And most recently, Dr. John Lott of the University of Chicago has published the results of an exhaustive 15-year study of crime in the U.S. and found that the most significant way to lower murder and violent crime rates in a state is to allow citizens to carry firearms concealed.

Gun control has no place in a free society. The body of research is growing which shows that before the genocides of this century have been carried out by rogue governments, they first disarmed the target population.

Civilian disarmament is based on the assumption that people are irresponsible (unless they work for the government). This country was founded on the opposite premise. Rather than suspect the people, we are to suspect the government and keep it under control. As George Washington said, "Government is not reason; it is not eloquence; it is force! Like fire, it is a dangerous servant, and a fearful master." We don't need gun control, we need government control.

(Lead Statement for the America On Line Debate, March, 1997)

The State of the Second Amendment

Freedom everywhere is under attack. One of the main targets of freedom-haters is an armed citizenry. We are not surprised when we learn that dictators disarm their subjects. What should positively alarm us is when political leaders in the United States advocate the same policies as did Hitler, Stalin, and many other mass murderers of the last century.

Democratic presidential contestants Al Gore and Bill Bradley have joined the Congressional clamor calling for registration and licensing of guns and gun owners. It has to be said, even though it is not politically correct, that these were the very laws that enabled disarmament of Germans, Russians, Armenians, and many others prior to the great waves of genocide.

"But wait," it is objected, "that will never happen here! Are you suggesting that our government would ever confiscate guns?" Frankly, I don't have to suggest it. All I need to do is point to the confiscations in New York City and in California that have followed gun registration and licensing of owners.

While most of America was celebrating the new millennium, thousands of California gun owners were wondering when the knock on the door would come for their SKS sporter rifles. These guns had been purchased and registered. Now the rules have been changed and these gun owners were told to surrender their guns by the end of last year or become a felon this year. Happy New Year, California style!

The Founders spelled out the Second Amendment, along with the other freedoms protected in the rest of the Bill of Rights, because they did not trust government. After Richard Nixon and Bill Clinton, to name just two, why should we now?

Most Americans still believe that the Founders meant for the Second Amendment to protect our individual right to keep and bear arms. Certainly, the Founders who had fought a war to keep the British from collectively owning American guns were not of a mind to give away that for which so many had fought and died.

If we are serious about protecting our freedoms we had better be serious about getting the anti-freedom crowd out of office. One of the best ways to sort out the good guys from the bad guys is the gun issue. If they are not for you having a gun, they are not for you at all.

Moving Forward on the *Emerson* Case

One of the most insidious and outrageous attacks on the Second Amendment right of individuals to keep and bear arms is the attempt to exercise so-called "prior restraint" by denying a person a firearm when there is no reason whatsoever to do this.

One such case we at Gun Owners Foundation (the litigation arm of Gun Owners of America) are involved in, a very important case, involves a citizen in Texas. This case is before the U.S. Court of Appeals for the Fifth Circuit (No. 99-10331). It's known as *United States v. Emerson.* We're on the side of Timothy Joe Emerson, the defendant.

Under federal law, Emerson was indicted for possessing a firearm while under a routine restraining order issued in the course of a Texas divorce proceeding between him and his former wife. The district court dismissed the indictment on the grounds that the statute was unconstitutional under both the Second and Fifth Amendments. The U.S. Government appealed this dismissal.

Our argument is very clear: The Second Amendment codifies a fundamental— we would say a God-given—right, an individual right to keep and bear arms, independent of and unrelated to any power of the States to create and maintain a military force, and independent of and unrelated to any power of the government to regulate commerce.

Thus, this right is severely infringed when the mere passive possession of a firearm is criminalized by the issuance of a boiler-plate domestic relations restraining order not based upon any evidence or finding of a threat directed toward the person protected by the order.

In our legal brief defending Emerson, we document in detail, with scores of references, the fact that the Second Amendment says what it means and means what it says. And we note that what is most impressive about this almost total academic consensus is that many of the scholars we quote are either self-identified "liberals" or unconnected with the pro-gun movement.

But, in a tribute to the intellectual honesty of these scholars, they tell the truth about the Second Amendment and what it means—even though some of them are for gun control. And by agreeing with the true meaning of the Second Amendment, these scholars are in line with members of the U.S. Supreme Court who from 1857 to 1990 have said, in what is known as dicta, that the right to keep and bear arms is a personal and individual right of free citizens.

This brings us back to Timothy Joe Emerson who is, obviously, a person, an individual. As we argue, his personal, individual Constitutional right to possess firearms was not merely infringed. At the instant the state court judge entered a domestic relations restraining order against him, his Second Amendment right to possess firearms was destroyed, negated, nullified.

Emerson was instantly transformed into a Federal felon and—this must be repeated—this was done even though there was no evidence and no judicial finding that he was a threat to his wife.

The Second Amendment is unfairly and repeatedly singled out for "prior restraint" attacks that would be found totally unacceptable—and have been so found by the courts—if they were launched against any other amendment.

For example, nobody would even think of going to court to try and deny, in advance, someone's First Amendment free speech right because of what that individual might say if allowed to speak—whether that person were a public speaker, a preacher in a pulpit, a talk show host, an editorial writer, or even a judge.

The courts have stated that one cannot use his "freedom of speech" to yell "Fire" in a crowded theater. And yet, no one argues that officials should gag everyone who goes into the theater, thus placing a prior restraint on moviegoers.

The proper response is to punish the person who does yell "Fire." Likewise, citizens should not be "gagged" before exercising their Second Amendment rights; rather, they should be punished if they abuse that right.

In defending our freedoms guaranteed in the Bill of Rights, we must tell the Congress, "No prior restraints!" We, of course, have no idea how the U.S. Fifth Circuit Court of Appeals will rule, but we hope and pray they will uphold the true meaning of the Second Amendment. This is a bell tolling for all of us.

The Gun Owners Foundation brief, along with the Emerson opinion by Judge Sam Cummings, can be found on the web at *http://www.gunowners.com/legal.htm.*

U.S. v. Emerson: From the
Fifth Circuit to the Supreme Courts?

A Second Amendment case is likely to end up in the Supreme Court. If the court as it is now constituted hears the case, it is likely to strike another anti-gun law. It all started when Dr. Timothy Emerson was going through a divorce. A routine restraining order was placed against him without a hearing or any opportunity for him to defend himself, nor was there any allegation of violence.

But that was enough under a 1994 federal law to bar Emerson from owning a gun. Dr. Emerson ended up in court and a federal prosecutor wanted to put him in jail for the mere possession of a firearm. Federal Judge Sam Cummings ruled that the law is unconstitutional because it violates the individual right to keep and bear arms.

Judge Cummings has launched a torpedo into the already sinking ship of anti-firearms rights scholarship that argues that the Second Amendment only protects a state's right to have a militia. This is the so-called "collective rights" view.

Well, if Judge Cummings launched one torpedo, the Fifth Circuit Court of Federal Appeals launched three more during the oral arguments over the *Emerson* case that is now before that court which sits in New Orleans.

Judge Harold DeMoss told the government lawyer that he was mistaken in his view that a case in the last century (the *Miller* case) established the collective rights view. In fact, he argued that the 9mm Beretta pistol that Dr. Emerson owned was in fact a militia firearm and specifically protected under the terms of *Miller*.

DeMoss went on to ask this question for which he is still awaiting an answer from the government: "I have a 12 gauge and a 16 gauge shotgun, and a .30 caliber deer rifle in my closet at home. Can you tell me how those affect interstate commerce?"

This question goes to the heart of all federal gun control laws. They are all based on the false assumption that the interstate commerce clause justifies federal gun control. The Supreme Court has already shot that assumption down in two other cases.

After that argument, it did not get any better for the government. Judge Robert Parker, originally appointed by President Carter to the federal judiciary and elevated to the Fifth Circuit by President Clinton, told this to the government: "I don't want you to lose any sleep over this, but Judge Garwood (the Senior Judge) and I, between us, have enough guns to start a revolution in most South American countries."

THE IMPORTANCE OF THE SECOND AMENDMENT

Section Three

＞—◆—○—◆—＜

POLICE AND
THE RULE OF LAW

From Peace Officer to
Law Enforcement Personnel

In the 1830's, a French nobleman, Alexis de Toqueville, came to the U.S. to find out how a bunch of frontiersmen were able to operate a government in such an orderly fashion—especially in the light of the terror and violence accompanying the French Revolution that occurred shortly after the American War for Independence. De Toqueville's book, *Democracy in America,* contains some penetrating insights on the nature of American government and how policing functions were carried out. The following comes from the 1945 Vantage Press edition of his book:

> The duties of private citizens are not supposed to have lapsed because the state has come into action, but everyone is ready, on the contrary, to guide and support it. This action of individuals, joined to that of the public authorities, frequently accomplishes what the most energetic centralized administration would be unable to do....
>
> In America the means that the authorities have at their disposal for the discovery of crimes and the arrest of criminals are few. A state police does not exist, and passports are unknown. The criminal police of the United States cannot be compared with that of France; the magistrates and public agents are not numerous; they do not always initiate the measures for arresting the guilty; and the examinations of prisoners are rapid and oral. Yet I believe that in no country does crime more rarely elude punishment. The reason is that everyone conceives himself to be interested in furnishing evidence of the crime and in seizing the delinquent. During my stay in the United States I witnessed the spontaneous formation of committees in a county for a great crime. In Europe a criminal is an unhappy man who is struggling for his life against the agents of power, while the people are merely a spectator of the conflict; in America he is looked upon as an enemy of the human race, and the whole of mankind is against him.

We should at least pause to consider de Toqueville's observations in light of the "Europeanization" of America's policing function. Could we give the same report today after the centralization, professionalization, and the bureaucratization of law enforcement here? Have we really gained as a result of getting away from our original model?

The Changing Views of Government and the Police

The idea of government popular with the elite in America now views their function as the ruler of the people, indeed, even the creator of the people at least regarding our rights. The creator/creature distinction has just about been reversed. Now we see, without any modification of the Constitution, government asserting itself in areas off-limits under our Constitution. In order to enforce this usurpation, the government has created a class of law enforcement employees to increasingly supersede the peace officer of the local community.

Rather than keep the peace by trying to apprehend malefactors who have allegedly broken the peace, law enforcement personnel come from the government to tell the people what they must do—or else. The use of military force to attack the Weaver family in Idaho and the religious followers of David Koresh in Waco are violent examples of the extremes to which government presumes to assert its power. Worse still, the government is increasingly unconcerned about laws prohibiting its choice of methods. The federal law prohibiting the use of military personnel and equipment against Americans was brazenly disregarded at Waco and Ruby Ridge, Idaho. This law, the Posse Comitatus Act (meaning full power of the county), has been on the books for over 100 years to reaffirm the superiority of local police powers over those of the national government.

H.R. 666

We should not be surprised that the federal government will brazenly break a law when the Constitution itself is held in little or no repute. The recent debate over H.R. 666 indicates that the problem is a bipartisan one as well.

H.R. 666 is a move to eliminate the exclusionary rule. This rule has been in existence most of the twentieth century. It is widely regarded as the guideline for applying the principle articulated in the Fourth Amendment. This amendment requires probable cause and a warrant in order for the government to invade our persons, homes, possessions, and effects. The exclusionary rule says that evidence obtained in violation of the Fourth Amendment cannot be used in trial.

Opponents of the rule, primarily but not exclusively many law and order, pro-gun Republicans, claim that the exclusionary rule is used to allow guilty persons to escape conviction by throwing out incriminating evidence just because it was obtained illegally. In truth, this problem occurs less than one percent of the time.

But to hear opponents of the exclusionary rule, one would think that the rule is the cause of the crime problem plaguing America's cities. In fact, it is hard not to conclude that these advocates of law and order view the Bill of Rights as a set of loopholes foisted upon an unsuspecting Republic by a clique of proto-ACLU conspirators. In other words, the Bill of Rights, and the Fourth Amendment in particular, are just a set of loopholes for crooks.

The Founders had another view. Their idea of the Bill of Rights derived from their search for effective obstacles to government tyranny. The Second Amendment was intended to insure that the people would always have military firearms so the government would never have a monopoly of force. The Fourth Amendment was intended to protect the general population against the occasional rogue officer that can plague any police organization. The Fourth Amendment also protects us from rogue policies the government might otherwise seek to impose.

The Redcoats Are Still Coming

The colonists' experience with King George III's redcoats was a schoolroom full of reasons why government must be strictly controlled. The king's troops, using the unconstitutional power of Writs of Assistance, thought nothing of violating the English common law tradition of "a man's home is his castle." Warrantless searches were the order of the day in the years leading up to the War for American Independence.

It is no surprise then that we have a Fourth Amendment. What is surprising is that President Clinton and conservative, pro-gun Republicans think it is good public policy to have police making random stops of automobiles and warrantless searches of peoples' homes—sometimes for the same reason, to confiscate another item subject to constitutional protection, namely firearms. It is worth noting that King George's troops sparked the War for American Independence by their efforts to unconstitutionally confiscate the people's militia firearms.

H.R. 666 is intended to enshrine all this and more into federal law. The law would be unconstitutional, but that would not be the first such violation. Specifically, H.R. 666 is written to give legislative approval to the current judicial chipping away of the exclusionary rule. As long as a police officer thought his warrant was valid—even if it were not—the evidence so obtained could be used in a trial. But what are we to do under this doctrine if one police officer knowingly gets a warrant on false grounds? As long as the evidence is gained by other officers unaware of this deception (wink, wink) the evidence must be admissible against an accused.

H.R. 666 then gets worse. It establishes the "objective" standard of an officer's good faith in gathering evidence without a warrant as long as he thought he had probable cause. How is a defendant to ever prove a state of mind? That is as objective as a dream.

Among the attacks on our liberties that we could expect from the passage of H.R. 666 is an expansion of warrantless searches of homes and random stops of cars looking for guns. Confiscate now, ask questions later. After all, the government knows that the people are better off without guns. This attitude is exactly 180° opposite of the role of government in the Constitution.

This cavalier attitude regarding the authority of the federal government to legislate away constitutionally protected liberties has surfaced in the war on drugs. The doctrine of forfeiture is simply a euphemism for confiscation, or government theft. In the name of fighting to stamp out drugs (with a singular lack of success in that regard) the government is winning another battle—the war against the Constitution. Over 50,000 confiscations have been occurring annually, but in eighty percent of the cases, no charges are ever filed.

Forfeiture means that police departments are able to sell the loot and use the money for whatever pleases them. No charges need be filed, for after all, that simply costs money to prosecute. We should not think that this license to steal only gets used against drug kingpins. It gets used against ordinary Americans who, following an illegal search, have "too much money" on them. Or guns. Or whatever target is attractive to a rogue officer or department. The 1994 Crime Bill extended this concept to include multi-jurisdictional task forces of local, state and federal police agencies. Moreover, that Crime Bill also cuts prosecutors in to a share of the loot. This pretty well insures that there will be hardly anyone in the criminal justice system looking out for the interests of the citizens and the Constitution. Why should they look out for them? They will have all been bought off with fenced merchandise.

Are Federal Agents Out of Control?

At the Waco hearing in July, 1995, one of the few worthwhile panels provided two Texas Rangers an opportunity to testify. They made it clear that rather than launch a military assault on the Davidians they would have taken Koresh up on his invitation to the Bureau of Alcohol, Tobacco and Firearms to come and inspect his premises—something the BATF did not want to do since they had other plans. The Rangers also indicated that they would have walked up to the door and knocked to serve a warrant.

Ranger Captain David Brynes made an eloquent plea at the hearing to warn against a federal police force. Byrnes pointed out that "we federalize everything. Right now, everything from carjacking to evading child support is a federal crime in this country, and that really worries me...." Byrnes continued that "as a law enforcement officer, I worry about that. I think that for law enforcement to be effective it has to be accountable, and to be accountable it has to be controlled at the lowest possible level....[W]e seem to be vesting a tremendous amount of authority in the FBI to take over every aspect of civil law enforcement in this country....I think it's detrimental to our continued freedom in this country."

We should not lull ourselves into thinking that the Waco slaughter and the Ruby Ridge murder of some of Randy Weaver's family were aberrations. Gun Owners of America produced a video, *Breaking the Law in the Name of the Law,* several years ago in an effort to get the Congress to take a look at the Bureau of Alcohol, Tobacco and Firearms. Even then they had a long career of lying to get search warrants and tampering with evidence to try to get convictions. But the BATF has not been the only agency to run roughshod over the Bill of Rights.

In 1992, 31 agents from eight federal and local law enforcement agencies raided the Malibu home of Donald Scott, the Scott paper heir. The agents of the multi-jurisdictional task force claimed to be looking for marijuana. They shot Scott dead. No marijuana was found. A 1993 report on the incident by Ventura County District Attorney Michael Bradbury said a "primary purpose of the raid was a land grab" by the Forest Service who coveted Scott's land.

Just last year, another multi-jurisdictional task force comprised of agents from the FBI, Environmental Protection Agency, Coast Guard, Army Corps of Engineers and California Fish and Game Agency raided an herb farm in southern California. Paul Friedman, owner of Greenhouse Fine Herbs, is a member of the Self-Realization Fellowship. During the raid, supposedly over charges of river pollution and threats to an endangered species, agents asked the employees if they were a member of Friedman's church and where they hid the guns. Workers at the farm indicated that the agents were more interested in their religious beliefs than in the environmental complaint.

The Washington Times reported that U.S. Attorney Alan Bersin views the pollution indictments against the herb farm as "a significant step in the government's commitment to improving the quality of life." Mr. Friedman denies polluting the river which he called a "sacred place," and claims the garbage washed there during heavy rains was dumped by local residents.

Even if Friedman were totally guilty, one can see the problem to which Captain Byrnes drew our attention. Does littering a local river really justify 70 agents standing ready to shoot the suspects?

Obituary for Posse Comitatus

The Posse Comitatus law which was enacted over 100 years ago to prohibit the use of military personnel and equipment from being used against Americans has already been whittled down in the name of fighting the war on drugs. An exception has been made to the Posse Comitatus prohibition in cases where federal police want to use the military in a drug bust. Barbara Kennelly (D-CT) proposed legislation that would establish a 2,500-man rapid deployment attack force. Whatever the name, this is still a military group, but since the rapid deployment force would not be under the control of the military, the Posse Comitatus Act does not apply (wink, wink).

President Clinton, along with Rep. Charles Schumer (D-NY), immediately saw the hysteria about the horrible crime committed by the Oklahoma City bombers as a way of demonizing all gun owners and militia members. The effort was a dream situation for the anti-gunners. They could accuse law-abiding gun owners of being no different than the murderous bombers in Oklahoma. It is doubtful, though, that the President would welcome a similar comparison to be made between the Weathermen who bombed a building at the University of Wisconsin and anti-war protesters like then-student Clinton. Lawful, constitutionally protected action should not be equated with criminal activity just because it is unpopular. Otherwise, we would have no defense of the Civil Rights movement under Martin Luther King, Jr. because of the sometimes murderous assaults of the Black Panthers, or no defense of Earth Day marchers because of the environmental extremists who have put spikes in trees to kill or maim loggers as they cut trees down.

The attack on the Bill of Rights flying under the title of counter terrorism would seriously violate the First and Fourth Amendments. The President would then be able, on his own, with no appeal permitted, to classify any organization as a terrorist organization. That organization's assets would then be under government control, along with all of their papers. Their fundraising could be shut down, thus strangling their voice of communication with the public. And the bill greatly expands the government's ability to snoop on our telephone conversations.

Such legislation would have been objected to if directed against the civil rights or the anti-war movements of the past or the environmental movements of the present. Surely the right to organize and march does not end because militants and murderers choose to utter some of the same words used by peaceful groups operating lawfully.

Our view of government determines what kind of, and how much, freedom we will enjoy. If we understand America to be a land where the people are largely self-governed, then the civil government will be small and a servant of the people. If we understand America to be like the other countries of the world, then an elite will be in charge of managing the people, and the police will be their enforcers.

(written for Guns & Ammo in 1995)

Sheriff Supremacy

The supremacy of the sheriff as the chief law enforcement officer in a county is in decline. The biggest culprit is the federal government that has bestowed upon itself such police powers as it thinks it might need.

The sheriff is what the Founders intended. The sheriff is elected and thus accountable to the people. The Constitution prohibits federal police powers outside of counterfeiting, postal matters, piracy, and treason.

Too many states have cooperated in the drift toward federalizing the country's police powers by vesting federal agents with those powers.

In a report filed by former Sheriff Richard Mack, GOA's Director of Public Affairs, we learn of a welcome reversal of the federalization of police work. This happened in Big Horn County, Wyoming, under the tenure of Sheriff Dave Mattis.

Before Sheriff Mattis was elected to office, the IRS, in conjunction with the Sheriff's office, pulled a raid at the home of a Big Horn County couple. As they frequently do, the feds messed up, and that became clear as they finally realized they had no grounds to do a no-knock raid on the Castaneda family that had done nothing wrong.

The Castanedas sued and won. To their great credit, they asked only for a nominal amount of cash for damages. What they really wanted was the good news I have to report. With Sheriff Mattis's full cooperation, the Castanedas got a policy mandate that greatly restored the supremacy of the local sheriff.

The policy in Big Horn County for federal agents is to check with the sheriff before taking any action in Big Horn County. The sheriff of a county of 12,000 people has become the overseer of all federal agencies present in his county. Every one of the some 3,500 counties in America needs a Sheriff First policy in force.

When the federals show up in Big Horn County, they not only have to notify the sheriff, they must follow some other guidelines, as well. They must show that they have done the proper paperwork and establish that they have probable cause to be in the county at all.

Think of the ramifications of this policy. Sammy and Vicki Weaver might still be alive had there been a Sheriff First policy in Boundary County, Idaho. Ditto for some 86 Davidians in Waco, Texas.

What if the sheriff rubber-stamps the missteps of the feds? The sheriff might well be held accountable by the voters of his county for waving the Federal Leviathan into his county without exercising due diligence to keep the feds under control.

Three cheers for Sheriff Dave Mattis of Big Horn County. May his numbers multiply exponentially.

King Clinton's Legacy:
Rampant Lawlessness

Without a doubt, the so-called "legacy" of Bill Clinton and his administration will be lawlessness—his violation of the Laws of God and violation of the laws of men, specifically the U.S. Constitution.

One example of the latter is Clinton's blatantly un-Constitutional Federal power grab, the American Heritage Rivers Initiative (AHRI), which he announced in his State of the Union address in 1997. Gun Owners Of America has joined with others to oppose the AHRI in a case pending before the U.S. Supreme Court.

While this case does not directly involve firearms, the question of unchecked presidential powers extending from the hand that writes executive orders does concern every gun owner in the United States.

The title of this case is: *Hon. Helen Chenoweth, Hon. Bob Schaffer, Hon. Don Young, and Hon. Richard W. Pombo v. William J. Clinton, President.*

The stated purpose of the AHRI is to designate certain rivers as "Heritage Rivers" to "help communities alongside them revitalize their waterfronts and clean up pollution." To do this, President Clinton directed several executive agencies to implement this initiative. Then—believing, evidently, that he was elected King not President—he refused to wait for Congress to act, issuing an executive order (13061) which implemented AHRI.

Commenting on this kind of clear abuse of power and Clinton's use of many other executive orders, one of his advisors, Paul Begala said, "Stroke of the pen. Law of the land. Kinda cool." But, of course, this is not kinda cool. This is patently un-Constitutional! And it is part of a protracted assault on the legislative powers that are given only to Congress under Article I of our Constitution.

Sen. Orrin Hatch (R-Utah), Chairman of the Senate Judiciary Committee, has said of Clinton, "This President has a propensity to bypass Congress and the States and rule by executive order; in other words, by fiat." And the *Los Angeles Times* (4 July 1998) has reported how King Clinton's White House was using "a blitz of executive orders" to make progress on their domestic agenda "with or without Congressional help."

Incredibly, in this same *Times* story, a presidential spokesman, Jack Siewart, said, "We've been fairly unapologetic about finding ways to act where we've found that Congress has not acted."

So, what's wrong with this picture? Well, let's start with the obvious. Article I, Section 7 of the Constitution sets forth the specific process by which an act "becomes a law" and details the respective roles to be played by the House, Senate, and President. Thus, it is for Congress to decide whether to take a presidentially-recommended "measure" and translate it into a "bill...order, resolution, or vote." The Constitution (Article 2, Section 3) expressly limits the role of the President in the lawmaking process to "recommending to their [Congress'] consideration such measures as he shall judge necessary or expedient...."

By initiating the AHRI, without any participation by Congress whatsoever, King Clinton has turned the Constitution upside down. He has completely nullified the vote of every member of Congress.

This case we are involved in is no small matter. The three branches of our national government were separated for the purpose of better securing liberty. As U.S. Supreme Court Justice Kennedy has observed, "Liberty is always at stake when one or more of the branches seek to transgress the separation of powers."

In another case, the high court said this separation of powers works to "assure full, vigorous, open debate on the great issues affecting the people." It ensures "that legislation should not be enacted unless it has been carefully and fully considered by the Nation's elected officials."

In implementing the AHRI by fiat, King Clinton has said, in effect, to our people, represented by Congress: Drop dead! But, there is hope. The courts have not totally disregarded Clinton's assault on Congress' legislative authority.

In at least one case (*Chamber of Commerce of the U.S. v. Reich*, D.C. Cir. 1996), a Presidential Executive Order (No. 12954) was struck down and invalidated for only the second time in history. Let's hope the U.S. Supreme Court does this for the third time in history with this case.

If Clinton's penchant for acting as if he were the Congress is not checked, gun owners may wake up soon to the news of an executive order to confiscate guns.

[The court ruled unconstitutionally to give Clinton a green light.]

Lessons Elian Can Teach Us

The saga of Elian Gonzalez's perilous pilgrimage to freedom has already produced a number of important lessons. Hopefully Elian can teach us about the rule of law. Certainly it sticks in the throat when President Clinton, a convicted perjurer and obstructer of justice, lectures the country about the rule of law.

The Florida family courts have always been the proper place to determine legal custody of a boy whose mother died bringing him to freedom. It would be relevant in such a court to point out that Elian's father has no parental rights because all such rights belong to the Cuban totalitarian state resting on the systematic murder of tens of thousands of people.

Evidence could have been entered that Mr. Gonzalez would have no more control over the education, religion, or disposition of Elian than a slave father on a Georgia plantation in 1835. Instead, Attorney General Janet Reno has sent troops she personally controls—agents of the Immigration and Naturalization Service—on a raid using a fraudulent warrant. During this time, negotiations between the government and the Gonzalez family were under way.

Of perhaps the greatest concern was the unwillingness of Miami Police Chief William O'Brien to reveal his advance knowledge of the raid to Mayor Joe Carollo. In fact, assistant chief John Brooks went on the raid to order the street cops to let the agents through police lines. Brooks' explanation is hauntingly similar for those who recall the Nazi defense after World War II: "I had a job to do. I did it in the most professional way I could." Brooks added, "This was a police issue, not a political issue."

No doubt Mr. Brooks would also have us believe another episode in the raid was just a police issue. A justification for the paramilitary style storming of the Gonzalez house was that one of the Gonzalez friends was known to have a concealed carry permit. Mario Blas Miranda earlier told the cops that he has such a permit. Mr. Miranda is a private investigator and a former police officer. To handle this dangerous man during the raid he was knocked to the ground, forced spread eagle and doused with pepper spray while a shotgun was put to his ear. Agents never even bothered to search Miranda for his gun.

Hopefully the people of Miami will not rest until Chief O'Brien and Assistant Chief Brooks are fired. Hopefully also, all Americans will not rest until we rein in and fire federal officials who abuse their authority.

The Rule of Law

Much was heard of the rule of law during the election aftermath. The debate revealed many misunderstandings of this concept. This should help gun owners understand the perversion of the rule of law which has been used to justify more calls for more restrictions on firearms.

Almost lost in the discussion was the idea that voting is a means, not an end. Majorities are not ultimate in the American constitutional system of a democratic republic. Our system of government was set up to frustrate majorities and protect minorities.

That is why we have two Senators from North Dakota, the same as we have two Senators from California. The Electoral College reflects this weighting in favor of small states. Both the Senate and the Electoral College were set up to frustrate majorities—particularly if they were achieved by theft or purchased by a well-financed propaganda campaign.

The Founders wanted majorities to be checked every step of the way. That is why they did not provide for initiatives and referenda. They intended for representatives to make law, not for law to be made through direct democracy. That is also why it is so hard to amend our constitution.

The people's will is to be heard in the selection of Representatives to the U.S. Congress, and now in the selection of Senators as well (originally Senators were to be chosen by state legislatures which had been popularly elected).

Al Gore's post-election legal strategy did not even truthfully pursue his oft-stated goal of having "every vote count." Gore only wanted certain (heavily Democratic) counties counted, wanted those counties counted in ways that would most benefit Gore, and wanted military ballots discarded.

Al Gore was looking for a way to change the rules to get a favorable majority.

Does that sound similar to arguments for gun control? We are told that we have a living, evolving constitution. In fact, Al Gore himself has espoused such a position.

We are told that while nine amendments of the Bill of Rights protect individual rights, the Second Amendment protects the right of a state to have a militia. This would have come as a great surprise to the Founders.

We are told that rights must be balanced (particularly when talking about the right to keep and bear arms). At this point "shall not be infringed" seems to be no obstacle at all to restricting firearms ownership in the name of balance.

Even supporters of the Second Amendment can be confounded by the corruption of the rule of law. How else do we explain the call for enforcing the existing infringements of the right to keep and bear arms known as Project Exile?

The post-election contest is a powerful teaching tool to educate gun owners and the population at large. If you did not like what you saw being done to the integrity of the voting process in Florida, perhaps it will be easier to understand just how much has been done to corrupt the integrity of the Second Amendment.

Al Gore is a staunch proponent of restricting the right to keep and bear arms to that of the protection of recreational shooting. He is also a strong proponent of counting only those votes that count for him.

The rule of law is all about protecting citizens from rulers such as Al Gore.

The rule of law does not work in a vacuum. It must be upheld by enough of the population that the rulers are constrained to adhere to it, too. We have our work cut out for us.

The King Is Above the Law?

The English Civil War of the 17th Century produced a flood of refugees from royal tyranny that ballooned the colonization of America. Those who remained in Britain thought they put an end to government run amuck by executing King Charles I. But after a brief respite, his kids were back on the throne and the same old dictatorship came with them. Finally in 1689, the Stuart kings were given the boot and William and Mary of Orange were invited to ascend the throne after signing a Bill of Rights that, among other things, protected the right to keep and bear arms.

The kings believed that they were the law. Whatever they said was law. They did not believe that they were accountable to anyone. They called this doctrine the divine right of kings, but the doctrine is actually contrary to the teaching of the Bible.

A Scottish theologian, Samuel Rutherford, wrote a book entitled *Lex Rex*. Rutherford was so hated by the monarchy they wanted to burn him at the stake. Having been uncooperative with royal tyrants during his life, Rutherford's last act of defiance was seen as dying before he could be burned. Not to be deterred by his death, the crown ordered his bones dug up and burned along with his books.

The story makes you want to read a book that had a bunch of tyrants so upset, doesn't it? If it does, the book is still in print by that title. It is nothing more than two Latin words that mean *"the law is king."* Rutherford laid down an historical and Biblical foundation for limiting the power of government and holding the government accountable to the people when proper limits were exceeded, especially when limits were violated repeatedly over time.

Well, the old divine right of kings theory (or *Rex Lex*) is alive and well in the U.S. Federal Government. It has raised its tyrannical head in the case before the Ninth Circuit Court of Appeals. The feds have taken the same position as the British government following the Boston Massacre—their agents are immune from prosecution.

The case involves the Boundary County, Idaho prosecutor's attempt to press charges against Lon Horiuchi, the FBI agent who shot Randy Weaver's wife in the head while she was holding a baby in her arms on Ruby Ridge in 1992.

The lawyer for Horiuchi, the Solicitor General, Seth Waxman, told the justices that it did not matter whether Vicki Weaver's death was the result of excessive force: "These federal law enforcement officials are privileged to do what would otherwise be unlawful if done by a private citizen. It is a fundamental function of our government."

In other words, Horiuchi's defense is that he was simply following orders. That defense resulted in the execution of numerous Nazis following the Nuremberg trials held after World War II.

What a dark day that a mere 45 years after seeking the death of other murderous government agents, the American government has taken the Nazi position in defense of its own murderous agents.

The Tyranny of Good Intentions

How we view government has a profound affect on our liberties. Our Founding Fathers looked upon government as a shield to protect individual liberties. Most of our politicians today look upon government as the engine for doing good.

This framework is described masterfully in a very important book entitled, *The Tyranny of Good Intentions: How Prosecutors and Bureaucrats Are Trampling the Constitution in the Name of Justice*, by Paul Craig Roberts and Lawrence Stratton.

The English liberty tradition of the law as a shield to protect individual liberties traces back to Alfred the Great in the ninth century. The notion of the law as an instrument of the policy of the rulers was articulated by, among others, Jeremy Bentham, a 17th century political philosopher.

One of the more visible abuses of the law in our day is the ever-expanding number of reasons why police agencies are allowed to take people's cash, cars, houses, and other property without a warrant and without ever pressing charges. Justified in the name of giving police and prosecutors effective crime-fighting tools, the reality has become a license to steal because the proceeds of confiscation go to the very officers who carry out the forfeiture.

The Tyranny of Good Intentions describes how the Communists made the law a weapon of the ruling elite. A process to seek justice was consciously rejected in place of a process to achieve the political objectives of the Communist Party. With that in mind, the authors paint a very disturbing picture of the perversion of the legal process in the United States that is now operating all too much like that of the Soviet Union.

What is the end of this? Well, consider that one of the most horrifying features of totalitarian government is the concentration camp. Jeremy Bentham believed that people who might, because of their economic and social status, commit a crime should be apprehended and reformed through heavy labor. Hitler and Lenin must have had Bentham on their nightstand.

So, too, might today's English Prime Minister, Tony Blair. He is proposing that the government be allowed to confine people proactively, based on the fears of their potential danger to society.

The Bible says that only God knows the hearts of men. Our Benthamite politicians obviously believe they share that divine knowledge.

Fuhrman Tapes Reveal Danger of H.R. 666

The disgusting statements by former Los Angeles police detective Mark Fuhrman should be mandatory reading for members of Congress. The revelations contained in Fuhrman's taped statements indicate that some officers routinely beat innocent people, plant evidence, and lie to get convictions. Such actions underscore why Congress must reconsider H.R. 666.

Earlier this year the House of Representatives passed H.R. 666. The bill now awaits Senate approval. H.R. 666 would gut the exclusionary rule which has given teeth to the Fourth Amendment protection against illegal searches and seizures for most of this century. While this bill would at first affect only federal agents, no one doubts that state and local laws would soon follow.

The rationale for gutting the exclusionary rule is that crooks avoid conviction when evidence is excluded from trial because it was obtained with faulty warrants or without probable cause. However, efforts to blame our crime problems on the exclusionary rule are absurd. According to the American Bar Association, scarcely one percent of those facing trial escape conviction because of the exclusionary rule.

Proponents of H.R. 666 say that evidence should not be excluded, no matter how flagrantly the suspect's constitutional rights have been violated, as long as the officer obtained such evidence in good faith. These proponents tell us that the good faith of the officer is an objective standard.

It should be obvious to all that the good faith of an individual is not an objective standard. How does one prove the state of mind of another person? H.R. 666 would place the burden of that proof on the defendant—an impossibility. If an officer knowingly broke the law in gathering evidence, all he has to say is that he did it in good faith.

Would the police ever lie? While we would like to think not, America's Founding Fathers assumed that government should never be blindly trusted. That is why they gave us a Fourth Amendment along with all the rest of the Bill of Rights.

Recent revelations from both federal and local police actions should renew our confidence in the judgment of the Founders rather than those members of Congress who recklessly assume that all that is needed to fight crime is to give the police a free hand without any accountability.

In addition to the Fuhrman revelations, Philadelphia has recently been rocked by allegations that some police in that city conspired to convict

Mumia Abu Jamal of murder. But racism is not the only motive for this kind of behavior.

The Bureau of Alcohol, Tobacco and Firearms agents entrapped Randy Weaver into a minor firearms violation in Ruby Ridge, Idaho. U.S. Marshals lied about the circumstances of how they killed Weaver's 14-year old son, and FBI agent Ron Horiuchi lied about circumstances surrounding his killing of Weaver's wife, Vicki. Subsequently, FBI officials have lied to cover up their criminal actions during the siege on Weaver's home.

Other BATF agents lied to get a search warrant in Waco against the Branch Davidians and lied to cover up their misdeeds in the initial raid. The Davidians and the Weavers were targeted for their religious and political views, not because of any racism of the agents.

We need more accountability for law enforcement officials, not less. This is the only way to protect the honorable majority of officers from the Mark Fuhrmans of the world. Congress needs to strengthen the exclusionary rule, not gut it.

The Power to License Is the Power to Ban

"Can I still get a Federal Firearms License (FFL)?" I get asked that question a lot these days. Bill Clinton's endless war on gun owners has made many of us reconsider questions such as, "How can I be sure I can always legally purchase firearms?"

The short answer to the FFL question is yes. FFLs are still being obtained by both first-time applicants and being renewed for long-time licensees. FFLs are more costly. The Bureau of Alcohol, Tobacco and Firearms (BATF) is working overtime to reduce the number of licensees. Depending on where you live, new BATF policies could affect your chances. But for most people in most places, an FFL is still available.

I am also asked how this whole mess happened. People are concerned, correctly, that as long as we have an anti-gun President, the BATF will be encouraged to run wild. Yet they also want to know if there were something our side did to cause the FFL troubles. I have been forced to say these problems have been caused by both our friends and our foes.

The Danger of Asking the Government for a Monopoly

The man who owns a store specializing in firearms faces many challenges. Some of them are common to any business: taxes, paperwork, meeting a payroll, and making a profit. There are also additional costs. The labor costs at a quality firearms shop are higher. Unlike a fast food restaurant, the firearms store can't just hire anyone off the street and pay them the minimum wage. They have to hire knowledgeable people who can answer technical questions about a wide variety of firearms. The staff must also remember all the laws regarding firearms sales, know something about gun safety, and, sadly, keep cool if someone decides to rob the store.

It is a tough business. And there are people in it who have decided to ask Congress to make their business more profitable. Every time the firearms industry asks the government to do something to eliminate "competitors," it asks for trouble. There are those who believe that private FFLs should be abolished. They forget that every time they say FFLs should cost more and be harder to get, Dianne Feinstein will agree. Our enemies will gladly raise the price of FFLs—to the point nobody can afford one.

License costs jumped from $30 for three years to $200 ($90 for renewals) in the last Congress. And there were bills introduced to make these costs much higher. Where did the notion come from to raise FFL fees? There are two people who deserve the credit: Josh Sugarmann of the Violence Policy

Center and Bill Bridgewater of the National Alliance of Stocking Gun Dealers.

Josh Sugarmann began making his place in this debate as an employee of the National Coalition to Ban Handguns. In 1988, he had an insight: if it looked like a machine gun, most people would think it was a machine gun. And the debate over banning certain semi-automatic rifles and shotguns (so-called "assault weapons") began.

In 1992, Mr. Sugarmann issued documentation suggesting a new form of gun control. If there are no places to legally purchase firearms, then firearms are effectively banned. Thus the BATF should make FFLs much more costly and harder to obtain. His monograph, "More gun dealers than gas stations," became the source for the debate on FFLs in the next Congress. (Mr. Sugarmann is listed as the holder of two FFLs himself —both stating Washington D.C. addresses, one being that of his Violence Policy Center.)

Mr. Sugarmann is a smart man, but a review of his study suggests that he picked up some of his ideas from "friends" of the gun movement. On page 21, Mr. Sugarmann begins a discussion of "the kitchen table dealers." He talks about the difference between the wholesale and the retail price of firearms. He refers to people using an FFL "for personal use or resale, [and] kitchen-table dealers can also broker sales between wholesalers and retail purchasers for a 'handling fee.' " Mr. Sugarmann cites other sources for this discussion, but the term "kitchen table dealer" is a stock complaint from Mr. Bill Bridgewater and his National Alliance of Stocking Gun Dealers.

The April, 1994, issue of Mr. Bridgewater's magazine, *The Alliance Voice*, is a relevant example. The cover shows Mr. Bridgewater shaking hands with the hero of Waco, then-Treasury Secretary Lloyd Bensen. Inside, readers were reminded, "How in the world can a gun retailer make money when there are tens of thousands of people who are ordering guns wholesale and bypassing the legitimate gun shop?" The National Rifle Association (NRA) was attacked, "Their sole concern with the industry is that there be enough extra FFLs issued to keep prices down to factory cost for their members."

The featured theme of this issue? An agreement signed by Mr. Bridgewater and several anti-gun "police" organizations calling for an increase in FFL fees and requiring that any FFL holder must comply with "state and local laws and ordinances." This agreement would soon be enforced by the BATF with a vengeance.

Those who see the interests of stocking gun dealers as being somehow distinct from other portions of the shooting community forget one thing: Our enemies see us as different parts of the same problem. If it goes bang, they want to ban it, be it hunting rifle or AR-15. They want to shut down every gun store everywhere. And they are succeeding.

BATF Harasses Home Businessmen

Anyone who begins a business tries to hold down unnecessary costs. Apple Computer began in a garage, not an expensive office. In today's decentralized workplace, computers, faxes, and other technology have even created the "virtual office" and "virtual corporation"—workplaces that exist wherever the coworkers may happen to be. Many Americans earn extra money (or obtain more time with their children) by running all sorts of home-based businesses.

The "kitchen table" firearms dealer is no different than the "kitchen table" computer shareware manufacturer or the "kitchen table" Mary Kay saleswoman. The business may be the beginning of something much bigger. Or it can be as much a hobby as a business, allowing a person to make a few extra dollars doing something he or she enjoys anyway.

Generally, these efforts are conducted in a fairly law-abiding manner. But if a person wishes to do business from his home, he generally does so even though his home is not zoned for commercial purposes.

The mechanic may fix cars for friends on Saturdays. So long as automobiles do not overflow onto his yard and elsewhere, the neighbors do not mind. In fact, they may not even know. A newly divorced woman may run a telephone answering service from her home. Again, this may not be strictly legal according to zoning laws or some ordinance, but it bothers no one and provides her with an income.

Under President Clinton, the BATF has taken it upon itself to become the national enforcer of local zoning laws, state sales tax laws, and state and local licensing laws. This is flatly unconstitutional. The federal government has no Constitutional authority to enforce local ordinances. In fact Article 1, Section 8 of the Constitution prohibits the federal government from usurping powers that belong to the states.

The BATF is persecuting the FFL holder who has not obtained a retail store and other licenses. Consider the following letter I received from the City of Melvindale, Michigan:

> The Bureau of Alcohol, Tobacco and Firearms is attempting
> to limit the number of Federally-licensed firearms dealers.

One way in which they are attempting to limit the number of licensees is by requiring all future renewals to be sent to the local municipality for zoning approval.

Currently all local Melvindale licensees are NOT zoned for retail sales. In order for the City of Melvindale to approve the zoning on your future licenses (sic) renewal you must apply for and receive special approval from the City of Melvindale Planning Commission for a home occupation involving retail sales of ammunition and firearms.

Applications for special approval are available from the City of Melvindale Building Department. The fee is $200.00 and a Public Hearing will be required. This does not guarantee that special approval will be granted.

It looks like there will be no more FFLs in Melvindale for a while. The minute politicians or bureaucrats must affirmatively approve something is the minute few things will be approved. They will offer reasons which sound good—liability concerns, public complaints, whatever. But the bottom line will be no FFLs.

A chat with Robert Lesmeister of American Firearms Industry reveals Melvindale is not alone. The city council of Honolulu, Hawaii, has just passed an ordinance banning the sale of firearms and ammunition from residentially-zoned districts. FFL holders in Detroit's residential zones have been threatened with a $500 fine for failing to get a variance from the Board of Zoning Appeals. FFL holders in Maryland are being similarly harassed.

Curiously, though everyone seems to know about this BATF change of policy, the BATF has not bothered to follow the procedures required to make this policy legal. In a discussion one of my staff had at a meeting between firearms dealers and the BATF, we were told that no Notice of Proposed Rulemaking had been printed in the Federal Register, no public comment took place, nor was a Final Rule published. Requests for any documentation at all have been met with either silence or hostility.

Commercial Dealers Are Not Safe

Bill Bridgewater and his allies may think that fewer FFLs mean bigger profits for those that remain. What they do not realize is that Bill Clinton has no love for retail gun shops either. Honolulu firearms stores in commercially-zoned districts are being required to provide BATF with a letter from their landlord specifically giving the dealer permission to conduct a firearms business.

When Jonathan Low told BATF agent Gerry Kim getting such a letter would be no problem, the agent disagreed. Two days after the landlord had agreed to write the needed letter, he changed his mind. The reason? A federal agent had visited the landlord and warned him of all kinds of "liability concerns" the landlord might face for allowing the store to operate. When Low found a new location for his shop, agent Kim spoke to the new landlord, and Low lost another letter of permission.

The BATF will eagerly put a store out of business for recordkeeping errors. Yet when the BATF itself could not account for 152 firearms during a 1991 inventory, the missing firearms were simply removed from the computer. Had an FFL holder tried that, he would be in prison.

FFL Not the Only License Needed These Days

The BATF is not only willing to help localities enforce zoning laws, it is eager to help states and localities enforce all kinds of licensing and tax laws. While FFL holders have been required to comply with state and local laws, determining what those laws actually are can be a task worthy of Sherlock Holmes.

Given that states and cities are eager to find new sources of revenue for their reckless spending, the honest businessman had better expect to keep up with ever-changing rules in this area. State governments have found a friend in the BATF when it comes to learning who should be licensed and who should be paying sales taxes.

North Carolina asked for and received a complete list of FFL holders from BATF. A North Carolina firearms dealer is required to have a state license (cost: $50 annually) as well as an FFL. Roughly 3,900 did not. The licenses are issued by the state's Revenue Department, which also enforces income tax and sales tax laws. Some of these FFL holders could be looking at extensive audits in a search for "unreported" business income—even if they sold no firearms to anyone else.

North Carolina's policy seems motivated by anti-gun sentiment as well as greed. Jean Kossoff of the department was reported as saying, "We're going after them. We've made them a priority."

What You Can Do

For some people, getting an FFL may well be more trouble than it is worth. If you live in an urban Northeastern area or an anti-gun community, it may be a costly struggle. If you live in most other places, getting an FFL will cost a bit more but, otherwise, is easily attainable.

Some people argue that groups like Gun Owners of America should support whole new categories of FFLs. While this argument has some merit from the perspective of the prospective pistol smith, it could further divide our splintered community. We are all in this together. It is time we started to act that way. We should all support the end of federal licensing of firearms dealers for which there is no constitutional authority.

In the meantime, write your Congressman and Senators. Demand that the BATF get out of the zoning business, and encourage your local firearms stores to fight with you, not against you.

Section Four

>—I—❯—❯—⊙—❮—❮—I—≺

WACO

Waco Hearings: A Rush to Judgment

One of the most important questions emerging from the Waco tragedy never got considered by the Waco committee even though an eloquent appeal to consider the dangers of federalizing police work in the U.S. came from Texas Ranger Captain David Byrnes. Byrnes pointed out the trend to federalize everything from carjacking to those evading child support. He warned against passing repressive laws in the wake of the Oklahoma bombing.

Byrnes continued, "For law enforcement to be effective it has to be accountable, and to be accountable it has to be controlled at the lowest possible level. It worries me to think that we're vesting...a tremendous amount of authority in the FBI to take over every aspect of civil law enforcement in this country....I think it's detrimental to our continued freedom in this country. I don't believe anybody wants a national police force in this country. I certainly don't."

Byrnes was in the right place to issue his warning. Last year it was the Democrats with their Crime Bill of 1994 who fought to weaken local control over the police. This year it is the Republicans in their Terror Bills offered in response to the Oklahoma tragedy. Those anti-Bill of Rights bills of 1994 and 1995 are the very legislation that Capt. Byrnes was warning against.

Other issues seemed to preoccupy the members of Congress, or at least it seemed that way as Representative Charles Schumer virtually hijacked the hearings single-handedly. Was David Koresh a teacher of wacky religion? Was he a sexual pervert and child abuser? These were the issues that Schumer wanted to focus on. No one bothered to point out to Mr. Schumer that his oath of office does not give him, or anyone else in the federal government, authority in these areas. Instead of trying government agents for a disastrous action, Kiri Jewel was brought in to spin a lurid tale of how Koresh sexually abused her. No one asked *London Daily Telegraph* reporter Ambrose Evans-Pritchard to testify regarding the few easy phone calls he made to find out that Ms. Jewel was never in Waco during the time she claims to have been molested. But, like the tendentious affidavit sworn out by BATF agent Davy Aguillera, which read like a supermarket tabloid, the hearing record was distorted by the irrelevant, and probably untrue, statement allowed from Ms. Jewel.

Another part of Schumer's hijacking was based on his unrebutted hypocrisy. He made a huge case out of the NRA's willingness to pay a group of experts to X-ray the supposedly full-auto guns taken from Mt. Carmel. Somehow, Schumer alleged, this tainted the whole committee process. Where was the

Republican rebuttal to point out that the Cult Awareness Network attorney, David Bardin, was visibly consulting with the Democrats on the first day of the hearing right in front of the cameras? Congress has traditionally used outside groups to supply information. But only Schumer can make it seem, because of Republican ineptness, that something is wrong with what Schumer himself has done for years with Handgun Control, Inc. when he was the top dog on the same committee.

The evidence that there was no ambush planned by David Koresh was glossed over or even ignored by the committee. A fifty caliber Browning—even a semiautomatic .50 caliber—had it been used in an ambush, along with the rest of the guns the Davidians had at their disposal, would have left the BATF invaders a lot worse off than four dead. As attorney Jack Zimmerman pointed out, the BATF had to drive hundreds of yards down a flat, wide-open driveway. The Davidians had the high ground. Had they planned an ambush, it would have been like sheep going to the slaughter. But even before the hearings were over, Chairman Bill McCollum was pronouncing as fact that the Davidians had ambushed the government.

Also, the Committee never explained a photograph Gun Owners of America supplied them. The photo (which can be found in the Gun Owners Foundation's book, *The Davidian Massacre* by Carol Moore) shows five BATF agents firing blindly at will into the Davidians' building without any cover whatsoever. If those agents had been ambushed, their casual shooting posture would have left them vulnerable.

If there had been an ambush and the Davidians had fired through their front door at the unsuspecting agents lawfully delivering a warrant, where is the door? One of the agents at the trial said he had seen splinters showering out of the door during the Davidian fusillade. Splinters from a metal door? All of this corroborates the testimony of attorneys Jack Zimmerman and Dick DeGuerin who saw the door and who said that the bullet holes showed entry from the outside. They also saw the same pattern in the roof of the building that was being ground into the dirt by the tanks before the fire started. And any evidence that might have survived the fire was filmed being pushed into the fire by the FBI's bulldozers.

It is clear from the record of the trial and the hearings that there was never any intention of serving a warrant on David Koresh. The raid commander could not even say who he had designated to serve the warrant. Koresh could have been arrested on any number of occasions in town. Firearms dealer Henry McMahon has told of David Koresh's offer, seven months before the raid, to have BATF agents come to Mt. Carmel and inspect the large quantity of guns he had bought legally from McMahon. The Davidians made a fair amount of their income from selling guns at gun shows throughout Texas. The BATF was not interested in inspecting Koresh's guns or arresting him the way real cops would; they just wanted to carry out their Rambo-raid.

Another disturbing piece of testimony was overlooked by Chairman McCollum in his rush to judgment that the Davidians were to blame for what happened related to the CS gas. The hearings did not give a seal of good housekeeping approval for CS gas. It turned out that the FBI had declined to use it against the survivors of their attack on the Weaver family for fear of killing the baby. Dick Sherrow, a former BATF agent and expert witness, contradicted other experts who claimed that CS gas was as good as a vitamin pill. Amnesty International has reported on cases of children dying from CS gas, but they were not invited to testify. Failure Analysis Associates, the firm retained by the NRA, found that the CS gas was, depending on the location in the building, between two and ninety times the concentration used on soldiers. It would seem that the FBI did not want the Davidians to get out of the building.

If fact, Sherrow had warned two years before the BATF assault on the Davidians that something like Waco was going to happen. Corroboration could have come from Mike Wallace of CBS's *60 Minutes*. Wallace found from his contacts with the BATF that the decision to attack Mt. Carmel was based on a desire to improve its tarnished image. In other words, it had nothing to do with the charter the BATF supposedly has from the 1968 Gun Control Act—to combat violent street crime.

The unanswered questions of the Waco hearings still beg for answers. Why did the videotape the BATF made of the initial raid not record? Where is the missing front door with all of its mute testimony as to who shot first? Why were the Davidians' bodies allowed to decompose in the morgue, thus preventing any follow-up autopsies? Why did 4 1/2 minutes of the infrared tapes for the period just prior to the outbreak of the fire mysteriously get erased? Why were the walls bulldozed into the burning fire?

Representative Schumer was of the opinion that gunfire or fire killed all the Davidians. Yet there were six women and children who died of blunt trauma, almost certainly from the concrete wall that fell on them after the tank knocked it over, according to Harvard physician Alan Stone.

The hearings gave the overall impression that the government's honor was being defended, although the evidence of a cover-up is abundant. The FBI was allowed to charge Koresh with having broken his word during the course of the negotiations. Yet the congressmen did not seem interested in the FBI's lack of good faith that resulted in the Davidians not trusting the government. The Treasury Department's report on Waco said that there had been no guns on the helicopters. At the hearings, however, it came out that at least one airborne agent did have a gun. And of course, it is now quite clear that the BATF lied to the military about there being drugs at Mt. Carmel. And we know quite well that the raid commanders lied about losing the element of surprise. (Lying is a serious issue, but it should not obscure the even worse offense of deciding on a military raid to begin with.)

And worst of all, something Texas Ranger Captain Byrnes underscored—the need for accountability—is still almost totally lacking. Eighty people are dead, and nothing has happened to those in charge.

The next time the government has a mess like Waco, the feds should be required to call upon the SWAT team of almost any major U.S. city. Had that been done in Waco, it is very likely that nobody would have died on April 19, or any day after that. The Davidians would have almost certainly come out if real cops had been involved.

Of Conspiracies—Politically Correct and Otherwise

Much has been made of the 50-year anniversary of the atomic bomb. Richard Rhodes's book, *The Making of the Atomic Bomb,* has been the source for much of this discussion. According to Rhodes's book, another anniversary is upon us. Fifty-two years ago, on August 28, 1943, the Nazis ordered the Danish government to ban arms and to create a death penalty for those who harbored arms. The Danish government refused. The following day, the Nazis reoccupied Copenhagen and confined the Danish King.

Once again, we are reminded that those who seek to control a people or a nation must first seek to disarm them. Such a statement is merely common sense. Yet in the wake of the tragic events at Oklahoma City, it is no longer politically correct to say such things. Those who do are denounced as conspiracy theorists or even as lunatics who have no place in politics.

However, some folks were able to talk about conspiracy without being criticized in early August. They alleged that the entire Philadelphia legal system conspired to frame Mumia Abu-Jamal for killing a cop and were accorded a respectful hearing for their theories. It is politically correct to oppose the death penalty, so not surprisingly, a conspiracy that might discredit capital punishment was favorably reported.

Some conspiracy theories, long criticized, have turned out to be true. Until recently, people who believed there was an organized effort by the Soviet Union to undermine the American government were dismissed by the same politically correct crowd. Now Soviet and American Communist Party documents proving precisely that are a matter of public record in books like *The Secret World of American Communism.*

The far left in this country has a history of dismissing any criticism until presented with incontrovertible evidence. This technique allows them to pursue their agenda unhindered for years and even decades. Just as Alger Hiss has many defenders, so do the actions of the federal government at Ruby Ridge, Idaho and Waco, Texas.

One need not be Oliver Stone to ask questions about those events. Most fair-minded critics are rightfully concerned as to why the enforcement of this nation's gun laws took an unusually deadly turn in 1992. The upcoming hearings on government excesses in Idaho should answer many questions, such as, What kind of government is so paranoid that it would equate Randy Weaver's move to Idaho as evidence that he was conspiring to kill federal authorities? Why did the Justice Department cover up evidence that it had illegally set in place a shoot-on-sight policy that led to the killing of Weaver's wife? Was the killing of Weaver's son (who was shot in the back) justified?

The investigation into the Weaver killings comes on the heels of the Waco hearings in July. Congress discovered the Clinton administration had engaged in an extensive cover up to suppress exculpatory evidence that would implicate government officials of wrongdoing in the aftermath of more than 80 men, women, and children being killed.

This administration and its allies go out of their way to whip up hysteria against law-abiding gun owners and anyone else who criticizes any act of the federal government. Like the Nixon Administration, this administration seems willing to do anything, fair or foul, to discredit its opponents in the pursuit of a cover-up. Perhaps this is why a recent poll found 52% of the American people believe the government to be an immediate threat to their liberties.

Those who ask questions about the Clinton administration's gun policies are responsible citizens with reasonable concerns. As even Congress discovered during the Waco hearings in July, conspiracy theories sometimes turn out to be true.

Waco: Still No Justice

Seven years after the government's lethal assault on the Branch Davidians at Waco, the country still waits for justice to be rendered. David Hardy, an attorney from Arizona, has authored *This Is Not an Assault*, which is a fascinating account of his efforts to find out what really happened at Waco.

Hardy has filed a series of Freedom of Information Act (FOIA, pronounced "foya" inside the Beltway) in an effort to get to the bottom of the Waco tragedy. What he has uncovered is very damaging to the government's insistence that, except for a few honest mistakes, BATF and FBI agents did nothing wrong at Waco.

Hardy has an eye for detail. It was the BATF and FBI Waco reports plus the 1995 hearings that, thanks to Hardy's eye for detail, showed the government's account of what happened at Waco did not add up. For example, photos of one of the victims of the fire that ended the siege of the Davidians were curious. The victim, Jimmy Riddle, had been photographed amidst the ashes of the fire, yet most of his body and clothes were not burned. Had his body been moved? And why?

Hardy's findings from the FOIA documents progressively revealed government perjury. The BATF denied that Koresh could have been arrested by nabbing him in town even though plenty of witnesses saw him off the Davidians' property. Well, BATF agents had gone shooting with Koresh nine days before the assault.

Audiotapes made on the first day of the assault revealed the sound of shots being fired from helicopters that buzzed the Davidians. Sifting through the disclosures made to Hardy enabled him to state categorically that the Davidians did not ambush the BATF attackers and that the BATF fired first.

Forward Looking Infra Red (FLIR) tapes were pried out of the government grudgingly. Denials that tapes existed were finally given up when Hardy was able to show that the government referred elsewhere to the tapes' existence. These tapes were made on the last day, the day of the fatal fire.

Some twelve tons of evidence had been stored by the Texas Rangers. When an examination of some of that evidence revealed that, contrary to repeated FBI denials, pyrotechnic rounds had been fired into the Davidians, the Justice Department sent Federal Marshals to the FBI's facility at Quantico, Virginia. The Marshals took possession of FLIR tapes made from approximately 6:00 a.m. to 10:42 a.m.—tapes that an FBI official had told Hardy in writing and under oath did not exist.

Mr. Hardy was able to piece together a picture of two FBI's—one, represented by the negotiators during the siege and the other represented by the paramilitary Hostage Rescue Team (HRT). On at least three occasions, the negotiators had gotten the Davidians to agree to leave their building and surrender. Each time, the HRT foiled a peaceful solution by aggressive, offensive, and, finally, fatal behavior.

The Waco siege ended in tragedy, Hardy found, because the FBI's HRT had run amuck.

(*This Is Not an Assault,* by David Hardy, is available from Gun Owners Foundation.)

Lessons of Waco:
Government Control, Not Gun Control

Abuse by the federal government of gun owners in the name of enforcing federal gun laws is not news to GOA members. About a decade ago, Gun Owners Foundation documented abuses committed by the BATF in its video *Breaking the Law in the Name of the Law: The BATF Story.*

Revelations of FBI lies and cover up have been steadily coming to light as a result of "smoking guns" found in the Waco evidence room. Attorney General Janet Reno has pledged a vigorous investigation, even while her own department's civil division continues to stonewall the plaintiffs' efforts to get at that evidence in the wrongful death suit brought by Davidian survivors and families.

Adding to the impression that the cover up continued as the actual policy of the Clinton administration, the U.S. Attorney for Waco, Bill Johnston, has been removed from any contact with the case.

Johnston aggressively prosecuted the Davidians and may have even gone too far when he took part in the 1993 raid decisions. But the times may be changing, and Johnston let the producer of *Waco: Rules of Engagement* see some of the evidence the Justice Department has been illegally hiding from the Davidians' lawyers.

That led to the proof that the FBI had been lying about not using any pyrotechnic rounds the day of the fatal fiery end of the government's 51-day siege.

(Note: Both the BATF and the Waco tapes are available from Gun Owners Foundation and can by ordered from the GOA web page at *http://www.gunowners.com/videot.htm* or by calling 703-321-8585.)

BATF Caught in More Lies

The BATF's mendacity has been exposed again with renewed calls to include their actions in the congressional reviews that are cranking up. The BATF had an undercover agent with a colleague in the Davidian buildings, shooting with Koresh and handing over the agent's .38 revolver, some two weeks before the military-style raid conducted by the BATF. Its kidnapping of Karen Kilpatrick and her gun-store business partner is also emerging as a factor.

Kilpatrick was kept in "custody" and incommunicado while the siege was under way. She would have publicized that Koresh had been on the phone with her when the BATF was in her store and that Koresh had invited the agents to come and inspect his inventory.

Such information would certainly have brought the government's actions under closer scrutiny during the raid. There were obviously plenty of opportunities to act like real cops and search Mt. Carmel and arrest David Koresh. But the BATF lied about drugs being present.

Their lie was used to get military equipment from the armed services, so they could conduct a military attack, presumably for making a good impression during the appropriations hearings that were to be held shortly after the February 28, 1993 raid against the Davidians.

Video films taken by the government of the last day of the siege are also finally available. As the *Washington Post* has asked, Who was firing machine guns into the Davidians' building shortly before the fire? The FBI has denied they fired a shot all day.

Is There a Distinction Between the Police and the Military?

The tragedy of Waco can result in good if we resolve that commando raids on American citizens are entirely inappropriate for police tactics.

The scandal of the Delta Forces goes beyond their being at Waco and perhaps even beyond being involved in the operations of the last day. The scandal is that any American police agency would want guidance from the military who are trained to kill people, not arrest them and bring them in for a trial.

As General James Scott, a post-Waco Delta Force commander who is now teaching at Harvard, told the *Dallas Morning News*, "If any good comes out of these new investigations, it will be to redraw a bright line between the military function and the police function."

Another good that can come out of Wacogate is the realization that the FBI and the BATF are so ethically challenged that they have no business keeping registration lists of American gun buyers. Not only is this unconstitutional, it is subject to great abuse.

We have seen abuse from the data collection efforts of the FBI in Filegate. It has never been explained why the FBI was keeping files on over 1,000 politicians and people in public life who have broken no laws and then turned the files over to the Clinton White House. If the Republicans cannot get to the bottom of politician registration, should we expect better results from gun owner registration?

(Note: Over 3,000,000 gun buyers have already been added illegally to the FBI and BATF registration lists since the inception of the Brady Instant Registration Check in November, 1998.)

The politicians need to hear from their constituents that we need government control, not gun control.

Section Five

BATTLEFRONTS IN THE GUN WAR

Clinton's War Against the Constitution and Guns

When you stop and think about it, President William Jefferson Clinton has probably been more effective in destroying the rights of Americans than was King George III. For a man as famous for lying as President Clinton is, he has been surprisingly open about his desire to disarm the civilian population. Clinton answered a question by *Rolling Stone* (December 9, 1993) regarding the possibility of banning handguns rather straightforwardly: "I don't think the American people are there right now.

"But with more than 200 million guns in circulation, we've got so much more to do on this issue before we even reach that. But there are certain kinds of guns that can be banned and a lot of other reasonable regulations that can be imposed." In that same interview, Clinton outlined his desire to pass the Brady Bill, the ban on semi-automatics (the so-called "assault weapons") and step up regulatory harassment and reduction of federally licensed firearms dealers (FFLs).

After pushing hard for it, Clinton signed into law the Brady Bill which requires a national permit to buy a gun and, adding insult to injury, imposes a period for us to wait while the government decides whether or not we can exercise our constitutionally protected right to keep and bear arms. The Brady Law's implementation resulted in an immediate abuse of police power as thousands of denials were issued for unpaid parking tickets and other supposedly off-limit reasons. The Brady Law, in addition to being quite unconstitutional, became one more method of tax collection.

Can you see it now in your mind's eye? There is George Washington, huddled in a freezing tent at Valley Forge with many of his men shoeless, writing in his diary that all of this suffering would be worth it if Americans were able to throw off the yoke of London's tyranny so there could be a brave new world of government approval of who can buy a gun—especially if it could be done instantly. No doubt he would have appreciated, in this line of thinking, the fascist propaganda of making the trains run on time. Hey, do what you want as long as there is no wait. If you can't see that in your mind's eye, neither can I.

The Brady instant check has an additional charm for advocates of civilian disarmament such as President Clinton. As a justice department task force stated in 1989, "Any system that requires a criminal record check prior to purchase of a firearm creates the potential for the automated tracking of individuals who seek to purchase firearms."

Most background check laws, including the Brady instant check provision, have no effective way of preventing the authorities from compiling a registration list of gun owners. To believe that the government is not making a registration list is to believe people such as Clinton when they tell us, "I'm from the government, and I'm here to help you." In fact, a registration list is already being compiled—illegally—by the Bureau of Alcohol, Tobacco and Firearms. Operation Forward Trace has involved the BATF in a massive sweep of the country's gun dealers' books to record the names and addresses of buyers of so-called "assault weapons." A BATF agent told a reporter on the national TV program *Day One* (on ABC) that the out-of-business records that are sent to the BATF are being computerized—in spite of an explicit congressional prohibition.

Happily, one effort to build a computerized gun registry was blocked when a Pennsylvania court this spring stopped Pittsburgh from using a grant from the U.S. Justice Department. It was to be a pilot project to design a computer program that, when fully distributed, would have linked all local, state, and federal agencies together to access information on gun owners nationwide.

Passing the Brady Law did not stop Bill Clinton and the gun grabbers any more than British Prime Minister Chamberlain's appeasement of Hitler by inviting him to invade Czechoslovakia prevented World War II. Senator Bob Dole fits the Chamberlain mold well. The habit of offering a deal—"Here, you take only half of what I have instead of all of my investment"—for nothing in return and calling it a compromise has been a powerful self-deception throughout history. And such appeasement has always resulted in worse losses. Such compromise only whets the appetite of the aggressor.

Bob Dole had cut deals with the Democratic leadership of the Senate to allow the semi-auto ban to go through so as to focus on the Brady Bill. He capitulated again and did the same thing to let the Brady Bill through the Senate. Clinton and his allies had an agenda, and they pressed on relentlessly toward their goal of eventual civilian disarmament. Having already passed the House, once Brady got out of the Senate, the way was clear to push for the gun ban as well.

Clinton was able to get more than a gun ban as part of the 1994 Crime Bill. He also stole a march toward a national police force and a rape of the Fourth Amendment in the same bill. The Crime Bill, which banned nearly 200 specific guns from civilian possession if they were made after the effective date of the law in 1994, also banned magazines of over 10 rounds.

What a state of affairs. King George's troops sparked the start of our War for

Independence when General Gage's troops tried once too often (they had been at it for months) to confiscate colonial powder and arms. Only the government should have such weapons, it was argued. Is it not interesting that the same argument that was answered with lead 200 years ago has been met with a sporting smile in our age?

Even many gun owners bought Clinton's idea that guns are only legitimate if they are "suitable for sporting use." Thanks to the research of Jews for the Preservation of Firearms Ownership we know that this notion originated in Nazi Germany and was imported into our country in 1968 as part of Senator Tom Dodd's version of the Nazi law within his 1968 Gun Control Act. Actually, Hitler did not think that idea up all by himself. It was rooted in European history as a way of banning weapons to keep the peasants from hunting on the king's lands. Of course, the same bans also worked nicely to keep the peasants under control otherwise, say at tax time. In the tradition of European tyranny, Clinton and his allies made the same arguments that the people cannot be trusted with the means needed to keep the government from having a monopoly of force.

In the *Lopez* decision, the Supreme Court finally (after 50 years) admitted that it had been wildly unconstitutional to use the interstate commerce clause of Article I, Section 8 of the Constitution to regulate and ban guns. The court threw out the federal prohibition on possessing a gun within a 1,000 feet of a school, not on the grounds of public policy, but strictly because the Constitution does not give the federal government the authority to act in this area. Too bad the Republican Congress in 1995 did not take up on that idea, because they should have been repealing all the federal gun control laws. They could have started with the 1994 Crime Bill with its gun ban.

One of the shortcomings of the repeal of the semi-auto ban passed by the House was the refusal of Gingrich and the other House leaders to act on the version sponsored by Representative Steve Stockman (R-TX). Stockman's repeal bill would have not only done away with the ban on guns and magazines; it also would have checkmated the rest of the agenda Clinton had announced to *Rolling Stone,* namely, getting rid of as many gun dealers as possible. The 1994 Crime Bill, in effect, set the BATF up as the national zoning czar. It empowered the BATF to require dealers to show they have zoning variances to do business. Most of America's gun dealers have been part-timers operating at home. The Crime Bill does not seek to make Amway and Mary Kay dealers get proof of local zoning variances—just gun dealers. The result has been the reduction of the number of dealers from a high of nearly 290,000 in 1993 to 161,000 by April of this year.

Increasing fees, requiring photos and fingerprints, and the zoning hassle have served as additional disincentives for people to seek to be FFL's or to renew their licenses. Pressure on dealers has also come from an arbitrary regulation with no statutory authority (not to mention that there is no constitutional authority) to require burdensome paperwork of dealers operating at gun shows. If a dealer from out of state wishes to do business at a gun show, the BATF is now requiring him to sign over all of his show inventory to a local dealer at the beginning of a show. Then, after the show, the dealers must go through all of the same paperwork in reverse, minus any guns that were sold and transferred off the local dealer's books.

Heretofore, it was enough for an out-of-state dealer to take just the gun he was selling to a local dealer, transfer it to that dealer's books, and then have the local dealer transfer the gun to the buyer. Of course, if there were no unconstitutional licensing of dealers by the federal government (another Nazi idea), none of this hassle would take place. Clinton would object that he would then have no way of knowing who was buying a gun. The answer would be what I am sure our Founding Fathers might have replied, "That's the idea."

The Crime Bill also expanded the ability of police agencies to profit from forfeited property. Forfeiture is often a euphemism for government theft of private property. About 80 percent of the more than 50,000 property seizures every year have no charges filed. The property just goes into some police department's control, or is sold so they can buy military-style armament or whatever they desire. The Republicans have really been asleep at the switch to let Clinton grab such unconstitutional and dangerous power.

We are forgetting at our peril that almost no police powers are vested in the United States, these being reserved to the individual states. James Madison, architect of the Bill of Rights, pointed out that the Constitution delegated to the national government police powers only in the areas of counterfeiting, treason, piracy, and offenses against the laws of nations. Generally speaking, Madison stated that the powers of the United States are few and well-defined.

But Clinton was not interested in the Constitution. He was interested in aggrandizing his own power, and he was willing to use any shameless excuse to do so. For an example of this, one need look no farther than the explosion that rocked the Murrah Federal Building in Oklahoma City killing 169 men, women, and children. Clinton threatened the Republicans with a bucket of mud if they did not bend the knee before the President's demands that an Anti-Terrorism Bill be passed in response to the tragedy. Amazingly, the

Republicans gave him much of what he wanted—more money for the BATF, a study that will be used to justify the banning of hunting ammunition, and several due process violations that stripped the Fifth Amendment guarantee of that right.

One due process violation enacted into law in the Government Terror Bill was a standard-of-knowledge rule governing those selling explosives, meaning black and smokeless powder and probably ammunition, that will be a prosecutor's dream. Sellers can be convicted of a minimum mandatory sentence of five years if a jury can be convinced that they "should have known" that the buyer would commit a criminal act. How do you prove that you did not know? Putting the burden of proof on a defendant is to turn upside down our presumption of innocence until proven guilty.

Another violation of due process involves the virtual destruction of the Great Writ of Habeas Corpus. This is the right of judicial review, and even the power to free one convicted unjustly. Now, thanks to the passage of the Government Terror Bill, for practical purposes, a defendant will have to show that the trial court violated one of his constitutional rights in a wholly unreasonably unconstitutional manner in order to get an appeal heard. If a prosecutor withholds evidence that would have led to acquittal but was only 95 percent unreasonably unconstitutional, what's the big deal? Let the prisoner rot in jail, right? Well, consider that a lot of judges and prosecutors like convicting gun owners just because they are gun owners. Gun Owners of America has used habeas corpus lots of times to seek redress for the unjustly convicted. Probably no longer, though, thanks to King William I.

To fully appreciate what Clinton got in his Government Terror Bill's assault on the Great Writ, consider that habeas corpus dates back at least to the Battle of Runnymede in 1215 when the barons of England wrested the recognition of this right from King John. With a majority vote of our Congress, Bill Clinton was able to take back what King John was forced to give up.

But this is not all. Clinton actually delivered more than he promised to Sarah Brady's Handgun Control crowd in Congress. As a fan of what President George Bush referred to as the New World Order, Clinton has been seeking to turn over U.S. sovereignty to the U.N. and other international bodies. This has been from the beginning the dark side of NAFTA and GATT. These treaties have had the result of placing U.S. laws under the World Trade Organization and other international bodies' approval. When Cuba shot down two private planes full of U.S. citizens, there was strong sentiment to tighten the economic sanctions against Cuba. Nothing of the sort happened.

Why? Because Canada and the European Community warned the U.S. that they could not do that under GATT and NAFTA.

So, why is the U.S. continuing to participate in the U.N. Crime Commission? This group has called for the harmonization of world gun laws—meaning, dragging the U.S. down to the level of most of the rest of the world. The Japanese and Canadian governments are pushing for an international convention to disarm the U.S. the way they have disarmed their own people. Were the U.S. to ever sign such a convention, it would become the law of the land. Perhaps the scenario would be similar to how forced busing was imposed when the U.S. Courts made rulings and the politicians simply said, "Well, there is nothing we can do." Actually, there was plenty the Congress could have done. Under Article I Section 8, Congress could have withdrawn jurisdiction for busing cases from federal courts. Clinton could have easily pulled the same charade—sign up for U.N. gun control and then whine that there is nothing he can do since civilian disarmament would then be the law of the land. It is similar to the defense used by the guy that killed his parents and then pled for the court's mercy since he was an orphan.

All this happened in Clinton's first term in spite of what he admits was the heavy political price he paid for pushing gun control in 1993 and 1994. Clinton publicly acknowledged that gun control cost his party control of the Congress.

(Originally written for Soldier of Fortune magazine, 1996)

Instant Registration Check

The instant registration check is one of the worst things that has been done to the Second Amendment and to gun owners. This became law as part of the Brady Bill, having been designed to replace the waiting period after the first five years of the act. The waiting period was unconstitutional because it infringed on the people's right to keep and bear arms protected by the Second Amendment.

The waiting period encouraged local law enforcement agencies to convert our Second Amendment right into a privilege. A right does not exist if the government gets to give permission for us to exercise the right.

The instant registration check also converts a right into a privilege—both presume that the government should control the exercise of the right.

"But," gun control advocates will ask, "what about all the bad guys the Brady Law has kept from getting guns?" The answer is that those who are actually disqualified from owning a gun (less than half of those initially rejected) can easily get a gun elsewhere if they are intending to commit a crime.

The Brady Law has not lowered crime. Crime started to decline before the law went on the books. Armed citizens keep crime down, and making it legally easier for the average person to carry a concealed firearm must get a lot of the credit for our decline in crime.

Meanwhile, the instant background check not only converts a right into a privilege, it registers gun buyers at the same time—over 3,000,000 since the FBI started doing the checks. The FBI says they need to keep the names of gun buyers (who have broken no laws) for law-enforcement purposes.

What? Files on non-criminals? What paranoia! The FBI evidently thinks the same way Sarah Brady does—the civilian population cannot be trusted to keep and bear arms.

Am I being paranoid? What's wrong with registering gun owners? Ask those who bought an SKS sporter rifle in California at a store and had to register it. Now they are a crook if they did not hand it in by the end of last year. And the state of California has had plans to go door to door to get the more than 90% that were not turned in.

Isn't that a good reason to be against registration?

Trigger Locks

Those who want civilian disarmament—the true objective of gun control—tell us how dangerous it is to keep a gun in our house. We are told that locking up our safety is necessary to protect the children. Well, let's put this emotional argument into perspective. Of the 1,400 accidental firearms deaths in 1995, 200 were children under 15.

When you hear figures higher than 200, remember that the gang-banger age group is included—sometimes up to 22 or even 24 years old being considered a "child."

Also consider that 2,900 kids that same year were killed in motor vehicle crashes, 950 drowned, and more than 1,000 children died from fire and burns. Hundreds more children die in bicycle accidents every year than die from all types of firearms.

Well, the anti-self-defense crowd argues, cars and water have social benefits whereas guns are only made to kill.

Really? What about the 2.5 million people who use a gun each year in self-defense? That is not a social utility?

The Wall Street Journal reported last year that Beretta tested a "Saf-T-Lok" which caused 18 of 27 rounds to "totally malfunction." And when Handgun Control's chief attorney, Dennis Hennigan, attempted to demonstrate the same trigger lock at an HCI-sponsored event, he found, to his embarrassment that he was unable to disengage the lock.

Now, we might want to laugh at the egg on Mr. Hennigan's face, but it would have been no laughing matter if the trigger lock kept a homeowner from using his gun against an assailant.

Locking up our guns is a way to help criminals kill their victims. It is an insanity borrowed from Britain where cumbersome and eventually expensive storage requirements led many to give up their guns.

After all, most of us urban dwellers have little opportunity to hunt. And if a gun cannot be used for self-defense, why own one?

Atlanta Buy-Back Scheme:
Public Relations Only

Many so-called "gun control" efforts are nothing more than feel-good public relations schemes for which there isn't the slightest evidence that they work, which is to say that they do not reduce crimes committed with guns.

Take, for example, a recent "buy-back" program in Atlanta, Georgia, where the city, using private funds, would buy guns ($50 each, no limit on the number of guns bought) from anybody, no questions asked. In this particular program, which lasted four hours, 520 guns were purchased for a total cost of $26,000.

Now, the first thing wrong, and stupid, about such a program as this is that obviously—since no questions are asked—this is a financial incentive for people to steal guns, sell them, and make some quick cash, and, perhaps, a lot of cash since there was no limit on the number of guns the city would buy.

Was this possibility considered in Atlanta? It was not, according to Bonni Ware, Community Affairs Manager in the office of Mayor Bill Campbell who supervised this program. In an interview, when asked if buying guns with no questions asked might not be an incentive to steal guns, she says this possibility never occurred to her. "It did not. I guess any program you have could have some sort of improprieties."

At this point, Ware was asked why those who turned in firearms were not required to prove that they were, in fact, the real owners, as this would greatly reduce the likelihood that stolen weapons would be purchased. The idea of government officials running background checks on its citizens is certainly an idea that is repugnant to the Constitution. But as long as officials like Ms. Ware are conducting a buy-back program for guns—an idea that is also contrary to sound constitutional doctrine—why should they draw the line at a solution that might keep criminals from stealing guns and then cashing them in?

So, why wasn't such proof of ownership required before any gun was paid for? Ware says, "Because we don't want people to fear coming to City Hall to turn in their weapons and fear that they may be incarcerated for coming down."

Now, this is a truly amazing statement. Because what Ware is saying, in so many words, is that they wanted to protect any possible criminals who were turning in guns! She's saying that any such background check might have discovered that some turning weapons in were criminals who should be jailed. So, no such check was made.

It is, of course, highly doubtful that any criminals would be voluntarily giving up their guns, right? Right. And even Ware seems to agree. She says, "Maybe not. That's why they're criminals, because they don't obey the law." Exactly.

Still, Ware insists her program was an "overwhelming success." How so? Because, she says, there are 520 less guns on the streets of Atlanta "and this makes it less likely that people will be killed from dangerous weapons." But, more guns doesn't necessarily mean more crime. Besides, as Ware has said, they have no idea who exactly was selling the guns, much less whether these guns had been "on the street" or in homes.

When asked about the Second Amendment to the Constitution, the right of people to bear arms and defend themselves—particularly poor people in the inner city where the crime rate is high—Ware says, "Well, you know, we're hoping we can appeal to people's sense of trying to find other ways of solving their differences rather than using guns."

Great. But, what about this Constitutional right to have guns? Is she against people using guns in self-defense? She's already admitted that the crooks aren't turning in their guns. "I'm not in favor of guns, period," she replies. "I'm not an advocate of guns, period."

So, here we have it, at last. This is the real agenda of the gun-grabbers. They are against guns—all guns—period. And they couldn't care less about what our Constitution allows.

Clinton & Wesson Agreement

In 2000, the Clinton administration shocked the nation when it announced a historic agreement with the venerable firearms manufacturer, Smith & Wesson.

But if all you knew of the Clinton & Wesson agreement was what the mainline media told you, you would think that Smith & Wesson only agreed to require people to buy trigger locks with their guns.

Since they were already doing that, you might think that Smith was pretty clever.

As is often the case, the media version is far from the truth. The Clinton & Wesson agreement is a black-booted step toward the stomping out of the rule of law.

The Clinton & Wesson deal is actually a contract to be enforced by court order. It is a piece of unconstitutional legislation that never went before a legislature. It will result in tax monies being spent without legislative appropriation.

The Clinton & Wesson deal is taxation without representation. Ever hear that phrase before? Probably not if you're a recent graduate of a government school.

The Commission will be comprised of four bureaucrats and one industry representative. There is no information in the contract about how they will be chosen or financed. One thing is certain: Congress will have no say in the matter. And these folks will not be working as volunteers. But if there are any infractions of the yet-to-be determined edicts of the Commission, the violators can be put in jail for contempt of court.

The Clinton gun control agenda is enacted in this contract, and it will apply to ALL gun sales, not just sales of Smith products. There will be no sales at gun shows where there is still the freedom of private sales; no sales without a certificate of consumer training; no purchases of more than one handgun every two weeks; no sales of self-defense magazines above the politically correct number of 10 rounds; no sales of politically incorrect semi-automatic rifles and shotguns.

The dealers will have tremendous costs as well, including electronic security, huge safes, out-of-reach ammo displays, and more. If you were a dealer, would you submit to these terms? No wonder Smith & Wesson is being dropped like a hot rock by dealers.

Concerted action by dealers is an anti-trust law violation? Hardly. These are the spontaneous decisions of rational, freedom-loving Americans in the gun business.

Why not tell your dealer you want him to drop Smith and that you do not want to buy any gun from a dealer who has bowed the knee to a tyranny on a par with what George III attempted?

Boycott Smith & Wesson. Support the Constitution.

Clinton & Wesson Update

When Smith & Wesson capitulated to the Clinton administration and signed the gun control deal with Housing and Urban Development, the agreement reached well beyond the two parties.

It is important to boycott Smith, not just to send them a message but also to save the Second Amendment.

The Clinton & Wesson deal is a contract. As such, it cannot be reviewed by any court. But this contract is legislation that never went through a legislative process. Let us leave aside the fact that gun control is unconstitutional.

The Clinton & Wesson deal takes us right back to the days of King George III when our colonial forbearers cried out against taxation without representation. How so? Very simple.

The contract establishes an Oversight Commission to be staffed by four bureaucrats and one industry representative. Those bureaucrats will be paid by taxpayer funds not authorized by Congress or any other legislative body.

The Oversight Commission gets to enforce the broad and vague terms of the contract, but where the contract is vague, the Commission can invent its own specific regulations.

For instance, the Oversight Commission will establish what kind of a certificate of competence you must have before being allowed to buy a gun. Why not require you to be able to hit a bullseye with a snubby .38 at 100 yards? Or set a $500 fee for your competence testing? Any dealer who sells Smith & Wesson would have to impose that requirement on you no matter what kind of gun you bought through the Smith dealer.

The same broad sweep would affect all firearms sold by Smith dealers in the case of handgun sales—only one every two weeks will be allowed. If enough dealers come into the Clinton & Wesson gun control program, there is a built-in way to shut down virtually all gun sales in the country. Under the Clinton & Wesson deal, dealers may not transfer a gun until they hear back regarding the customer's background check.

Currently, the law allows a transfer after three days from the time of initiating the check. But if the FBI decides to shut down the whole process for an indefinite system overhaul, then no gun sales would be made through dealers subject to the Clinton & Wesson deal.

Fight for freedom. Boycott Smith & Wesson, and urge your Representatives to support Congressman John Hostetler's efforts to amend various spending bills to neuter the implementation of the Clinton & Wesson deal.

[*Hostetler was successful in attaching a rider to the defense department appropriation bill that prohibited the purchase of firearms on a non-competitive basis, that is on the basis of political correctness.*]

The Fraud of Gun "Buy-Backs"

Of all the ridiculous schemes put forth by the gun-grabbers, few are more expensive and fraudulent than the so-called "buy-back" scam where police departments pay people—usually with our hard-earned Federal tax dollars —to turn in weapons, no questions asked.

President Clinton was, of course, an enthusiastic supporter of this wrong-headed idea. Ditto, the lady who organized the Million Mom March. And now a "buy-back" has been held in Washington D.C.

A press release from the D.C. Metropolitan Police Department announces, proudly, that during its recent 3-day "buy-back," 1,787 firearms were purchased at a total cost of $141,000. Police Chief Charles H. Ramsey says this "buy-back" (an absurd name since his department is "buying-back" nothing; they never had these guns) will "significantly reduce" the likelihood that some minor disputes will escalate into shootings and homicides.

But even he admits in this release, "We will never know for certain just how many lives will be saved by getting these firearms off our streets and out of our homes."

Indeed. In fact, even the ultra-liberal, rabidly anti-gun, vehemently anti-Second Amendment *Washington Post* (19 May 2000) has run an article quoting experts as saying that "buy-backs" have had little impact on crime.

This article says, "Studies show that [surprise!] lawbreakers rarely surrender their weapons to buyback programs and that many people who do sell their guns have other firearms at home, or soon buy new ones."

The *Post* quotes Garen Wintemute, director of the anti-self defense Violence Prevention Research Program at the University of California at Davis as saying, in part, about "buy-backs", "The guns that are removed from the community do not resemble the guns used in crimes in that community. (*There has never been any effect on crime results seen*)." (Emphasis mine.) Still, the President's administration set aside $15 million to be thrown down the "buy-back" rat hole.

When we called the D.C. Police Department and asked spokesman Joe Gentile if he knew of any evidence that "buy-backs" actually reduced crime, and that we questioned the wisdom of this program, these were, obviously, not his favorite questions. Here's the way it went.

> Q: What evidence is there that these buy-backs have any
> impact as far as reducing crime?

A: Don't know. Gotta' check because I don't know if they've run all the guns through yet. One of the reasons we did it was to safeguard people, to get guns out of their houses, to prevent the possible death of someone during an argument or accidental discharge. This wasn't just to fight crime.

Q: But some of these buy-back studies show that those who do turn in guns don't turn in all of their guns. They still have a gun or guns at home.

A: They might not. We don't know. We don't know. But it's an opportunity to allow people to get rid of weapons that are lying around their house.

Q: But you don't really believe that criminals turn in their best gun or guns, do you?

A: I'm not saying that. I'm saying I can't tell you what's behind someone's door. So, I won't get into that ...

Q: Do the people turning in the guns you buy have to prove that they actually own the guns?

A: No.

Q: Then how do you know these guns came from anybody's house?

A: That's not the point. There are no questions asked.

Q: But, those who turned in guns could have stolen them.

A: Are you calling to get into a debate with me or to ask me a question?

Q: You just said that one purpose of your buy-back was to get guns out of the houses of some people. But, if you don't ask for proof of ownership, how do you know they brought the gun or guns from their home?

A: I didn't say where they were bringing the guns in from. Those are your words. I said *some* of these people don't want the weapons lying around in their homes.

Q: Right. But, I'm saying that, in actual fact, you don't know if *any* of the guns turned in were from *anybody's* home because you don't know, and don't ask, where they got the guns!

A: No, I don't.

Q: Why would no questions be asked? This would seem to be an incentive for people to steal guns and sell them to you.

A: Because that's the way the law is.

Well, now. If Gentile did check about "buy-backs" reducing crime, he never got back to us. But, incredibly, he is right about the law.

He sent us the text of a D.C. law (Firearms Control, 6-2375) which says that if a person voluntarily and peaceably delivers and abandons to the Chief any firearm, "such delivery shall preclude the arrest and prosecution of such a person...[and] no person who delivers and abandons a firearm...shall be required to furnish identification, photographs, or fingerprints."

Yikes! This is crazy!

Can you imagine any program nuttier than one in which guns are purchased —*no questions asked*—in a city full of violent criminals, and no one turning in a gun is asked to prove that he even owns the gun! This is truly insane!

Washington D.C. Mayor Anthony Williams says his town's "buy-back" program is another "important step" toward the goal of reducing "the scourge of gun violence." And Andrew Cuomo, Secretary Of Housing and Urban Development, says this "buy-back" will make Washington, D.C., "safer."

But, these assertions are hogwash. Instead of calling their "buy-back" program by the ludicrous name of "Operation Save A Life," it should be known as "Operation Lie To The People And Waste The Taxpayers' Money."

Finally, there is no answer from the "buy-back" crowd to those who could have been one of the nearly 7,000 people a day who use a gun in self-defense but could not—because they were scammed out of their safety or their life for a measly $50.

Brady Law Study: No Effect on Crime

An anti-gun researcher has produced an amazing (to him) finding. The Brady Law does not work. It has had no impact on crime. Jens Ludwig, a Georgetown University scholar, published this finding in the usually rabidly anti-gun *Journal of the American Medical Association* (itself led by anti-self-defense zealots).

Ludwig has been—at least until now—one of the academics that Handgun Control, Inc. liked to point to in an effort to put a scientific spin on their drive for gun confiscation.

Long before Ludwig's research, Dr. John Lott of Yale University Law School had convincingly proven that more guns means less crime. But the impact of Lott's research, although highly regarded by other academics, has been minimized by the media and the Congressional anti-self-defense crowd.

Ludwig's research—if honesty were in ample supply—would require even Sarah Brady to demand repeal of the Brady Law. But Sarah Brady wants to ban guns, as her continued support for the District of Columbia gun ban proves.

We cannot wait for Sarah Brady to admit that her law does not do what she says it will do. Let us be clear. The Brady Law does not, to use the Brady mantra, "keep guns out of the wrong hands."

We must demand of our lawmakers that they dismantle the entire Brady Law with its dreaded instant registration background check. Criminals get all the guns they want and the decent, peaceful citizens who buy guns through dealers are getting registered by the instant registration check computers maintained by the FBI in Clarksburg, WV.

All we will hear from the likes of Senators Feinstein, Schumer, and company is that we need to register guns and license owners. Since the Brady law does not work, we should find their agenda rather transparent.

The anti-self-defense crowd is not interested in reducing crime. That is only a smokescreen for finding out who has the guns, so the government can come and get them.

This has been the history of England, Australia, Canada, and New York City. The state of California is poised to do the same.

Does anybody really think that the rest of us are next?

Let the politicians know. No more Brady Law. No more instant check. No more gun registration.

Oops! The Trigger Lock Trap

The stampede was on in 2000. Gun locks. Trigger locks. They are good things. Politicians gave them away—using taxpayer funds, of course, and forced gun companies to sell them. Motherhood and apple pie! Well, not quite.

It turns out, even assuming trigger locks are a good thing—an assumption Gun Owners of America vigorously rejects—they don't work as intended! Government safety tests have found that all but two of 32 models of gun locks tested recently could be opened without a key according to a February 8 *Washington Post* report.

The Consumer Product Safety Commission (CPSC) found that the locks could be opened with paper clips, a pair of scissors or tweezers, or you could whack them on the table and they would open. Of course the other two could probably be opened rather quickly with a hammer and a screwdriver.

Now, Gun Owners of America thinks that the best gun lock is no lock, and the next best one is one that can be opened with paper clips, or a pair of scissors or tweezers, or a whack on the table. You might almost be able to get to your personal protection device before an assailant gets to you!

But here's the rub: a de facto gun ban. Happily, the CPSC is prohibited from regulating guns. But gun locks are considered accessories. As such, they can be regulated by these bureaucrats. Now if a federal law is passed—and some state laws have already been put on the books—requiring that some kind of gun lock be sold with a gun, the sale of guns can be banned if no suitable locks are available to be sold with the gun.

Meanwhile, Houston, Texas, announced a recall of thousands of gun locks it had distributed at taxpayer expense. The city offered no apologies for their role in endangering its citizens' safety. The National Shooting Sports Foundation also has a red face, having put forth about 400,000 of the bum locks. Hopefully the firearms community will leave the politicians to go it alone in such a misguided endeavor.

If one wants to prevent theft of a gun, a gun lock is a poor choice. To keep a gun from unauthorized use, hiding it well or using a safe is the way to go.

Gun Owners of America would plead with gun owners not to use trigger locks, especially for a gun the owner depends on for personal security. It is for sure that the assailant will not be so encumbered.

If trigger locks are widely used, expect the murder rate to go up.

Defense Department Blocked From Gun Confiscation

It's nice to be able to report a battle with a happy ending. Had we lost, the consequences would have been catastrophic. Defense Department authorization bills are not likely places to look for gun control, but that's where a monster gun grab had been tucked away.

Supposedly, the problem to be solved was an attempt to close the barn door after the horse was out. Namely, the Clinton administration allowed the sale of a fighter plane assembly line to the Communist regime of mainland China.

The solution involved using a wrecking ball to kill a bug. The Defense Department would have been authorized to confiscate and destroy any military surplus item that had ever been sold by the government.

They could have destroyed .45's, MI-A's, uniforms, ammo, scopes, antique planes, anti-aircraft guns in front of VFW posts, and much more. It was pretty sneaky, too, because the definition of munitions was not in the bill. Munitions were defined as the same as in the Export Import Act. GOA had to go there to find the list, and it is a long one.

Gun Owners of America put out e-mail and fax alerts asking our members to contact their congressmen and demand removal of this incredible gun grab. The bill had already passed both houses of Congress by huge margins (nobody reads the bills) and was in a conference committee to iron out differences.

One of the members of that committee, anti-gun Republican Senator John Warner of Virginia, was crucial. GOA mailed postcards to our members in the state urging them to put the heat on Warner. Two days after the mail went out, Warner's office called asking what was going on. We told them they were on the verge of angering not only gun owners but veterans as well. The message evidently got through.

Thanks to the tireless members of Gun Owners of America, who are always ready when called, Congress felt the heat. The Pearl Harbor attack on the Second Amendment was averted by the flood of calls and e-mail directed to Congress.

GOA Members Help Another
Senator "See the Light"

Senator Everett Dirksen was fond of saying, "When I feel the heat, I see the light." Dirksen's aphorism is still valid today. The latest validation of Dirksen's connection of vision and heat occurred in Utah.

Senator Orrin Hatch was not pleased to have his vision corrected, but Utah gun owners applied a tremendous amount of heat and greatly improved the Senator's eyesight.

GOA members are familiar with Sen. Hatch's increasing embrace of gun control.

During the last Congress, Hatch was forced to drop several anti-gun provisions from his crime bill after GOA activists flooded the Senate with thousands upon thousands of postcards, thus encouraging seven Senate co-sponsors to remove their names from his bill.

Hatch reintroduced his juvenile crime bill (S. 254) in 2000 and brought it before the Senate right after the Colorado shooting. Not surprisingly, his bill was loaded down on the Senate floor with several anti-gun provisions—many of which had Hatch's support.

For example, S. 254 would now put gun shows out of business by setting promoters up for jail terms and loss of their property if even one attendee was not notified of his responsibilities under the Brady Law.

Of course, the object is either to stop gun shows altogether or to eliminate firearms transactions the government has not registered, which is what happens when people buy guns through dealers.

Hatch's bill would also require the sale of trigger locks, even though they are the same as locking up your safety. Trigger locks might also be known as Home Invader Protection Devices.

In addition, S. 254 would ban the importation of self-defense magazines of over 10 rounds and prohibit people under 21 from having semi-automatic rifles and shotguns.

Despite the anti-gun provisions included in the bill, Hatch voted for it in May of 1999. But more than that, he voted to break Senator Smith's filibuster of the anti-gun crime bill two months later.

GOA Keeps Utah Citizens Up To Date on Hatch's Voting Record

GOA informed its Utah members of Hatch's increasingly anti-self-defense voting record. We also mailed this information to key Republican activists and those who had been delegates in past Utah State Republican conventions.

Hatch's support for all but two of Clinton's judicial nominees, some of whom have been flaming anti-self-defense candidates, was also made available to convention delegates in Utah.

The Senator responded in a very predictable fashion typical of most politicians when they are confronted by voters who are unhappy with their record in office. He first tried to charm convention delegates, even phoning them individually. One GOA member was kept on the phone so long by the Senator that she finally had to say goodbye and hang up in order to catch up with her domestic responsibilities.

Next Hatch tried to "shoot the messenger."

Hatch was quite critical of Gun Owners of America, perhaps thinking he could get away with attacking us since GOA was the only national gun group to hold him accountable. (Thankfully, some local gun groups were equally involved in keeping the heat on the Senator.) When shooting the messenger did not work, Sen. Hatch tried re-inventing his record. After all, Al Gore re-invents things all the time, so why shouldn't others get in on the fun?

Hatch and Other Gun Compromisers Get Booed at Conventions

At one county convention held a week before the May 6 state convention, many delegates gave the Senator a very unfriendly welcome. This was not uncommon in other such meetings. The state convention was not a happy day for the Republican establishment in Utah.

All of their statewide candidates were booed and heckled when they addressed the assembly. Governor Leavitt, who had convened a special session of the state legislature just to ram through gun control (happily he was largely unsuccessful), was not able to finish his speech because of the loud booing.

Senator Hatch was barely able to avoid a primary by getting just one percent more than the 60 percent required of the convention vote. Governor Leavitt did not fare so well, being forced into a primary with pro-gun Glen Davis. And Mark Shurtleff, the establishment Attorney General candidate, did not even quite get a majority and was forced into a primary with Frank Mylar who is pro-self-defense.

The experience shook the Utah Republican establishment as if they had had a near-death experience.

Senate Leaders Pressing for Gun Vote

Since the convention, Senator Hatch has publicly stated that he has been resisting pressure from Senate Majority Leader Trent Lott (R-MS) and Assistant Majority Leader Don Nichols (R-OK) to pass the bill and get it off the agenda well before the elections.

Lott and Nichols are talking the same way Senator Bob Dole did when he was the Majority Leader: "Let's get this issue behind us."

But Hatch has stated that he will not allow his bill to move out of the conference committee where it is now stuck unless all the gun control provisions are removed. And that from the man who voted for almost all of them!

The entire country owes a debt of thanks to Utah gun owners. They took the time to become delegates to the Republican convention, and they made a difference.

And we at GOA also want to thank the members who supported the GOA Political Victory Fund to enable us to be politically active in Utah.

And while thanks are being properly extended, I want to thank all the GOA members who sent in their post cards during the three-year battle against the Juvenile Justice bill. The seven senators that bailed out from sponsorship of Hatch's bill in 1998 felt enough heat from you that they saw the light.

So, the next time you are a little tired and wonder, "What's the use of sending in another postcard, or e-mail, or making another phone call?" please remember the Utah Republican state convention where another chapter in vision restoration through heat application was written.

Nix Project Exile

How did the defenders of the Second Amendment get into the business of calling for enforcement of gun laws to control street crime? After all, we opposed the passage of all the federal gun laws now on the books because they are all unconstitutional.

It is beginning to look as if state legislators have set gun owners up for walking into the indefensible position of calling for the enforcement of federal gun laws that should not be on the books. States have the exclusive jurisdiction over street and domestic crime. It is the failure of states to install judges who are tough on violent criminals that needs criticism. We should not be asking President Clinton and Janet Reno to do a job they have no authority to carry out.

What are we going to say when a teacher is convicted of having a gun for self-defense at a school—a federal felony? Should we call for the incarceration of Joel Myrick, then, of Pearl, Mississippi, for having pulled his gun from his truck to stop the killer's rampage?

Do we really want to incarcerate fathers for giving a handgun to their sons in another state without going through the federal registration process via a gun dealer? These are both federal felonies.

Do we really want to call for Bill Clinton to handle those cases with zero tolerance?

Let's take a deep breath and go back a step or two. Let's look at England. Guns were registered for decades. Virtually all of them were confiscated two years ago. England now has 3,000,000 illegal guns in the hands of criminals —on an island! What has happened to the violent crime rate? It has now surpassed that of the United States. And England's murder rate is also on the rise.

Forcing people to be checked out by the government before they buy a gun is not going to keep criminals from getting a gun. A gun ban in England has not kept criminals from stocking up, so what makes us think a Brady instant check in the U.S. will get any better compliance than a ban in England?

For that matter, the handgun bans in Chicago and Washington have also led to skyrocketing crime rates. Imagine that, criminals on both sides of the Atlantic behave the same. Disarm the victims, and the criminals are more vicious than ever before.

The problem is not that Clinton has failed to enforce the unconstitutional gun laws currently on the books. Let us hope he never does.

The problem is that Clinton wants to take away guns from the civilian population. Clinton is for victim disarmament. That is the issue. Dead, disarmed victims. The issue should not be Project Exile.

Instead of Project Exile, let's have Project Repeal—of *existing* gun laws. Let's have Project Victim Rearmament.

Gun control kills. Guns save lives.

Project Exile:
Do We Really Want to Enforce These Laws?

Project Exile has been heralded as the way to do something about crime without succumbing to demands for more gun control. Project Exile legislation recently swept through the U.S. House of Representatives by a vote of 358 to 60.

I believe that 358 Representatives voted wrong.

Project Exile is not going to decrease the demand for gun control. It is a call for zero tolerance and five-year prison terms in the enforcement of existing gun control laws.

Here are some existing illegal gun-related activities:

- Attaching a 2 or more round extension to a post-ban Glock pistol magazine.

- Attaching a flash suppresser, folding stock, or bayonet lug to certain household firearms.

- Accidentally carrying or possessing a weapon (with or without a state license) into a federally prohibited area, such as near a school.

- Driving to another state to give a family member a handgun without going through the instant check registration scheme.

- Possessing a gun while subject to a restraining order, regardless of the absence of violence, and without a trial or any legal adversarial process having taken place.

- Committing any minor infraction of any unconstitutional federal gun law.

Two very well known cases of the zero tolerance-type approach embodied in Project Exile are Ruby Ridge and Waco. At Ruby Ridge, federal agents killed a boy and a mom holding a baby. They came down on the Weaver family because Randy had sawed off a shotgun 1/4 inch under the federal limit. And the jury found that Weaver sawed it off because a federal agent persuaded him to do so, and thus was not guilty.

At Waco, 85 church members were killed over the possibility of a non-registered machine gun on the premises. All that carnage was based on federal records that the head of the records department admits are wrong 50 percent of the time.

Project Exile also represents a transfer of street crime jurisdiction to the federal government even though the Founders very clearly intended for it to be excluded from federal control. The Project Exile bill gives money to states which agree to meet federal standards or turn their jurisdiction over to the federal government.

Rather than Project Exile, how about a zero-tolerance for all Second Amendment infringements? Let's have Project Repeal of *all* federal gun control.

Exile Project Exile

Project Exile is a crime-fighting tool that is proving to be a cure worse than the disease.

The disease, as it were, is soft-on-crime judges in the various states. Project Exile assumes that the cure is to prosecute criminals in federal courts and incarcerate them in federal jails because there are fewer protections of the rights of defendants in federal courts, and the sentences are tougher.

The cure should be to get rid of criminal-coddling judges at the state level. It is unconstitutional to try criminal cases at the federal level because the constitution gives no such authority to the federal government.

It is doubly unconstitutional to be calling for enforcement of federal gun laws which are all unconstitutional. For gun owners to call for such prosecutions is self-destructive.

The unintended consequences of Project Exile are becoming apparent, and they are horrible. One example from Arizona should by itself convince every gun owner—indeed every freedom-loving American—to call for the exiling of Project Exile.

Jerry Michel's Specialty Firearms in Mesa, Arizona, was raided on October 25 by a multi-jurisdictional task force of local police and the BATF. He was accused of not having complied with local zoning requirements and not having taken out a $100 license for being a second-hand dealer. The affidavit for the search warrant also alleged straw purchases had been made by Michel, something he adamantly denies.

The agents threw his guns into trash barrels, damaging many by this negligent practice. Several of the guns were collectors' items, and one was taken unfired from the box it came in and hurled into a barrel.

The BATF was unconstitutionally given jurisdiction for whacking gun dealers for "violations" of local zoning requirements by the Clinton-Gore gun ban of 1994. In effect, the BATF was made the national zoning and business-licensing agency for firearms dealers.

Thousands of dollars of damages were incurred by a pack of criminals posing as police agents. No charges have been filed, but Michel is out of business—his inventory is gone, and that means his life investment is, too.

The next time you hear a gun owner call for the zero tolerance enforcement of federal gun laws, ask him or her if they are glad Project Exile was used to wipe out Jerry Michel's livelihood.

Project Exile: No Impact on Crime

The big reason for supporting the enforcement of federal gun laws (all of which the gun lobby opposed) called for by supporters of Project Exile is to lower crime and take the "oomph" out of gun control. It turns out that the data do not support the claims of Exile supporters.

Richmond, Virginia, was the flagship city for Project Exile. It was launched in 1997. The trouble is crime went up that year, according to FBI crime records. A review of Richmond's murder record shows that the murder rate did start dropping in 1995 and 1996 and resumed the downward trend in 1998.

What happened in 1995? Virginia's concealed carry law was vastly improved in that year, forcing judges to issue concealed handgun carry permits to applicants unless they could prove they were criminals, insane, fugitives from justice, or drug abusers.

Philadelphia is another city that followed suit in 1999, kicking off their Project Exile program with much ballyhoo. What did the crime rate do that year? It went down. A review of Philadelphia's murder statistics shows that the murder rate started declining in 1997 and 1998.

Exile can hardly take credit for either the Philadelphia or the Richmond decline.

What happened in Philadelphia in 1997? It was the first year that the anti-gun politicians of the city were forced to comply and come under the "shall issue" concealed carry law as in the rest of the state (and in Virginia).

Dr. John Lott has shown from his massive 18-year study of all the jurisdictions in the U.S. that crime rates are only impacted by concealed carry laws. Namely, the easier it is for citizens to legally carry what they have a constitutional right to bear anyway, the lower the violent crime rates. Or, as Lott put it in his book title, *More Guns, Less Crime.*

Supporters of Project Exile (or its sequel, Project Safe Neighborhoods) would better spend their time working for reforms in the nation's concealed carry laws rather than enforcing laws that not only are unconstitutional but also have nothing to do with fighting crime.

Gun owners certainly do not want to unleash more federal gun prosecutors (as called for in Project Safe Neighborhoods) with the attitude of U.S. Attorney James Comey as reported in the May 21, 2001 edition of *U.S. News & World Report:* "[G]un possession itself is a crime of violence."

Crime will go down when more good guys are packing on the streets. The criminals already are carrying concealed. It's time for the rest of us to follow suit.

Section Six

SELF-DEFENSE

Let People Choose How to Protect Themselves

It's been said the definition of a fool is one that redoubles his efforts, even when his methods have proven ineffective. Such foolishness has plagued the gun control debate.

Despite the failure of gun bans in Washington D.C., New York City, and other places, gun haters continue to call for more and more restrictions. But there is a silver lining in all of this madness. Congress is currently revisiting the ban on more than 180 types of semi-automatic firearms. And it should. The law must be repealed.

The statistics certainly tell us that so-called assault weapons are not the criminals' weapon of choice. The Bureau of Justice Statistics reports that violent criminals only carry or use a "military-type gun" in about one percent of the crimes nationwide.

And according to the FBI, people have a much greater chance of being killed by a knife or a blunt object than by any kind of rifle, including an "assault rifle." In Chicago, the chance is 67 times greater. That is, a person is 67 times more likely to be stabbed or beaten to death in Chicago than to be murdered by an "assault rifle."

One can't have it both ways. If we want to ban truly dangerous weapons, then we should start by banning knives and baseball bats. But why, the skeptics ask, would someone need an "assault weapon?" Surely, one doesn't need such a gun to hunt deer.

First of all, the Second Amendment was never about hunting deer or any other game. To quote a U.S. Senate Subcommittee report from 1982, the purpose of the Second Amendment was "to create an armed citizenry... considered essential to ward off tyranny."

Those who think that the government could never act in an excessive fashion only need to look to Waco, Texas, and Ruby Ridge, Idaho—to name just a couple of instances. The armed assaults by government agents against law-abiding, non-violent citizens in both places resulted in dead women and children and the subsequent attempts by officials to cover-up their actions.

Secondly, semi-automatics are especially good for women and for those who must defend themselves against multiple offenders. Consider the testimonies of two citizens who appeared before a House Judiciary Subcommittee in March:

- Sharon Ramboz is a small, frail woman who hardly looks anything like a "Rambo." Nevertheless, she chose to defend her three young children one morning with a Colt AR-15 rifle—a firearm covered by the 1994 gun ban.

  Ms. Ramboz stated that she chose this gun because, unlike a shotgun, the kick of the AR-15 when fired is not overpowering for a woman of her stature. Happily, she reported that the mere presence of her gun was enough to "send multiple perpetrators scurrying" without a shot even being fired.

- Gary Baker is a jewelry store owner in Virginia. He and his employees were forced to defend themselves against two offenders last December. Both attackers were career criminals—one was on parole while the other was wanted by the FBI. In defending their store, Mr. Baker and his workers spent 35 rounds of ammunition before the thugs finally put down their weapons.

  "If I was the only person responsible for defending my employees or even myself, I would never have had enough ammunition with a five-shot revolver," Baker said. "I would have needed a semi-automatic firearm and several high capacity magazines."

  Clearly, one does not have to be a jewelry store owner to find multiple offenders threatening one's life. Riots and natural disasters typically bring out roving gangs which terrorize unarmed citizens who simply rely on police. Unfortunately, the "thin blue line" is usually overwhelmed during such emergencies.

  Mr. Baker's point should be well taken. The police are rarely present during the commission of a violent crime. Thus, one needs to be adequately prepared. But if one must face multiple opponents, one needs a gun that shoots more than just five or six bullets.

  The ban imposed by Congress will only work to disarm decent Americans. Criminals should not be expected to obey a gun ban any more than they obey a drug ban. Congress should repeal the semi-auto ban and allow law-abiding Americans to decide how they want to protect themselves. After all, it's Congress' job to protect people's rights, not to decide what Americans do or don't need.

Stephanie Kuhen's Murder Could Have Been Prevented

Three-year-old Stephanie Kuhen came to a violent end when the car in which she was riding inadvertently turned into a dead end in a Los Angeles ghetto. Seconds later, the gangs who rule that neighborhood riddled the car with bullets, killing Stephanie and wounding her brother and the driver.

The tragedy goes well beyond the senseless murder of Stephanie Kuhen. The street was unofficially known as the "Street of Killers." Neighbors for a long time have lived barricaded in their homes, trying to escape the terror of the gangs.

The police do not have the manpower to protect the residents of the Street of Killers, nor to make many other similar areas safe. Is the solution to get more police on duty? Not with the budget constraints most localities are looking at. Usually the localities that have the most violent conditions have a declining tax base that makes increased police manpower highly unlikely.

There is a way out, although it will not be willingly chosen by most of the rulers in America's cities where they have worked to disarm the civilian population. There has been one notable exception, however: Maurice Turner. When he was Chief of Police in Washington, D.C., he decided that the people could not continue to be a spectator in the battle to make the city safe.

Chief Turner decided to reach out to the decent people of the "Streets of Killers" in Washington, D.C. He put a number of men through the police academy, giving them the very same instruction that a sworn officer would have—including firearms training. His intention was to provide an armed volunteer police auxiliary to work alongside of the paid officers. The volunteers would be the eyes and ears for the regular force, making it much more likely that the good guys could be sorted out from the bad guys.

Without the means to protect themselves, few have been willing to work with the police in Washington D.C. After all, who will protect the citizens after the squad cars leave the neighborhoods and the regular officers return to their own homes?

When the D.C. City Council heard that Chief Turner was going to graduate his first class, they held an emergency session and passed an emergency ordinance prohibiting the auxiliaries from having firearms. Naturally, the program fell flat and the D.C. crime rate continued climbing to new heights.

In the mid-eighties I had the opportunity to travel to Guatemala and the Philippines. In both countries I had a chance to see the success of programs rather similar to what Chief Turner had hoped to implement in our nation's capital.

Both Guatemala and the Philippines had nearly succumbed to guerrilla insurgencies. The guerrillas were seemingly able to win over the hearts of the people with acts of social service. But soon, the guerrillas were collecting taxes from the people, and the trap was sprung. With their tentacles surrounding every aspect of the people's lives—and with a monopoly of guns—the guerrillas gained control. The military governments got the impression that the people supported the guerrillas, not realizing that an unarmed and unorganized people had no choice. As a result the government response was terrible, and in Guatemala it amounted to genocide.

But in 1982, General Rios Montt emerged as the head of a military junta ruling the country. He opted for a radical policy—treat the Indian populations of the country's interior as people. He armed and organized them. All of a sudden the identity between the guerrillas and the people was broken. Within six months, the guerrilla threat was reduced to a problem of occasional banditry.

A similar result followed the downfall of the corrupt Marcos dictatorship in the Philippines. The government could not protect the people from the guerrilla scourge, so the people armed themselves through the underground gun market in the country and formed their own militias. Happily, the military leaders quickly saw the benefit of working with the people, rather than trying to disarm them.

In both countries, the people were emboldened to cooperate with the establishment once they were able to protect themselves from retribution of the guerrillas. Maurice Turner had the same hope for Washington, D.C., but the politicians were inflexibly wedded to the idea that disarmament brings peace.

America needs to learn the lesson that Guatemala and the Philippines learned —that only with an armed people is there victory over the criminal element.

Self-Defense Defended—On National Television!

Well, now. This is news! And good news, too. I mean, how often do you see anybody on national TV actually making sense when they talk about guns?

Right. Hardly ever. But, on ABC's *Politically Incorrect* program (11/3/1999), comedienne Vicki Lawrence and television's Judge Joe Brown had many common sense things to say about owning firearms. Judge Brown was raised in one of the toughest neighborhoods in South Central Los Angeles. He graduated with top honors from UCLA's Law School.

On this program, discussing the most recent workplace shootings in Hawaii by a man who legally owned the guns he used, Lawrence adamantly opposed taking guns away from responsible citizens saying, "You're not gonna ever get them off the streets. You're not gonna get them away from the gangs. You're not gonna do that. So, why are you gonna take them away from me?"

When the host of the show, Bill Maher, disputed the notion that victims of gun crime would have been safer if they had been armed, Judge Brown, said, "Well, let's put it this way. I tell you what. I would have felt a lot better if when (in Hawaii), somebody walked in and said, 'All right, this is going down. I'm going to blow you away,' that somebody else (armed) would have been able to say, 'Well, you know, make my day. I got my stuff. Let's see if it works.' See, that way you're not holding your butt in your hand. You got something else showing."

When another guest on the program suggested that the shooter in Hawaii should have been legally limited to only two guns (instead of the 17 he reportedly owned), Judge Brown said, to applause from the audience: "I mean, what difference does it make? If he had one or two, he could have done the same damage, but if you had your own, you could have stopped it. You want to give Big Brother more authority than he's already got? Goodness!"

When guest Peter Frampton, the rock-and-roll guitarist from England, said it is "ridiculous" to advocate that teachers in our public schools be armed, Judge Brown said, "Tell you what, down in Arkansas a few years ago, some kid went amok with a pistol, and he started shooting the school up. The principal went out, got his .45 out of the trunk, drew down on the kid, he threw the gun down, [and this] stopped the tragedy. "Now see, I've noticed this. I'll tell you as a criminal court judge, when you've got armed citizens, the crime drops."

What Judge Brown is alluding to—though his geography is a little off—is a

1997 shooting in Pearl, Mississippi, where Luke Woodham shot two students to death and wounded seven others at Pearl High School. During this carnage, Assistant Principal Joel Myrick got a handgun from his truck, blocked the road as Woodham was on his way to kill some other students, and ordered him to the ground at gunpoint until police arrived. Myrick has said he has no doubt Woodham would have killed more people if he had not been stopped since he had 36 rounds of ammo in his pocket when he was finally subdued.

Referring to the slaughter at Columbine High in Colorado, Lawrence said, "Okay, let's talk about teachers. What if somebody had had a gun at Columbine? Could they not have shot those guys instead of getting on a cell phone?...I ain't going into a public school unless I'm armed and dangerous."

So, let's hear it for Vicki Lawrence and Judge Joe Brown—two of our citizens who are not afraid to defend our Second Amendment rights. And on national television, too. What a breath of fresh air.

Israeli War Veteran Nearly Killed
by Chicago Gun Control

Born in America, Hillel Goldstein's family moved to Israel just in time for the Yom Kippur war in 1973. In 1983, Goldstein was drafted into the Israel Defense Forces, or IDF. He served in a combat unit for three years, seeing action in southern Lebanon.

Upon arrival in Israel, Goldstein had been surprised to see gun-toting men and women walking around all over Israel. By 1983, his M-16 service rifle was merely an extension of his own arms.

Back in the United States in 1986, Goldstein readjusted to the who-needs-a-gun view that is all too prevalent here. Worse still, he took up residence in one of the world's largest legislated gun free zones—the city of Chicago.

On July 2, 1999, Goldstein was on his way back from Friday evening worship at his local synagogue. He was quite conspicuous in his Sabbath garb. He was all too easy to spot for Ben Smith, a neo-Nazi on a private mission to kill blacks and Jews. Smith went on to kill several people before committing suicide and saving the state the expense of executing him.

Goldstein became one of his victims, taking five shots to his torso and arm. His time in the hospital was educational as well as therapeutic.

Goldstein did not respond to the media inquiries right away, spending the time to think through why a non-soldier should also have a gun. When he decided the issue affirmatively, he found that the media dropped him like a hot rock. So did many of his friends who mindlessly assured Goldstein that we don't need guns because we have the police to protect us.

That argument seemed to Goldstein as full of holes as his own body had been after Smith's attack.

Goldstein argues forcefully that self-defense is a biblical doctrine found in the book of Leviticus among other parts of Scripture. Those interested in this subject can find a piece I have done called, *"What the Bible Has to Say About Gun Control"* on the GOA web page at *http://www.gunowners.org* in the "Fact Sheets" section.

Goldstein has by now remedied his inability to protect himself and his family. He has procured firearms and reacquainted himself with their use.

He has also been given a life membership in Gun Owners of America.

Safe Streets and Cities

I suspect that most of you have heard of some city announcing a gun "buy-back" scheme to "get guns off the streets."

Well, of course, I agree that we do not want guns on the streets. We want them in the pockets and purses of the decent people of our country who otherwise, without the ability to defend themselves, are more likely to be victims of crime.

And before I go any further, let us be clear about the word game involved in the term "buy-back." How can a unit of government buy back something it has never owned? If we are not careful, these politicians will go from buying guns back to just taking them back. After all, we are saying that guns ultimately belong to the government if we accept the implication of "gun buy-backs."

This was one of the talking points I discussed with Memphis Councilman Brent Taylor when he called to discuss the gun buy back program his fellow councilmen had voted to kick off on Mother's Day.

Similar to other gun grabbers, the Memphis City Council, save one—Brent Taylor—wants to get guns off the streets. They assume that this will make crime go down, since they believe any gun out of circulation has to result in less crime.

The problem with the Memphis Council's collective logic is that the guns they would like to see out of circulation are never going to get surrendered. The criminals will hang on to their pieces no matter what is the law. Really.

In order to encourage citizens to carry guns on the street, Gun Owners of America launched a pilot project in Memphis. The Safe Streets and Cities Fund is being tested there to see how many people will take the training required to get a concealed carry permit in Tennessee. Major establishments that provide the training are getting the word out that a rebate of up to $50 is available for those taking the training course.

Let's hope that in the months ahead the balance of power will shift away from the criminals and toward their potential victims. Maybe someday a municipality will see the need for an armed citizenry. Then, rather than trying to scam the people's guns out of their hands, they will erect a sign like the one in my dreams:

"Welcome to Memphis. Thank you for packing."

Texas Concealed Carry Handgun Owners

It's bad enough that Handgun Control, Inc. has no facts to back up their claims for the gun control they want passed into law, but they also take data that supports gun ownership and twist it beyond recognition!

HCI put out a press release entitled "License to Kill," a play on the term "License to Carry Concealed." "License to Kill" claims that the 3,370 license-holders who were arrested for a crime means that license holders are 66% more likely to commit a crime than are non-license holders.

Here are the real numbers. There were 3,679 arrested among license-holders in Texas over a four-year period. The yearly average comes to 671 per 100,000 Texans. That compares to 9,508 per 100,000 arrests for all crimes per year among the rest of the population. In other words, non-licensees get arrested 14 times more than licensed gun packers.

By the way, getting arrested does not establish guilt. More than half of those arrested are acquitted. Also, about a quarter of the arrests are on felony charges, the rest for misdemeanors.

And how many murders, attempted murders, and manslaughters were committed by this group? Three—in four years. That's a license to kill? We should have such a crime wave in Washington, D.C. where guns are banned —or in Chicago, or L.A.

The only way I can explain the "66% more likely" number is this: HCI is 66% more likely to get it wrong than just about anybody else.

The Social Costs of Not Owning Guns

The steady barrage of fear-based propaganda against private gun ownership would have us conclude that we would all be better off if we got rid of our guns.

They want us to believe that we are many times more likely to be harmed with our own gun than to kill a home invader. Some of the anti-self-defense crowd appear to actually believe that an act of self-defense has not occurred unless the perpetrator has been killed.

In the real world, almost all self-defense uses of firearms do not involve firing a shot. Research by award-winning Florida State University criminologist Dr. Gary Kleck has found that we are 2.5 times more likely to be injured when we offer no resistance than if we use a gun against an attacker.

Another line of attack has been to point to all the health care and welfare costs engendered by taking care of the victims of criminals who use guns. Not only are those costs grossly exaggerated, the research of Dr. John Lott, now of the Yale University Law School, has shown that gun control has actually increased crime.

Not only do gun owners have nothing to apologize for, truth be told, those who have all the explaining to do are those politicians who have disarmed victims and thus made the criminals' job environment safer.

It is where armed gun owners are able to legally exercise their constitutional right that violent crime rates are lower. This automatically lowers health care costs because there are fewer wounded or dead victims and criminals alike.

Moreover, as crime goes down, there is less need for the police, thus allowing smaller police forces. This could result in huge savings in the anti-gun cities which have the highest murder and violent crime rates.

So, the most compassionate policy, the one designed to save social expenditures on health, welfare, and police, is to repeal gun bans, repeal gun free zones, repeal restrictions on people carrying concealed firearms, and in every other way make it so that the good guys can walk and drive and study and worship securely.

A Tale of Two Cities

It's a cautionary tale—or should be—of two cities. In one city, Wakefield, Massachusetts, it was the worst of times because only the bad guy mass murderer had the guns. But, in the other city, New York, it was the best of times since a good guy also had a gun, knew how to use it and, because of this, the bad guys are dead.

Describing what happened when seven employees of an Internet consulting company were murdered in cold blood, Middlesex County (MA) District Attorney Martha Coakley said: "There is an enormous amount of bullets and casings in the building. There was an enormous amount of fire power that occurred in that building today."

The *Washington Post* said that what happened was a "slaughter." And a surviving co-worker of the employees who were massacred lamented the fact that she was unable to do something "for the people who were there and couldn't get out of the way."

Meanwhile, in the other city, the Big Apple, things turned out quite differently.

Off duty but armed on Christmas Eve, Detective Michael Zeller went to the Two Flag Deli Grocery in Brooklyn. Zeller was accompanied by his wife, Marie, their three-year-old daughter, and a two-month-old son. They were going to pick up Mrs. Zeller's mother, who owns the deli.

It was just about closing time when Jonathan Lynch walked in and asked for a sandwich. Marie Zeller, who was closing up while her Mom left to get her bags from her nearby apartment, said, sure, she'd make him a sandwich.

But, as the New York *Daily News* reports it, the Zellers became suspicious when Lynch said he wanted to go outside and ask a friend if he also wanted a sandwich. The Zellers watched Lynch chat with his friend, who stood near the open trunk of a parked car.

Michael Zeller studied the two men but dismissed any distrust, telling his wife things looked okay. But, to be sure, he walked outside to take another look. Seconds later, when he headed back into the store, he was staring down the barrel of a .22 caliber revolver pointed at his head. As the first robber ordered the husband to lie on the floor, the second robber held a knife to Marie Zeller's throat, forcing her to empty a cash register.

Suddenly, the Zeller's three-year-old daughter Devin, who was at her Mom's side, ran from behind the counter and screamed, "Leave my Daddy alone."

Daddy yelled to Devin, "Go back." Startled, the robber gunman briefly took his eyes off of Michael Zeller—a big mistake.

Reaching into his waistband, Zeller pulled out his 9mm Glock pistol and squeezed off five shots. The first two bullets struck the 6-foot, 240-pound James Culbertson in the chest, mortally wounding him. Another shot ripped into the lungs of the 6-foot, 170-pound knife-wielder Lynch, who died at the scene.

Both of the two dead robbers had long criminal records. Police said Lynch's record dated back to 1986 with arrests for assault, grand larceny, and armed robbery. Culbertson had been arrested seven times, but six arrests were sealed, apparently because he was a juvenile at the time. In 1999, he was arrested in Queens for robbery and possession of stolen property but was allowed to plead guilty to a reduced charge of disorderly conduct and sentenced to "community service."

I say that all of this is a cautionary tale—or ought to be—of two cities. So what exactly do I mean? Well, in his novel, *A Tale Of Two Cities,* Charles Dickens notes, at the beginning, that he writes of a time when, "It was the age of wisdom, it was the age of foolishness." And so it is in our time regarding guns.

Over and over, *ad nauseam,* we are told foolishly by the anti gun nuts that guns are the focus of all evil in the world, that they must be banned, that concealed weapons always do more harm than good...blah, blah, blah.

This is a lie.

If just one employee at that Wakefield, Massachusetts Internet consulting firm had possessed a gun on the job and knew how to use it, there's at least an even chance there would have been no slaughter. But, a slaughter is what always occurs when only the murderer has guns and his victims do not.

We must be wise and allow our citizens to keep and bear arms because the lives of innocent people, literally, depend on this right.

It Matters Where You Live

Many people are familiar with the work of Dr. John Lott. His massive research of our country's crime data encompassed all 3,000 plus counties for an 18-year period.

Lott presented his work in a book entitled *More Guns, Less Crime*. His work has been subsequently corroborated by researchers in nearly four dozen of our country's institutions of higher learning.

Lott's work has been corroborated by Al Gore. Actually, George W. Bush also helped.

Most people have probably seen the map of the country's voting by counties. The one most of us saw showed the Bush counties in red and the Gore counties in blue. The Gore vote was primarily along both coasts as well as other urban pockets in the rest of the country. The Bush vote was the great expanse of the rest of the country.

Thanks to Professor Joseph Olson of Hamline School of Law in St. Paul, Minnesota, we now know something else about those counties.

In the Gore counties, the murder rate is 13.2 per 100,000.

In the Bush counties, the murder rate is 2.1 per 100,000.

What do urban centers have in common around the country? Try to get a concealed carry permit and you will find out. In fact, in Washington, D.C., New York City, Chicago, and a few others, just owning a handgun is impossible.

What had Lott found was the reason for the lowering of violent crime in various jurisdictions? Passage of concealed carry laws.

Indeed, the longer such laws have been on the books, the lower the violent crime rates go, including murder.

Where you live matters a lot. Thanks to Bush and Gore, making this decision has been made much easier.

Invade a Home, Invite a Bullet

A rash of home burglaries in South Carolina elicited a refreshing reaction from the state's Attorney General, Charlie Condon.

In a January statement, Condon sent a memorandum to all state prosecutors and law enforcement officials warning them not to arrest or prosecute people who defend themselves with "deadly force" against a "home invader."

Condon went on to say, "In South Carolina, would-be intruders should now hear this: Invade a home and invite a bullet." Not only was Condon putting the crooks on notice, he was letting homeowners know their rights.

Can you imagine the Attorney General of Illinois, California, Massachusetts, or New York making such a statement? No doubt they would be afraid that too many crooks would be killed. The anti-self-defense mind views protecting oneself as being a vigilante—even terrorism.

This, of course, was precisely what Handgun Control, Inc. was saying when they equated George Washington and other founders of American independence with Timothy McVeigh, the terrorist involved in the Oklahoma City bombing.

The anti-gun crowd is so opposed to self-defense that they cannot see that it was the Americans who were resisting British terrorism. Illegally attacking people, which the British did to the Americans, is the classic predicate for employing self-defense, but that's not good enough for Handgun Control, Inc.

It would have been better still if South Carolina's Attorney General had also told prosecutors not to bring cases against citizens who defend themselves outside the home with a concealed handgun for which they may have had no permit.

Prosecutors have that kind of discretion. They have the freedom to determine, case by case, whether to seek an indictment and prosecute.

We the People, as voters, should be looking to elect prosecutors who respect the right to keep and bear arms. Hopefully, enough of us will ask candidates about this that they will eventually get the point that this might be a key to their election.

Thanks to Charlie Condon, the door is now partially open for self-defense in South Carolina. Let's work to see this idea spread.

Concealed Carry Battles Revisit
Same Old Arguments

Utah and Illinois are two of the state legislatures that have had concealed carry bills introduced this year. In varying degrees the bills would tell the government to recognize the people's right to protect themselves by carrying a concealed handgun.

Whether highly restrictive or completely permissive, the arguments raised against these bills are always the same. Critics tell us that we cannot allow just anybody to carry a gun.

"It's our position that arming everybody is just not the solution," said Illinois Council Against Handgun Violence spokesman Kirsten Curley. "If someone has a gun on them, the opportunity to escalate a situation into deadly violence is exacerbated." (Springfield *News Gazette Online*, 11 February 2001)

A spokesman for the Illinois Association of Chiefs of Police said it even more clearly: "We're opposed to any concealed carry laws. Our big concern, of course, is the proliferation of handguns out there. That is a situation that we believe would not be safe for our police officers."

Utah State Representative Gary Cox—who is also a police officer, in violation of Utah law against serving in two public offices simultaneously—opposes bills that would recognize the constitutional right of anyone in Utah to carry a concealed weapon. Rep. Cox wants a very restrictive law to permit only a few in Utah to climb over the barriers he would set in their way.

Rep. Cox can carry a concealed firearm off duty, but he can't understand why anyone else would want to. He believes it would be too dangerous.

Let's think about this. Since the criminals are already armed, these opponents of self-defense are claiming that if the rest of us can pack a piece, we will also become criminals. Some people say that "the clothes make the man," but this takes that notion to a new extreme: "The guns make the criminal."

In my debates with gun control advocates, I have learned that many of them confuse self-defense with vigilantism. They actually think that self-defense is taking the law in our own hands. In other words, they think that self-defense is illegitimate.

The experience of states with permissive concealed carry laws leads to only one conclusion: The more citizens have the opportunity to arm themselves, the lower the violent crime rate in that jurisdiction.

Vermont is the ultimate test of freedom. In that state, anybody can carry a concealed weapon as a matter of right. That means there are no permits or licenses for those who carry concealed firearms. Vermont's murder rate is consistently at or near the bottom of the fifty states every year.

Since we can't all live in Vermont, let's bring Vermont's wisdom to where we live.

Section Seven

❧⟶◦⟵❧

BATTLES IN THE STATES

Colorado Governor Owens
Sliding Down the Slippery Slope

All too often "conservative" Republicans, who say they support the Second Amendment to our Constitution, are among the gun-grabbers who are working tirelessly to destroy our fundamental, God-given right as individuals to keep and bear arms. A case in point is Bill Owens, the GOP Governor of Colorado.

When Governor Owens spoke recently (2/29/2000) at the Heritage Foundation in Washington D.C., a flyer promoting his appearance noted that he was different from those "Liberals [who] screamed for stricter gun control" after tragedy struck at Columbine High School. And, in some ways, Gov. Owens is not like these liberal screamers. For example, he calls himself a conservative, and he *is* very soft-spoken. But still, Gov. Owens is calling for stricter gun control.

In his January 6, 2000, State of The State Address, Gov. Owens called for the following: A ban on all so-called "straw purchases" of firearms; juvenile record background checks for firearms purchases; the "safe storage" of all firearms in the home; a state background check for guns bought at gun shows; raising the age for buying handguns from 18 to 21; and making the state criminal background check system for gun purchases permanent.

Interestingly, Gov. Owens referred to these proposals as "common sense" gun control, words used by President Clinton to push his anti-gun, anti-Second Amendment agenda.

In an interview, when it is suggested that—whether he intends it or not—he is on a slippery slope and allying himself with the ducks who are nibbling the Second Amendment to death, Gov. Owens strongly denies this.

Rejecting a no-compromise approach to the Second Amendment, he says this approach "will lead us to more gun control, quicker than my approach which is able to be resilient and able to in fact hold ground for the future." He likens a no-compromise approach to the Second Amendment to the Maginot Line, a French fortification in World War I which was, supposedly, a colossal blunder.

Gov. Owens is sadly, and dangerously, mistaken. He can call his tactics whatever he wants to call them, but what they amount to, in reality, is surrender on the installment plan. He speaks of having to be "resilient" now in order to "hold ground for the future." But, what ground? Seriously, if Gov.

Owens and other supposedly "conservative" supporters of the Second Amendment continue to give ground on the gun issue at the present rate— "at the margins," as he says—then it is only a matter of time before there will be no more ground to defend!

But, in fact, Gov. Owens seriously misunderstands our strategy and tactics. Our no-compromise approach to the Second Amendment is not defensive. It is offensive—attack, attack, always attack the enemies of the Second Amendment.

Gov. Owens insists that he is yielding to gun control only where its advocates "have a point." But, is this true? He asks, for example, regarding his call for a ban on so-called "straw purchases," "Why on earth would we legally allow someone to buy a firearm for somebody who couldn't legally buy it for himself?"

But, when pressed and asked if he knows for a fact that "straw purchases" are really a problem and how many guns purchased this way have been used in crimes, he admits he doesn't know. Then why support such a ban? He says he's "not going to engage in a long debate on gun issues"—or, for that matter, obviously, give even a brief answer to this reasonable question.

As for Gov. Owens's support of the instant background check, this is nothing more than caving in to the wrong-headed gun control mentality which seems to believe that criminals will be participating in, and thwarted by, such a check, which is ludicrous.

He also seems totally oblivious to the fact that such an imposition and check on the non-criminal element—registering them on an FBI computer—will do nothing to control crime.

Concerning Columbine, one of the things that seems to guarantee that such tragedies will in fact become a slaughter is that the murderers can assume that they are the only ones with firearms. So, how about allowing school officials—principals, teachers and/or other designated personnel—to carry firearms in our schools?

Gov. Owens is against this saying, "You know, these things happen regard-less of whether you have concealed carry. I'm thinking of the killer in the Texas Baptist church, where they do have concealed carry in that state. This still doesn't mean that somebody is going to be—I'm not gonna', I don't think we ought to have concealed carry in the schools....I don't think that post-Columbine, in Colorado, more guns in schools are the answer." But, of course, the situation now is that where we have had "more guns" in some schools, the only ones with guns have been the murderers! As for that Texas church, just because no one there carried a concealed weapon doesn't mean that this would have been a bad idea. What is a bad idea is the status quo where, all too often, the only people with firearms are the murderers.

When Gov. Owens is pressed and asked why he is against school officials being allowed to carry firearms, he says he will not "debate" this issue. But, aren't people without guns always more vulnerable to people with guns? No reply.

In his talk at the Heritage Foundation about our culture—in which he said many good things—Gov. Owens made a very important observation. He said, "Great civilizations are not destroyed overnight." Amen! And the same thing can be said about our Constitutionally-protected rights and liberties. Historically, they, too, have been eroded, slowly but surely—as in the case of the Second Amendment.

Gov. Bill Owens may deny, as he does, that he is sliding down a slippery slope toward the destruction of our God-given, individual right to keep and bear arms. But, he's wrong. He's sliding much faster than he realizes—and in the wrong direction.

Rat Out Your Neighbor

New York City has been doing its history homework. The city's finest have adopted an official policy that can only remind us of King George III—or Lenin and Hitler.

The New York City Police Department has issued an official policy termed "Operation Gun Stop."

The idea is simple and disturbingly similar to the BATF campaign to dial an 800 number to report a gun.

In New York City, citizens are invited to call the cops when they see an illegal gun. Of course, in New York City, most privately owned guns are illegal because the law and the police have made it so difficult to legally obtain a personal protection device.

Here's the deal in the police memo's words: "Under this program, private citizens will be able to anonymously provide this Department with information regarding individuals or locations involved with illegal handguns. Individuals who provide information that leads to an arrest for such sale/possession will be eligible for a cash reward of $500."

Based on an anonymous tip, without any substantiation whatsoever, a search warrant will be issued and a search of the accused's premises will be carried out.

This is virtually the same as a general warrant. King George used them and the British still call them Writs of Assistance. These writs had a great deal to do with Americans taking up arms against British terrorism.

The King's thugs, posing as soldiers, would enter the homes of Americans to search for contraband. A suspicion was all that was required because the Writs of Assistance were the same as a search-anytime-anywhere authorization.

Twentieth century terrorists such as Lenin and Hitler took the Writs of Assistance one step further. They developed a formal network of secret neighborhood spies who would anonymously tip off thugs hired by the regime who would act against any politically incorrect behavior that needed to be suppressed.

Too bad that neither Lenin nor Hitler are around to issue a Certificate of Achievement to the New York City Police Department. Perhaps one might be issued by Fidel Castro, the terrorist who has oppressed Cuba for over forty years.

Massachusetts—Government by Decree

The anti-self-defense crowd has been finding innovative ways to impose unconstitutional gun control laws without bothering with the legislative process.

The recent agreement between the Clinton administration and Smith & Wesson has gotten the most attention because it affects all firearms sold by any Smith & Wesson dealer.

But Massachusetts has shown the wisdom of the federal law preventing the United States Consumer Product Safety Commission from regulating firearms. It was the equivalent of that commission that decided to ban the sale of most handguns in Massachusetts.

It was done in the name of safety. Then Attorney General Scott Harshbarger usurped some non-legislated powers to regulate the safety of handguns as an ordinary consumer product. Thirty-four other states have passed legislation allowing officials to regulate handguns as they would other consumer products.

But in Massachusetts, one official acting on his own wrote rules putting guns under the consumer product regulations of the state. Interestingly, the rules were not enforced until after the spontaneous outpouring of disgust at the recent Clinton-Wesson contract.

That enforcement came on April 3 of 2000, when the current Massachusetts Attorney General, Thomas Reilly, decided to drop the hammer. The Attorney General required all dealers to handle *all* of their firearms the same way— namely, only guns that have the safety technology of Smith & Wesson's latest guns. And only Smith has such handguns.

This becomes a powerful financial tool in the hands of the government officials who have been trying to extort the entire firearms industry. While they claim an anti-trust conspiracy on the part of other manufacturers, truth be told, the attorneys general have been threatening financially debilitating lawsuits if the manufacturers do not capitulate to their gun control agenda.

Massachusetts has become a lead collaborator in the effort to use public power to control a constitutionally protected industry. Massachusetts has gone one step beyond threatening a lawsuit if the firearms manufacturers do not buy into the gun control agenda of certain elected officials. Since Smith & Wesson capitulated, in Massachusetts they have been given a government imposed monopoly of handgun sales.

Isn't it great to live in a free country?

Massachusetts Legislature:
Blood on Their Hands

When Michael McDermott walked into the offices of an Internet consulting firm and shot seven people dead, he had an accomplice: the legislature of the Commonwealth of Massachusetts. Tragically, one of the victims was a legal gun owner who was licensed to carry in New Hampshire. Massachusetts law prevented him from carrying his firearm in the state and on the job.

There is no doubt that Sandy Javelle was bold. When the shooting started, Sandy ordered his co-workers to lock the door behind him and barricade it. He then confronted McDermott and soon became the third victim.

Had the Citizens' Self-Defense Act sponsored by Maryland's Roscoe Bartlett been on the books, Javelle would likely have been willing to carry his gun illegally in Massachusetts. He would have been able to seek an injunction and damages in federal court against prosecution for his violation of Massachusetts' anti-self-defense law. Lamentably, Javelle was more afraid of the Massachusetts cops than he was of Michael McDermott. He made a deadly choice.

What happened to Javelle and his six dead co-workers is but more data to validate the conclusions of Dr. John Lott in his book, *More Guns, Less Crime*. It is helpful to know that Dr. Lott bought his first gun *after* he finished the research that showed that concealed carry laws were the only thing that lowered violent crime rates.

Think about an observation Dr. Lott recently made about the inability of the police to be everywhere, thus increasing the risk citizens take when they are unarmed. He tells of a friend who dropped off his kids at a public school and outside the school was a sign that said, "This is a gun-free zone." Lott could not help but think that if he put up a sign on his home that said, "This home is a gun-free zone," it would make his home more attractive to criminals entering his home and attacking his family and himself.

It is easy for the media to report on a crime such as Wakefield. Seldom do they report on the 2.5 million times a year a citizen uses a gun in self-defense.

Don't expect the legislators of Massachusetts to ask for forgiveness for their deadly law that killed Sandy Javelle. If they do anything, it will be to make it easier for the next Michael McDermott to kill a bunch of helpless victims. If McDermott were not such a creep, we might ask him to thank the legislature for enabling him to have his 15 minutes of fame.

Maryland "Gun Safety" Law = Gun Ban

Poor Casper R. Taylor, Jr., the Democratic House Speaker in the Maryland Legislature. Obviously a slow-learner, he just doesn't get it. He just doesn't understand how the anti-Second Amendment gun grabbers work. But maybe he's a little wiser today. Let's hope so.

According to an Associated Press story in the *Washington Times* newspaper (28 December 2000) Taylor, "fearing that the state's gun-safety bill has turned into a ban on handgun sales," has written a letter to Maryland Attorney General J. Joseph Curran asking him "to move quickly to clear up confusion about the law that took effect three months ago." One section of the law in question prohibits handguns from being sold in Maryland unless the manufacturer includes a shell casing fired from the gun. Casings are then turned over to Maryland State Police where their "ballistic fingerprints" are entered into a computer data base.

This law was a major part of Governor Parris N. Glendening's legislative package during the 2000 session. When President Clinton himself came to Maryland to see this measure signed into law, he urged other states to follow Maryland's lead and enact similar laws. But—surprise!—there's been a problem because of this law. Taylor says gun dealers tell him that manufacturers are not shipping weapons with casings into Maryland. Thus, they are running out of guns to sell. So, Taylor has written to Attorney General Curran saying, in part:

> I am frustrated by the lack of a definitive, written answer to a number of questions posed by gun dealers from around the state....In good faith, many members of the General Assembly voted for this measure as a strong gun safety bill, and they, as well as I, were assured that it would not result in an outright ban on handguns.

Taylor adds that if this law had been seen as a handgun ban, it would not have passed. In an interview with the AP, he says, "The spirit of the law, as I voted for it and as many of my colleagues voted for it, was to gain gun safety, but not to gain a gun ban."

Well, now. Earth to House Speaker Taylor: Wake up, please!

First, when dealing with rabidly anti-gun, anti-Second Amendment people like Governor Glendening and Attorney General Curran, there's no such thing as "good faith." Forget it. Secondly, the precise purpose, goal, and/or effect of all such "gun safety" laws is to, ultimately, de facto, *ban the possession of all firearms by private citizens.* And to expect Attorney General J. Joseph Curran to answer your question and be concerned about the impact of the law in question is absurd.

Of all the public officials in the United States, Curran is one of the most vehement enemies of the Second Amendment and of private individual gun owners—as he made crystal clear, at length, in an October, 1999, report titled "A Farewell To Arms: The Solution To Gun Violence In America."

For example, on page 10 of his wretched report Curran is verbally foaming at the mouth and seething with hatred toward private persons who own guns—when he says that "owning and carrying handguns" must be stigmatized so that this Constitutionally-protected right is "seen as dangerous and aberrant behavior." One definition of the word "aberrant" is, of course, mentally unbalanced. So, Curran is saying, not so subtly, that he looks forward to a time when people who own and carry handguns are seen as crazy—as nuts.

On page 63 of this report, Curran says, "Our goal, then, must be to eliminate widespread handgun ownership through restrictive handgun licensing."

But, it is Curran's views about guns which are nutty. In an interview in February of 2000, Curran told how his daughter had been car-jacked in the early 1990s by a man with a handgun. He also spoke about how his father had been shot at in Baltimore's City Hall and later died of a heart attack.

When asked if there was any gun control law which would have prevented these crimes, Curran replied: "If there had been some, in other words, if the manufacturer, when they made these things, then had some understanding about how they would be distributed and what type of dealers they're going to go to, what criteria dealers use—rather than just because these guns are made—I don't think manufacturers can say, 'Well, I made them and I gave them to a distributor and what they do thereafter is their business.' I think that's nonsense."

But, what's nonsense is what Curran suggests. Seriously, how, exactly, would his proposal work in real life—for example, in the two personal crimes he mentioned? Before a gun manufacturer sells a gun to a dealer, should the dealer be required by law to pledge that these guns will be sold to no carjackers and that these guns will be sold to no one who will use them to shoot up Baltimore's City Hall? Please!

In the previously mentioned Associated Press story, it is said that Attorney

General Curran says he is "not aware of any problem" with the "gun safety" bill which has resulted in a *de facto* ban on handgun sales in Maryland. But, of course, for Curran there is no "problem"—*because he's for a ban on selling handguns to private individuals!*

Maryland House Speaker Taylor says that if the problem with this "gun safety" bill is not cleared up quickly, he will support legislation at the 2001 General Assembly session to amend the law so dealers can acquire and sell handguns. Well, terrific. Great. But, Taylor and those who favored it should have never voted for this dangerously stupid law in the first place. It should be repealed, not amended.

California Legislature: Blood on Their Hands

The California State Legislature has the blood of two murder victims on its hands. The victims would almost certainly still be alive were it not for California's "Lock up Your Safety" law.

John Carpenter was more afraid of the illegitimate law passed by the California legislature than he was of the harm his defenseless family could suffer from a criminal. Because of that, two of his little children, John William (7) and Ashley (9), are dead. All five children were home alone.

In a struggle straight from a B-grade horror film, Jonathon David Bruce cut the phone of the Carpenter home and burst in wielding a pitchfork. The naked intruder killed little John William as he lay in his parents' bed.

Ashley struggled with the killer as he attacked Anna (13). Bruce then turned his weapon on her and pinned her little body to the wall and stabbed her to death as she fell to the floor, begging for her life. This allowed Anna and Vanessa (11) to escape with the other sister.

Anna told her Dad from her hospital bed, "Ashley saved my life, Dad."

Meanwhile, Jessica tried to call 911 and found the line dead. She then tried to get one of the family guns, but the California legislators had made sure that would not happen. They were locked up. She was prevented from using a gun she knew perfectly well how to use.

A neighbor declined to get his rifle and stop the killer, but Jessica did manage to call 911 with his phone.

The cops finally put an end to the nightmare when they found Bruce still at the crime scene. As Bruce charged them, they killed him with a dozen shots.

Sixteen other states have these murderous laws. As Sarah Brady likes to say, "If we can save just one life, this bill should be passed." Well, two lives could have been saved if the California Lock-Up-Your-Safety law had been repealed. That's one gun law Gun Owners of America would like to see passed.

John Carpenter's mother, Mary Carpenter, has recorded a television spot for Gun Owners Foundation. She pleads with people not to lock up their safety. She has contacted several state legislatures urging them to defeat bills that would require people to face assailants with a gun lock.

Of Cars and Guns and Kids

When our kids approach the fateful age of qualifying for a learner's permit, most schools across the country offer driver's education. The courses are also referred to as driver safety classes. Indeed, many insurance companies offer discounts for taking a defensive driving course.

It makes sense to me. I can still remember the mixture of anticipation and fear when I first got behind the wheel of a car. Anticipation because, finally, I was about to be inducted into that great American fraternity of mobility and independence. But fear was also present. What if I lose control and ram a tree or shatter the garage door?

This same logic used to be shared by school administrators across the country when it came to guns, too. As late as 1969, even New York City schools had shooting ranges. Students would take their rifles to school to practice on teams. It was not uncommon for kids to take the subway to school with their rifles.

This logic is no longer politically correct. What works for cars—and what used to work for guns—is now only seen as valid for cars. Gun safety is no longer to be taught through the tried and true hands-on approach.

The Maryland legislature passed a gun safety bill that was vetoed by Governor Parris Glendening. The bill would have allowed educators to take middle-school and high school students to gun ranges and to work with pro-gun organizations to develop the courses.

The Governor said that he supported "efforts to create responsible gun-safety programs in our schools. However, this bill would create a clear appearance of the state encouraging young people to handle weapons and potentially furthering their interest in a time when we are trying to fight the scourge of gun violence."

Consider how ostrich-like the Governor's position is. Imagine that the state legislature had just passed a driver's education program with both class-room and behind-the-wheel training. Here is how Glendening's words would sound: "I support efforts to create responsible driver's education programs in our schools. However, this bill would create a clear appearance of the state encouraging young people to handle cars and potentially furthering their interest in a time when we are trying to fight the scourge of traffic fatalities." The Governor would actually be on somewhat less shaky ground if he were to oppose behind-the-wheel education in order to reduce the number of people driving cars. After all, many more people are killed each year in auto accidents, and, unlike firearms, very few automobiles are used to save lives. Firearms are used in some 2,500,000 self defense situations every year.

It sure seems that something is wrong with this picture.

Section Eight

＞－◆＞－◯－◆＜－＜

KIDS AND GUNS

What's Next: Hand-Control Laws?
Finger Registration?

I've got to admit that even though I know there's a lot of anti-gun hysteria in our country, this one I found hard to believe when I first heard about it. But, alas, it happened. And we can, no doubt, expect more such craziness in the future.

As reported in *Time* magazine (12/6/99), MeShelle Locke, 16, of Lacey, Washington, a National Honor Society student, was kidding around with a boy in her English class at North Thurston High School in early November. When he made some wisecrack to the teacher, Locke looked at him, made a gun with her thumb and index finger, and said, "Bang." The boy, with whom she often joked, wondered if what she said was a threat. "No," said MeShelle lightly, "it's a promise."

Following this incident—which was, obviously, a joke—two girls in MeShelle's gym class confronted her about her "threatening to kill" the boy, according to a story in *The News Tribune* newspaper (13 November 1999). Exasperated by this absurd accusation, MeShelle made the same thumb/finger "gun" gesture to them.

Well, the next school day MeShelle was confronted by a police officer who read Miranda rights to her (but didn't arrest her). She was expelled from school for four days.

The News Tribune quotes North Thurston High Principal Karen Eitreim as saying, presumably with a straight face: "I think schools are taking every precaution. And that includes looking at students' threats and really taking them seriously and analyzing whether there is a threat to safety or not."

But, this is idiotic beyond belief!

What possible "threat" is there from one student pointing his or her finger at other students and saying, "Bang"? Even the most cursory "analysis" of this incident would reveal that this is nothing more than—well, one student pointing her finger at other students and saying, "Bang." Period. That's it. By no stretch of the imagination, and by no definition, is this a "threat." No way.

Incredibly, Bob Locke, MeShelle's father, says that school district officials told him that his daughter fit the profile of a student who might hurt the school. And what, exactly, made them think this? Well, for one thing, she often ate lunch alone or in a small group!

Wow. A real profile of a potential terrorist, yes? No.

In an interview with Gun Owners of America (GOA), when it was facetiously suggested that maybe what we need now is a hand-control law and for all the fingers and thumbs of students to be registered, Bob Locke replied, with a laugh: "Right. Lethal fingers. We gotta have' em banned from the schools."

Locke—who says he's against gun control because it's unconstitutional— tells GOA that to get back into school his daughter had to sign a "behavioral contract" in which she promised "not to threaten any other students or to hold grudges against any other students." But, of course, he adds that MeShelle never really "threatened" any students in the first place. This is why he says that if his daughter had the whole thing to do over again, she would do nothing different.

Locke says their friends and acquaintances have been "shocked" by this entire affair. He says they originally found the school's actions to be "annoying, painful and embarrassing" to MeShelle. But, as it was resolved, it was "more of a joke."

Well, maybe, maybe not—a sick joke at best, to be sure.

It's all the sicker when we consider that the school would have never noticed MeShelle if she had chosen to extend her middle finger rather than her index finger.

But, this kind of thing is not funny, not at all. And it's sad to say, this sort of so-called "zero tolerance" lunacy appears to be happening more often across the country in our government-run schools. This same issue of *Time* magazine reports that a seven year old boy in Cahokia, Illinois, was suspended for having a nail-clipper in class.

And a high school in Nevis, Minnesota, turned thumbs down on a yearbook photo which showed an Army enlistee in the senior class posing atop a 155-mm Howitzer at a Veterans Of Foreign Wars post. The photo was approved when a U.S. flag was draped over this cannon.

Obviously, in many cases, this "zero tolerance" policy is being implemented by people with zero brains.

Guns in School

The occasional school shootings that have been magnified in the media, to proportions of epic disaster, can be greatly curtailed. But not by more gun control laws.

The solution is quite simple. Enable adults to carry concealed firearms in schools. Such an easy thing to do, of course, meets with howls of disbelief from those advocating civilian disarmament. Their disbelief is actually one of the best evidences that the aim of gun control is to disarm everybody but the government.

Gun control advocates claim that a gun in the hands of a teacher, principal, janitor, or some other adult at a school is more dangerous than is an armed killer with the *only* firearm at the scene of the crime.

Disarmament activists want to live in this fantasy world no matter how much their views do not match the real world. Gun controllers are convinced that all they need to do is pass more restrictions on gun ownership and the bad guys will get the message and stop committing crimes.

Another part of their fantasy world is an upside down view of who you can trust. Gun controllers are willing to trust bad guys to obey the law but insist on viewing the whole population with grave suspicion. You and I are viewed as too crime-prone and certainly too irresponsible to be trusted with a firearm—much less a concealed firearm at a school.

My recent trip to Israel yielded proof that guns save lives and that disarmament kills.

In 1974, there was a dreadful attack on a group of school kids, killing over 30. After a national debate, the country's parliament, the Knesset, decided that bad guys would not obey additional Israeli gun control laws. So Israel set about arming principals, teachers, and, in some of the conflict zones, parents to protect students at school.

When I was in Israel it was very common to see military-rifle-toting young men in their 20's protecting groups of school kids sight-seeing in Jerusalem or elsewhere in the country. The only time school kids have been killed since 1974 was when a group of students were touring a peace shrine on the Jordanian border and were told to leave their guns before entering. A Jordanian soldier was able to kill some of the defenseless students.

Guns really do save lives—but not if we insist on laws that ensure that only the bad guys will have them.

Columbine: One Year Later

On the last day a lawsuit could be filed stemming from the Columbine carnage, some real blockbusters were entered. The allegations provide new reasons—if we really need more—to refuse to rely on the police for our protection.

Parents had to sue the Jefferson County sheriff's department in order to see the report just two weeks before the one-year deadline on filing lawsuits.

Angela Sanders, daughter of slain teacher Dave Sanders, alleges that a sharpshooter had Klebold in his sights in the library, but his supervisors would not allow him to act. Sanders' suit also alleges that the sharpshooter saw Klebold and Harris commit suicide, and thus officers were aware the pair was dead three hours before Sanders died, but they still failed to rescue him.

The parents of Daniel Rohrbough allege that police, not the murderers, killed their son, based on reports from a police officer and teacher at the scene and the position of their son's body and trajectory of the fatal bullet. The Rohrbough suit, joined by five other families, also alleges that most of the deaths in the massacre could have been avoided. It says students could have easily fled the library early on, but a 911 operator had teacher Patti Nielson instruct them to stay put, and alleges they would have survived if they had not been told help was on the way.

Debates I have had with the gun ban crowd on radio and television reveal a uniform belief that self-defense is either futile or dangerous—or both.

My suggestion that we repeal the school zone gun ban so that adults working at the school would be able to carry concealed firearms was met with cries of outrage. "Why, that would lead to innocent people being killed in a cross fire."

Now we learn that one of the Columbine fatalities may have indeed been killed in a crossfire—by the police. Does that make the parents feel any better?

And the lawsuits only pose the question that was begging to be asked: "Why did no officers go in? Why the wait for so long?"

We Need More Kids with Guns

Typical of the anti-Second Amendment, anti-self-defense gun-grabbers is Brian Morton, Associate Director Of Communications for Handgun Control, Inc. who believes, and has said, that "guns and kids" are a "bad combination." But, he is dangerously mistaken on this subject. His incorrect view can be deadly.

In fact, just the opposite of what Morton says is true. *More* young people need to be knowledgeable about guns. They need to know how to use them safely and, most importantly, where they are in the house if needed. To not know where a gun is located when it is needed can be deadly.

A tragic case in point where "a kid" and a gun needed to be "combined"—and where such a combination would have saved lives—occurred in August of this year in rural Merced County, California. A murderous, pitchfork-wielding maniac entered the home of John Carpenter where he stabbed to death 7-year-old John William Carpenter and 9-year-old Ashley Danielle Carpenter.

The *Fresno Bee* (26 August 2000) quotes the children's great-uncle, the Reverend John Hilton, as saying of 14-year-old Jessica Carpenter, who survived this brutal attack: "If only [she] had a gun available to her, she could have stopped the whole thing. If she had been properly armed, she could have stopped him in his tracks." The *Bee* reports that the father, John Carpenter, "kept a gun in his home. His children learned how to fire it. *But he kept it locked away and hidden from his children*" (emphasis mine).

Rev. Hilton says of Mr. Carpenter: "He's more afraid of the law than of somebody coming in for his family. He's scared to death of leaving the gun where the kids could get it because he's afraid of the law. He's scared to teach his children to defend themselves." Hilton adds that the father feared over-regulation as well as laws that make gun owners criminally and civilly liable if their children or others are injured.

Dan Holman, who works at Gilman-Mayfield Firearms in Fresno, is quoted as saying that more and more people are changing their behavior because of gun laws: "The government has got people so scared. I agree wholeheartedly [with the Rev. Hilton]. If there had been a gun available, maybe nobody would have died."

The California legislature has to accept the blame for this tragedy. It was their bill requiring Carpenter to lock up his gun (so-called safe storage) that insured that the guns would be unavailable in a crisis. This is one more piece of criminal protection legislation that needs to be repealed so that more lives will not be lost.

In a letter-to-the-editor of the *Bee* (1 September 2000), Jason Hendrix of Clovis says he could not agree more with Rev. Hilton that Jessica Carpenter's siblings might have lived had she been armed. He adds: "As fast as Merced deputies showed up, it wasn't fast enough to stop the crime in progress. Regardless of what critics will say, Rev. Hilton was 100 percent correct. In fact, a firearm is the only thing that would have saved the day."

In another letter to the editor of the *Bee* (3 September 2000), Ron Shipman of Fresno writes: "The words spoken by Rev. John Hilton, 'If only,' cadence through my mind constantly. We let Ashley and John William Carpenter down, and it matters not if you are anti-gun or pro-gun. What matters is we are allowing our legislators and the courts to run roughshod over our Constitution and Bill of Rights. Ashley's and John's deaths need not be in vain—the death of these two children should be the biggest wake-up call this Valley has ever seen. No one in this Republic, of a responsible age, should have their right to self-protection challenged."

It's sad to say, in many ways, it seems that fewer young people are being taught how to shoot. For example, the *St. Louis Post-Dispatch* newspaper (4 December 1999) reports that "school rifle teams are on the brink of extinction." Chicago schools have discontinued rifle teams in their schools with junior ROTC programs. But, supporters of marksmanship programs in St. Louis "stress that none of the recent shootings in schools have been spawned by an in-school marksmanship team."

An example of the type of irrational, anti-gun hysteria which has led to a reduction in the ability of individuals, including young people, to defend themselves or others, are the remarks of Ellen Dennehy, a child psychologist and part-time faculty member at Southern Methodist University. In Texas, youngsters 12 and older can be certified for hunting licenses after completing a mandatory 10-hour course, according to a story in the *Dallas Morning News* (9 April 1998). There is also "no law that prevents a parent from teaching a child how to shoot or handle a gun at any age."

Kid-shrink Dennehy, however, is scandalized by all this. She says, incoherently, "We have a major problem in our country where we are pushing our children younger and younger and we are robbing them of their childhood." But, of course, in Merced County, California—because 14-year-old Jessica Carpenter could not get her father's gun—her younger brother and sister were "robbed of their childhood" *because they are dead!*

In the book *Guns: Who Should Have Them?* (Prometheus Books, 1995), edited by David B. Kopel, in a chapter titled "Children And Guns," Kopel notes, correctly: "The most important factor affecting how children deal with guns is how they are taught about them....To fail to teach America's young people responsible gun use, under the supervision of responsible adults, is to sow the seeds of a public health disaster, the murder epidemic that too many American cities have created for themselves."

Thomas Jefferson is quoted as having advised his nephew: "Games played with a bat and ball are too violent, and stamp no character on the mind.... [A]s to the species of exercise, I advise the gun." Kopel adds, "Other than hatred of guns, there is no strong argument against schools being allowed to offer target shooting as a sport, nor is there an argument against teenagers being encouraged to learn responsible attitudes toward firearms through participation in shooting sports."

Well, amen! This kind of thing and a lot more things must be done. As I say, we need *more* young people to be knowledgeable about guns. They need to know how to use them safely and—most importantly—where they are in the house if needed. The title of John Lott's excellent book says it well: *More Well-Trained Young People With Guns, Safer Families.*

California School Shooting Proves
Need for Armed Guards

Shortly after the most recent shooting at a California school, Sarah Brady, the head of Handgun Control, issued a statement trashing Attorney General John Ashcroft because, among other things, he did not take the "gun lobby" to task "for promoting the idea that guns make you safer and that guns are a vital form of protection for America's families." She also said it is "a tragedy" when leaders such as the Attorney General ignore "preventing children's access to guns."

But, what is a *real* tragedy is Brady's adamant, ignorant, and dangerous refusal to acknowledge that, in certain circumstances, guns *do* make things safer. A case in point, ironically, is the very shooting which prompted Brady's absurd attack on Attorney General Ashcroft.

According to the *New York Times* (24 March 2001), it was a man with a gun—a veteran police officer, Richard Agundez, Jr.—who prevented what could have been a mass slaughter at Granite Hills High School in El Cajon, California. As the *Times* reports it, Agundez, when he heard shots, "raced out with his weapon drawn and fired at Mr. [Jason] Hoffman five times, wounding him in the mouth and buttocks and apparently hitting and disabling his shotgun. Mr. Hoffman turned and ran, but fell about 20 yards away, near his truck. He had a .22-caliber pistol tucked in his waistband, the authorities said, but never fired it."

In an interview on CBS' *Early Morning* program, El Cajon's Chief of Police James Davis said that if Agundez—a man with a gun—had not been stationed at this high school things would probably have been "a great deal worse." Davis praised Agundez because he "reacted immediately by going to the sound of the gun fire."

Oh, and the alleged shooter, Jason Hoffman, is hardly a "child." He is six feet, one inch tall and weighs 210 pounds!

So, what this latest school shooting demonstrates is that Sarah Brady is flat wrong! What this latest school shooting proves is that guns *do* make things safer. In this case kids were safer, and not shot, since the alleged shooter was shot and disabled.

But, neither Brady nor her fellow gun-haters at Handgun Control understand or care about the importance of using firearms in defense of innocent human lives.

In a recent interview on *WMAL Radio* (3/22/2001) in Washington, D.C.—following the shooting in El Cajon, California—I debated Tony Orza, the legislative director of Handgun Control, Inc. Seemingly oblivious to the fact that lives had been saved thanks to the quick reaction of Officer Agundez at Granite Hills High, Orza attacked Gun Owners of America because we want, as he put it, "*more* guns, more people in schools with guns."

Well, *yes*! We *do* want this. We unashamedly thank God that there were "more guns" than just those of the shooter at Granite Hills High and that one of these guns was in the hands of a veteran cop who used it quickly to stop the alleged shooter and save lives.

Orza also asked at one point, rhetorically, "Do we really want bullets ricocheting around school hallways?" Well, no, if this can be prevented. But, what is Orza's alternative? If the good guys are not allowed to have guns in our schools then the only ones who will have them will be the bad guys, the shooters, the mass murderers. Does this make sense? Not at all.

Orza also spoke dismissively of Officer Agundez's heroic action saying that even though he was armed there were still two teachers and three students injured by the alleged shooter. But, he ignores the fact that had Officer Agundez *not* been there and immediately stopped the alleged shooter, things would probably have been much worse with many students and teachers murdered.

Orza says there are "a lot of risks when you have a gun." Well, yes. There are also a lot of risks by just being alive, just getting out of bed in the morning—or staying in it. But, sad to say, increasingly it seems, the *greatest risk* in our schools is having none of the good guys bearing arms for the defense of innocent students and teachers.

At one point in my *WMAL Radio* debate, a caller—another anti-gun nut—said, "Handguns are used for one thing: to kill other people." Well, some people ought to be killed, people like those who invade our schools and try to murder our students and teachers.

Section Nine

❧

DOCTORS AND GUNS

Guns Save Health Care Costs

Oxford University Press—from England—is offering a book entitled *Gun Violence: The Real Costs*. This book asserts that violence from Americans using guns is $100 billion per year. The previous exaggerated figure was $20 billion.

Several subjective criteria were used to bloat the numbers. One such non-objective issue was "emotional costs experienced by relatives and friends of gunshot victims and the fear and general reduction in quality of life that the threat of gun violence imposes on everyone in America, including people who are not victims."

So there you have it. Even if you have never been a victim of an armed criminal, you are part of the staggering cost of such violence each year because the emotional costs to the victims lower your quality of life. Isn't science wonderful?

Consulting the analysis of a doctor who has more of a grip on the tangible world, Dr. Edgar Suter, who is chairman of Doctors for Integrity in Policy Research, has put the true cost to victims and society at $1.5 billion per year. That is less than one percent of annual U.S. health care expenditures.

Dr. Suter makes this observation: "Claiming that gunshot wounds create costs of nearly half the annual U.S. health care expenditures requires estimates of 'lifetime productivity lost,' where every gangbanger is a brain surgeon and every rapist is a rocket scientist."

We also know that firearms are used some 2.5 million times a year for self-defense. Those are a lot of health care costs that never occur, especially since approximately 93 percent of defense uses of guns do not require discharging the firearm.

Dr. Miguel Faria, editor of the *Medical Sentinel* of the Association of American Physicians and Surgeons, calculates that between 25 and 75 lives are saved for every life lost to a gun.

The Harvard Medical School has estimated that 96,000 people a year die from physician malpractice. That is over three times the number of people murdered or committing suicide or dying accidentally with a gun. Hopefully doctors save 25 to 75 times the number of people they kill each year so that at least they are proportionately as socially beneficial as are firearms.

Beware of Pediatricians

If there were a "Chutzpah of the Year" award, I would nominate the American Academy of Pediatrics. Pediatricians are physicians, and according to the Harvard University Medical Practice Study, physicians collectively kill 96,000 people per year through malpractice.

Perhaps to draw attention away from a statistic that reveals physicians kill through malpractice 80 times more than those killed in firearms accidents, the pediatrics group has called for banning handguns from homes. Whatever the case, the pediatrician group issued a call in April of the new millennium for banning handguns to protect the children.

The AAP labels handguns a significant public health problem justifying a ban to stem what these doctors label an epidemic. The doctors claim that each gunshot injury costs $17,000, or $2.3 billion, for the 134,445 gunshot injuries in 1994.

The AAP totally overlooks the lives saved and the injuries avoided by firearms. The Clinton Justice Department—obviously not trying to produce material helpful to gun owners—found that guns are used nearly 3,000 times each day in self-defense.

A truer figure is nearly 7,000—a figure produced from the research of Dr. Gary Kleck of Florida State University. Kleck's work is so substantial that his fellow criminologists awarded him the coveted Hindelang Award.

If only half of the 7,000 people a day would have required medical treatment, then $22 billion is saved by guns—ten times more than the criminal costs of gun use doctors emphasize.

The doctors refer to the discredited study done by Dr. Arthur Kellerman used frequently by the anti-self-defense crowd. Dr. Kellerman supposedly found that we are 43 times more likely to be injured by a gun than to kill an intruder with that same gun.

The trick in his statistic is "kill an intruder." He completely eliminated all the other times a gun is used to frighten away an intruder. Only occasionally is a gun used to wound, much less to kill, an intruder.

As far as I am concerned, I would rather be one of the 7,000 who use a gun daily in self-defense than one of the 96,000 killed by incompetent doctors each year.

Doctors Against Guns

The American Academy of Pediatrics (AAP) has embarked on a strident campaign against gun ownership. In an article appearing last year in the *Medical Sentinel*, published by the American Association of Physicians and Surgeons, Dr. Timothy Wheeler explained what the AAP is fostering among its members. (*Medical Sentinel's* web site is *www.haciendapub.com.* The editor, Miguel Faria, has run several pro-gun articles over the years.)

The AAP is urging each of its member pediatricians to pry into the private lives of their patients and ask if they have guns in the home.

The pediatrician is urged to push on their patients the "gun safety instruction" patient materials the AAP adopted from Handgun Control, Inc. Since 76 percent of the pediatricians responding to an AAP survey support a ban on handguns, many parents are likely to encounter one of these physicians with their disarming manners.

Dr. Wheeler explains that this prying behavior is a boundary violation the same as doctor-patient sex. In other words, it is a violation of ethics. That means that there is something you can do about such a doctor (besides walking out immediately). An aggrieved patient can go to the Yellow Pages and find the phone number of the state Medical Society and file a complaint.

The doctor may be exonerated, but it may also reduce his ardor to confuse medicine with propaganda. And if several patients file complaints, the number alone could endanger his license to practice.

Keep in mind that the AAP is involved in a shameless exercise of blame-shifting. Physicians kill, according to the Harvard Medical School, 96,000 patients a year through malpractice. We are nine times as likely to be killed by our doctor than by someone murdering us with a gun.

Spread the word to parents who have children under the care of pediatricians.

Boys and Guns at Emory University

In an interview, Dr. Geoffrey Jackman says, with a straight face, that the study he conducted with three other doctors was simply about "common sense and education" more than anything else. But his study is junk science at its worst whose conclusions are designed to give the gun grabbers more "scientific evidence" to argue for banning the private ownership of firearms.

The study in question—titled *Seeing Is Believing: What Do Boys Do When They Find A Real Gun?*—was published in the June, 2001, issue of *Pediatrics* magazine. What these doctors, who obviously have too much free time on their hands, did was put together, in an outpatient center, 64 boys—in groups of two and three—ages 8 to 12. Two water pistols and a real .380 caliber handgun were concealed in separate drawers. These boys were observed for up to 15 minutes through a one-way mirror.

Well, guess what? As Dr. Jackman told us, "the obvious" happened. Seventy-six percent of the boys handled the real gun, 48 percent pulled its trigger. More than 90 percent of those who did this reported they had received "some sort of gun safety instruction." The conclusion: "Many 8 to 12-year-old boys will handle a handgun if they find one. Guns that are kept in homes should be stored in a manner that renders them inaccessible to children... ."

But this phony study proves no such thing about "homes." As one correspondent wrote to *Pediatrics* magazine, a correct conclusion would have been, "Guns that are kept in hospitals should not be stored in a context that suggests they are playthings, such as in a cabinet with toys, that test subjects have been encouraged to investigate." Amen! Bull's eye!

So, what's this study *really* about? Well, another correspondent wrote to *Pediatrics*, in part, "I suspect it is published more to further a political agenda than to offer discovery to the scientific community or the people in general." Again, amen! Another bull's eye!

Commenting on this study on the Cable News Network (6/5/2001), reporter Rhonda Rowland said, "These latest findings support the American Academy Of Pediatrics' recommendations that the best way to prevent gun-related deaths and injuries to children *is to get rid of firearms in homes and communities*" (emphasis mine).

And in an interview on ABC's *Good Morning America* (6/5/2001), Dr. Harold Simon, one of the doctors conducting the study, said, explicitly, "So, the best thing to do to prevent these injuries [to children] *is to remove the guns from the home*" (emphasis mine).

So much for Dr. Jackman's assertion that his study is simply about "common sense and education." In fact, when we pressed him, and asked if he agreed with Dr. Simon—that guns should be grabbed and removed from the home—he said: "Yes, if you have a child that would be our recommendation." Why? "Because they are going to play with it. Why not try to prevent something that is absolutely one of the easiest things to prevent and that is the death of a child?"

Is he aware that more children are killed by drowning in water buckets every year than are killed accidentally by guns? "Certainly. I get that argument all the time." Still, he says, guns are "the one item I picked."

Should all water buckets be removed from the home, too? "I think that more than anything else your children need to be kinda watched, especially around places where there is water, swimming pools for instance."

But should all water buckets be removed from the home? "I think that is a little bit extreme." Even though they kill more kids than guns? "You could argue anything. Children die from all kinds of things. They die in more numbers from other things." Indeed. So, why pick on guns?

How about self-defense? Studies show that every year as many as 2 to 3 million people use guns in self-defense. So, why would Dr. Jackman want to take all guns out of all homes where there are kids when among these 2 to 3 million there had to be kids whose safety was preserved by using guns? "Well, that's your argument. My situation is that I see the kids shot and killed."

But you don't see the kids defended by guns, right? "I haven't heard of a child that was defended by a gun for a while. I have not heard of or seen a child defended by a gun in my line of work nor have my colleagues for quite some time, I'm sure." Right. And I'm sure this is true, too. Because gun-grabbers like Dr. Jackman and his colleagues don't care about self-defense.

No doubt it has not occurred to Dr. Jackman, but the children who were defended by people with guns did not need a doctor!

Dr. Jackman says more than once that there's "a very good chance" a child will play with a gun if a gun is in the house. OK, so what, exactly, is this chance? What percent of homes with guns have kids in the home, and in what percent of those homes do kids play with guns and shoot themselves or others? He ignores this question. Instead, he says that in Georgia, between 20 and 30 percent of homes with guns have kids, and 23 percent of these gun owners said they could trust their child with a loaded gun. Dr. Jackman says that he considers someone a child up to the age of 18.

Does he believe the Second Amendment protects right of private citizens to keep and bear arms? "It's more of a privilege," he says, but "you can do what you want." But is there a *right* to keep and bear arms? "That's not part of my debate and that's not part of my study." His study "is all about the kids who come in to see me in the emergency department dead....I'm pro-child."

Evading questions about his view on the Second Amendment and gun control, Dr. Jackman says his study is "more about common sense and education than anything else." When asked what, precisely, was the kind of firearms instruction these kids had received, he replied, incredibly, "That was the one thing I did not specifically ask them."

It would have been interesting to know if any of their firearms training included how to determine if a gun is loaded, to always assume that it is, and to never point it at anyone.

Finally, let me share a few facts that render this absurd study even more ridiculous and unnecessary. First, according to the Centers for Disease Control, gun deaths for Americans under the age of 20 fell 35 percent in America from 1994 to 1998.

Secondly, according to the National Safety Council (NSC), as of 1996, the odds of dying unintentionally from a "firearm missile" is number 12 behind dying from accidents involving the following: motor vehicles; falls; poisoning by solids, liquids, gases, vapors; pedestrians; drowning; fire and flames; drowning by submersion (excluding water transport drowning previously mentioned); choking; complications, misadventures of surgical, medical care; and inhalation and ingestion of other objects.

Did you notice that medical category ahead of firearms? According to the NSC, the odds of dying unintentionally from medical mishaps is one in 1,194. The odds of dying unintentionally, during a lifetime, from a firearm missile is one in 3,096.

In addition, on this last point, which is particularly ironic and relevant, a 1999 study by the National Academy of Science's Institute of Medicine revealed that as many as 96,000 people are killed annually, just in hospitals, by medical mistakes—meaning malpractice. In 1996, 200 children under the age of five died accidentally from guns.

So, while it's true that guns in a doctor's office might be dangerous to those in the doctor's office, a far greater danger—many times over—would be the doctor!—especially if he treated you. Nothing, of course, is said about this deadly possibility in the study by Dr. Jackman and his fellow gun grabbers.

Remember, you are safer in a gun store than in a doctor's office.

Section Ten

ENEMIES OF FREEDOM

The Real Agenda

Sarah Brady of Handgun Control, Inc. says that her group only wants to get guns out of the wrong hands. From debating her and the other spokesmen from HCI, I can assure you that they think that the "wrong hands" belong to the entire civilian population of the country.

For example, when debating HCI spokesmen, I frequently challenge them to help repeal the Washington, D.C., gun ban which even makes it illegal to use a gun in self-defense! Surely, I ask them, you do not think that everybody in Washington has the wrong hands. "Well," they respond, "we respect local preference." Really, I ask, then why did you impose the Brady Law on the half of the states that had chosen not to have such legislation?

This exchange alone is enough to prove that they are for total civilian disarmament.

But there is more. Consider the frequent invitation to gun owners to accept such "reasonable gun control" as licensing. Why, we license cars don't we? Why should guns be any different?

To ask the question reveals a willingness to ignore the Second Amendment protection of the right to keep and bear arms. But they don't really mean they would treat a gun license like a driver's license. With my driver's license I can drive my car to the bank, to the bar, to church, to school—wherever I want. But the folks at Handgun Control, Inc. have opposed even much more restrictive concealed carry permits.

Gun controllers want total civilian disarmament because they do not believe in self-defense. I debated Representative Carolyn McCarthy of New York. Her husband was killed during the Long Island Railroad shooting. I asked Rep. McCarthy if it would have been wrong if someone had had a gun on that train and shot Colin Ferguson and saved her husband's life. I asked her the same question about the two adults who stopped school killers in their tracks because the adults were able to get their guns and stop the killing.

Mrs. McCarthy simply would not respond. No matter how I pressed her, she refused to answer the question. Her silence emphatically answered my question; she does not believe in self-defense.

Million Mom March

The Million Mom March provided a clear example of how the liberal establishment feels free to lie without fear of being held accountable. The hatred of self-defense seems to be a special justification for trashing the truth.

Aerial photographs of the moms march and the Promise Keepers gathering —a Christian men's group—make it possible to rather accurately estimate the crowd. Both assemblies were held in the very same place near the Capitol in Washington DC. The Promise Keepers were packed so tightly that one could hardly move, and they totally filled the mall ellipse. The moms were loosely assembled on picnic blankets with room to spare in between.

Had the moms gathered as tightly as had the Promise Keepers, the *New York Times* estimate of 100,000 might have been correct. More likely, the number of moms was about 50,000.

The moms themselves claimed 500,000, but many in the media headlined 750,000. The better to intimidate weak-kneed politicians, of course, into bowing to the demands for anti-self-defense gun legislation.

The leader of the moms, Donna Dees-Thomases, was not the soccer mom the media portrayed but a CBS public relations professional on leave from *The David Letterman Show*. Previously, Thomases had worked for six years for Dan Rather. She is also the sister-in-law of a Hillary Clinton attorney.

The media hype over the Misguided Mothers March (incidentally, they did not march!) provoked a number of women to form the Second Amendment Sisters. The sisters were stay-at-home moms and professional women alike. The sisters' main difference from the moms—other than their views on self-defense—was treatment by the media.

The moms were politically correct, so the media continually reported on them, even to the point of printing contact information about how to join up with the moms, meeting locations for traveling to the march, and more.

The City of Richmond, Virginia, spent $7,000 for school buses to send the moms to Washington. This was treated as not worthy of comment by the establishment, but imagine the outrage if public funds had been used to transport Ku Klux Klan members to a Washington rally.

Using the Internet and Christian radio, the sisters organized a truly grassroots effort and pulled off a very respectable presence of some fifteen hundred for their own rally the same day—Mother's Day, Sunday.

Thanks to the initiative of the Second Amendment Sisters, there was some media note of women who want to keep their guns for protecting themselves and their families. Texas State Representative Suzanna Gratia Hupp told the Second Amendment Sisters rally of the murder of her parents before her very eyes in a cafeteria in Killeen, Texas. A lunatic burst into Luby's Cafeteria and began methodically killing the lunchtime diners in the busy shopping center. No one there had a gun because it was against the law.

Hupp did have a gun—but it was 100 feet away in her car. The Texas law against carrying a concealed weapon provided the ideal environment for the murder of Hupps' parents. Her courageous crusading following the tragedy led to a law in Texas that legalizes what was a right all along—the right to protect one's own life and the life of others.

Another speaker was LaVerne Drayton who worked for Gun Owners of America at the time. She told of the anti-victim mentality that has repeatedly harmed her family.

LaVerne's brother was left paralyzed from the waist down by a gun-wielding assailant in Washington, D.C., where it is illegal to have a gun. Reduced to life in a wheel chair and repeatedly victimized by the criminal element in Washington, her brother took to keeping a handgun under the blanket over his legs. During a routine unconstitutional shakedown, police found his gun and locked up LaVerne's brother. Not only should he not have had a gun, according to the vicious D.C. law, but using one in self-defense is also illegal in Washington.

LaVerne Drayton told the truth about the ugly face of victim disarmament. The terror of living in Washington should not surprise us because the Bible, in Proverbs 8:36, tells us that those who hate God love death. And Washington gets plenty of what it loves, because the murder rate there is 35 times what it is just across the river in Virginia—where carrying a concealed firearm is perfectly legal.

A Million Mean Mommies?

The Million Mom March is in danger of being known as the Million Mean Mommies.

The most notorious case of a non-peaceful anti-gunner is that of Barbara Graham, who has been found guilty in the Washington, D.C., Superior Court of trying to avenge her son's death by shooting a young man whom she blamed for the killing.

Graham's son was killed in 1999, after which she joined the Washington-area group called Mothers on the Move Spiritually, which in turn helped sponsor the Million Mom March (so-called) in 2000.

The members of the MMM bill themselves as gun-control activists "dedicated to preventing gun death and injury and supporting victims and survivors of gun trauma." Indeed, at the Washington, D.C., march last year, Graham spoke out and helped memorialize the dead.

Evidently she didn't think there were enough dead to memorialize, so she tried to kill Kikko Smith, age 23. Graham did not kill Smith, but the shot she fired left him paralyzed and confined to a wheelchair for life.

Graham became frustrated with police efforts to apprehend her son's killer, so she took her son's .45-caliber handgun—which, by the way, is quite illegal in the District of Columbia. She and an accomplice then gunned Smith down as he tried to flee from them at his house.

Graham has subsequently received an object lesson about not being a private judge and jury vigilante squad. It turns out that the police already had in custody a suspect in her son's murder who had a similar-sounding name.

In a less tragic resort to violence, an ally of the Mean Mommies, Robert Howell, vice president of the Boulder chapter of the Bell Campaign, made it into the media in the Denver area. He assaulted a pro-gun concealed handgun carry permittee who was waiting to hear a Charlton Heston speech. Howell shoved a bullhorn into Shariar Ghalam's mouth and called him a dirty Arab (actually Ghalam is a Khurdish refugee from the oppression of Iran).

Incredibly, Gahlam restrained himself throughout this whole ordeal, even though he was legally carrying a loaded 9mm Glock at the time. He chose to run from his peacenik attacker, who then pursued him, pummeling him all the way. A police officer finally pulled Howell off of Ghalam. At no time did

Ghalam even brandish his gun.

Something may be in the water in the Denver area, because Fort Collins Mean Mommie Cherie Trine slugged George Keifer on the forehead with her clipboard outside a Mommie Meeting. The assault was witnessed by five people. Trine denies it, claiming that his head wound was there beforehand.

Another anti-gunner in the Denver area has plagued an Aurora gun show on two different occasions. He has been forced to pay restitution for the dealers' tables he has overturned during his rampage through the gun show.

Maybe the gun banners are right after all—to a point. They seem to be a violent bunch, so perhaps anybody with a membership in the Mean Mommies or some other anti-gun group should be prevented from owning a gun.

Now that's a background check Gun Owners of America could consider. (Just kidding.)

Ashcroft Confirmation: Rhetorical Lessons

One of the most decent men ever to come to Washington was treated by the Democrats as if he threatened the social order and the Constitution itself. Among those in the lynch mob were the strident voices of Handgun Control, Inc. Now, HCI's hysteria might have been understandable if John Ashcroft were an assault-rifle-waving militia maniac, if there is such a person. But Ashcroft's record on guns in the Senate was actually quite middle of the road. Indeed, Gun Owners of America graded the Senator with a C-. He earned such an anemic grade by voting to shut down gun shows and criminalize even the touching of a gun by someone under the age of 21.

On a non-binding resolution, sponsored by Barbara Boxer to free up the gun control bill that was stuck in the Senate, Boxer actually went to the Senate floor waving a letter from GOA. She was incensed that we refused to go along with her compromise. Only five Republicans agreed with Boxer, among them John Ashcroft.

That being said, it is all the more surprising that Ashcroft was likened by HCI Chairman, former Congressman Michael Barnes, to Timothy McVeigh, the Oklahoma City bomber. In case you are wondering what in the world Mr. Barnes and HCI were thinking, I will tell you right now. Senator Ashcroft had, in the past, said that he understood the Second Amendment to be a protection of an individual right intended by the Founding Fathers to insure that the people had the means to resist tyranny in government. This view was labeled by the Honorable Mr. Barnes as the "widely discredited, extremist insurrectionist view of the Second Amendment" held by Timothy McVeigh.

I was amazed to hear what HCI was doing to the history of our country. They have brazenly attempted to link the views of a terrorist to the beliefs of George Washington and Thomas Jefferson. Consider these words from the Declaration of Independence, penned by Jefferson and unanimously approved by the other 55 signers of the document:

> ...whenever any Form of Government becomes destructive of these Ends [unalienable rights], it is the Right of the People to alter or to abolish it....[W]hen a long Train of Abuses and Usurpations, pursuing invariably the same Object, evinces a Design to reduce them under absolute Despotism, it is their Right, it is their Duty, to throw off such Government....

What are we to think of an organization that thinks that the American Declaration of Independence is a terrorist document? If Handgun Control, Inc. had had its way, we all would still be British subjects of a tyrannical crown! HCI is so far from the mainstream of American history that they fail to see that it was the British who were the terrorists. They shot women and children—and worse. It was the Continental Army and the American militia who fought a defensive war. But then, HCI is against personal self-defense, too.

HCI Scorecard

Handgun Control, Inc. (HCI) issued its scorecard of how much gun control the states have imposed on their citizens. The scorecard came out just in time for the opening of school—for the safety of the children, you know.

HCI specifically stated that "each state was carefully rated for the existence of six types of legislation that protect children from guns."

I had the opportunity to debate an HCI spokesman on Fox Cable News. I pointed out some incredible inconsistencies in the scorecard. For example, Maryland got an A, but Nevada, with a slightly lower murder rate, got a D+. Illinois got a B+, but Alabama, with a lower murder rate, got an F. California got a score of B+, but Virginia, with a slightly lower murder rate, got a D. New York got a B+, but Wyoming, with a lower murder rate, got an F.

Connecticut got an A-, but Montana, with an identical murder rate, got an F. Hawaii, Maine, and Massachusetts all had the same murder rate, but Maine got an F while the other two gun control meccas got A-'s. And the three states with the lowest murder rates in the nation—New Hampshire, South Dakota, and North Dakota—all got D's.

Go figure.

Clearly, HCI is not interested in lowering crime. They are interested in keeping people from having access to firearms for self-defense.

I pointed out that the "loopholes" HCI wanted to close could end up like the ultimate "loophole" closure, to use their word, of English gun banning. And now England's violent crime rate has risen to a higher level than that of America.

The HCI representative did not like that and suggested that I was a conspiratorialist for suggesting that HCI wants to ban guns. I was able to show that "of course you do."

Indeed, in 1999, a bill was before the U.S. House of Representatives to end the gun ban in Washington, D.C. HCI opposed that measure. They would rather the people of Washington be legally disarmed even though the criminals of the city have all the guns they want and the results show it. In fact, Washington, D.C., has the highest murder rate of any jurisdiction in the country.

There is no doubt about it. The Handgun Control, Inc. Scorecard is a failure.

Parents should send it back to school without a signature. In fact, the teacher should be brought up on charges of incompetence before the school board and fired.

Surprise! Handgun Control Has No Facts

Nothing frustrates and angers the "gun grabbers" more than asking them to put up or shut up—to prove what they claim. Take for example some ridiculous statements made in a recent Fox Cable TV interview by Brian Morton, Associate Director of Communications for Handgun Control, Inc.

Trashing some states for supposedly not doing what they could "to protect children from guns," Morton said: "They have not tried to close the gun show loophole. They allow people to carry concealed weapons in all sorts of public places. They've taken away the right of individual cities to sue the gun industry for the damage their products do."

Well, now. These are new ones. I've never heard it charged before that the gun show "loophole" has harmed kids. Ditto laws that allow folks to carry concealed weapons. So, we interviewed Morton and asked him to put up or shut up. For openers, we asked for the evidence to support his first allegation.

Morton says one "classic example" is that the gun show "loophole" allowed a young girl (Robyn Anderson) to buy some firearms which she then gave to Eric Harris and Dylan Klebold who used them to murder some of their classmates and a teacher at Columbine High School. The only problem with this example is that Anderson herself has admitted that even if there had been a private-party background check at the gun show where she bought these firearms she would have passed the check! She would have passed because (a) she had no criminal convictions; (b) she wasn't a fugitive from justice; (c) she had never been adjudicated a mental defective or been in a mental institution; and (d) she was never dishonorably discharged from the military.

When asked if Robyn Anderson is the only example he has that gun show "loopholes" harm children, Morton says, testily: "I'm not going to sit here and go incident-by-incident through this with you. You clearly appear to have an angle you've latched on to." He accuses us of looking for "a tangible and explicit thing," of "seizing on an example of semantics to make a point you want."

When we continue to press Morton on this issue, he admits, finally, "I don't know that I could point you to any specific research on that."

Okay. So, we move on to Morton's charge that children have been harmed by concealed carry laws. We ask, again: Says who? What is your evidence to support *this* assertion?

Morton is not pleased by this line of questioning. He says that by asking this we are starting to get into "statistical things" and he sees where we are going. He tries, once more, to dismiss our question as mere "semantics." But, yes, he says, it is his contention that laws that allow the carrying of concealed weapons have harmed children. Unable to cite any specific evidence to back up his assertion, he refers us to Douglas Wile, head of research at Handgun Control, Inc.

When we ask Wile if he knows of any evidence showing that concealed carry laws have harmed children, he says: "Hmmmm, yeah. That's a good one. I don't think we know that." Does he know of any evidence that gun show "loopholes" have harmed children? Noting that this is a "difficult question," Wile says he "knows of no such data."

Another thing Morton complained about in his Fox TV interview—as previously noted—was that some states "have taken away the right of individual cities to sue the gun industry for the damage their products do." So, we ask, "And where does a city get the 'right' you assert?" He replies, "Home rule, sir." We ask, "But, a state has no 'right' to overrule a city?" "Yes," says Morton, "but not when the state does this at the behest of the gun industry."

In other words, for Morton, only the gun grabbers have a "right" to influence what a state does, but the "gun industry" and those law-abiding citizens who believe in the Second Amendment do not.

Morton insists that cities have the "right" to sue the gun industry just like cities should be allowed to sue Firestone for selling tires that caused 88 or so people to die because their tires were blowing up. But this analogy is no good. If people sue Firestone and win, it will be because Firestone was negligent and sold a product that was flawed. Cities that sue the gun industry do so not because certain guns were flawed and blew up when used, but because of the way the guns were used. This is a big difference from the Firestone tire situation.

Defending his absurd Firestone analogy, Morton says he doesn't think tires "are made expressly to kill people." Well, we say, neither are guns made expressly to kill people. There are a lot of other uses for guns. In fact, studies show that most guns used in self-defense never kill anybody and are never fired. Morton says, "I kind of find it hard to believe that when the Chinese invented gunpowder years ago they were thinking about plinking cans." But, he's probably wrong here, too. The *Encyclopedia Britannica* says that although black powder is thought to have originated in China, "there is, however, some evidence that the Arabs were the first to develop black powder."

Morton says, again erroneously, "Guns were made specifically to kill people. Handguns were specifically made to kill people." We ask, "But is *all* killing bad? Don't you believe in self-defense?" Morton says, "I see no reason to continue this....I don't think this is going to have any constructive purpose." He hangs up the phone.

But, again, Brian Morton is wrong. Our conversation with him has served a *very* constructive purpose. It has demonstrated, with a vengeance, that he doesn't know what he's talking about; that he has no facts to back up what he has asserted on national television.

A footnote: Morton was on Fox TV to talk about his organization's "report card" which gave "failing grades" to states which, basically, refused to enact the vehemently anti-gun, anti-Second Amendment agenda of Handgun Control, Inc. This "report card" paid no attention at all to the crucial issue of whether states had or had not reduced crime. In fact, this omission was so glaring that Morton's interviewer asked, incredulously, "But, isn't the point of gun control laws to lower crime?" Well, yes, said Morton lamely, but the populations of various states are so different that "you can't exactly compare apples to oranges here."

Despite this diversity, however, Morton and his ilk seek to impose *federal* gun control laws on *all* these "apples and oranges."

What a hypocrite.

Section Eleven

❧

ANTI-GUN NUTS
OF THE MONTH

John Guernsey

A drum roll and cymbal clash, please, as we begin a series called "Anti-Gun Nut of the Month," the title of which is self-explanatory and indicates the dubious achievement being noted. This month's winner: John Guernsey of Takoma Park, Maryland.

But, before we get to Mr. Guernsey, here is a little background regarding his place of residence. Takoma Park is the East Coast version of the radically leftist West Coast city of Berkeley, California. It is a hotbed of lunatic politics. For example, in 1983, the Takoma Park City Council voted unanimously for an ordinance making the city a "nuclear-free zone"—despite the fact that, at the time, the city was in no way involved with nuclear weapons.

Now, back to Guernsey. In late 1999, he organized an unofficial referendum to ban the sale and/or possession of handguns within his city's limits. This was done even though a county circuit judge had ruled that this referendum could not be put on an official ballot because it conflicted with state law. The result of this outlawed referendum was 409 to 85 against handguns. There are 18,600 people living in Takoma Park.

So what exactly is it that causes Guernsey and his ilk to be so hysterically and un-constitutionally gunophobic? Well, for openers, he says 85 percent of all armed robberies are with handguns "and this should be enough right there" to ban them. But, what about all the good, self-defense uses of guns every year, including handguns? Guernsey says this happens only "a very few times." To support what he says, he refers GOA to the Johns Hopkins Center For Gun Policy And Research (JHCGPR) in Baltimore, Maryland.

OK. But, Emile Lebrun, Coordinator of the JHCGPR, tells GOA that the figures they use for annual self-defense with guns, including handguns, are 108,000. This data, from a U.S. Justice Department National Crime Victimization Survey (1994), means that Americans use firearms to defend themselves or others 9,000 times a month, 2,077 times a week, 296 times a day. This is not exactly "a very few times." And it should be mentioned that this 108,000 figure is the lowest of several national surveys—one such survey showing this annual number to be as high as 3.6 million!

In any event, when confronted with the 108,000 figure, Guernsey says, "Well—uh, uh, well, OK. I mean, you got me there, you know with statistics." Still, he says, regardless of how many lives are saved by the use of handguns, he is still for banning all of them.

Now, to put it charitably, this position of Guernsey's is very odd because another one of his arguments for banning all handguns is that some are used to commit suicide and accidentally shoot people—which is true. But, if he really cares about saving human lives, why doesn't he care about all those lives saved by the use of guns every year, including handguns? If the data show—as they do—that tens of thousands, indeed hundreds of thousands, more people defend themselves with guns (including handguns) than commit suicide or accidentally shoot somebody, why don't these lives count?

But, clearly, to Guernsey, these human lives saved do not count—which is why his position is nutty.

In fact, when pressed, Guernsey admits that he personally had an argument with a woman who said her life was saved by the use of a handgun. He says that when he was seeking signatures for his handgun ban, this woman vehemently attacked him verbally "but because she was so irate there was no room for discussion."

When it is suggested that this is understandable because if his ban had been in effect this woman believes she would have been dead, Guernsey says he thought about this "but this doesn't come up as much" as people who use guns to commit suicide or accidentally shoot people. He criticizes this woman because her focus was solely on herself "and not on the rest of the country."

But, one more time, when you look at the statistics regarding the rest of the country, hundreds of thousands more people annually use firearms, including handguns, to defend their lives, the lives of friends and family and property, than use these firearms to commit suicide or accidentally shoot other people or themselves.

The sad fact is that in advocating, as he told GOA, a national law to ban all private ownership of handguns, John Guernsey does not care about this Constitutional right. He does not care how many innocent lives are saved yearly by the use of handguns. Guernsey's position is, literally: Don't confuse me with any facts. It is because of his aggressive and dangerous ignorance that he is our first—but, alas, not our last—winner of our "Anti-Gun Nut of the Month" award.

Joseph Curran

Maryland Attorney General Joseph Curran has issued a 63-page report titled *A Farewell To Arms: The Solution To Gun Violence In America.* Curran's report is a "solution" to nothing. Instead, it is a brazen, blatant, ignorant, erroneous, brass-knuckled, knee-in-the-groin attack on the Second Amendment.

Curran has circulated his Farewell to Arms to the other 49 attorneys general hoping to gain their support in his war against the Constitution he has sworn to uphold.

His proposals, if enacted into law (God forbid), would have the effect of doing to the Second Amendment what the explosives did to that federal building in Oklahoma. That is to say, Curran's proposals would, if they became law, demolish the Second Amendment.

And—like in Oklahoma—lives would be lost because millions of law-abiding Americans would be denied the right to defend themselves with handguns.

About one thing, however, Curran is absolutely correct. His proposals are none of those "small, timid measures" or "band-aid" solutions he denounces. No, siree.

Curran says, flat out: "Our public policy goal should be to restrict the sale and possession of all handguns to those who can demonstrate a legitimate law enforcement purpose or can guarantee that the use of such guns will be limited to participation in a regulated sporting activity....We must institute a plan that will move us to a point where people are ready to accept an end to unrestricted private handgun ownership."

Unrestricted?! I wish! In our country today, we have more than 20,000 so-called "gun control" laws!

There is so much in Curran's wretched report that is false, half-true, and intellectually dishonest that one hardly knows where to begin in trying to correct the record.

But, let's start with his false view of the Second Amendment. Curran says: "This notion of an individual constitutional right to own firearms is a myth. The Supreme Court and all lower federal courts have unanimously held, since the first decision in 1886, that the Second Amendment is about the states' right to maintain a militia, and has nothing whatever to do with an individual's right to bear arms outside the context of a state militia."

Wrong! In a case called *United States v. Miller* (1939), the U.S. Supreme Court noted that the militia reference in the Second Amendment alludes to "civilians primarily, soldiers on occasion," that "the Militia comprised all males physically capable of acting in concert for the common defense" and that ordinarily when called for service "these men were expected to appear bearing arms supplied by themselves and of the kind in common use at the time."

As Stephen P. Halbrook notes in his book, *That Every Man Be Armed: The Evolution Of A Constitutional Right* (The Independent Institute, 1994): "The Supreme Court's historical review demonstrates that the 'well-regulated militia' referred to in the Second Amendment meant the whole people armed and not a select group, that each private individual had the right and duty to keep and bear arms, and that the people were to provide their own armed protection rather than depend upon a militarist and oppressive standing army."

Maryland's constitutional history shouts against Curran's pro-civilian disarmament policies. In his book, *For The Defense Of Themselves And The State: The Original Intent And Judicial Interpretation Of The Right To Keep And Bear Arms* (Praeger, 1994), Clayton E. Cramer quotes a member of the Maryland convention considering ratification of the U.S. Constitution (Alexander Contee Hanson) as referring to the militia, "which is ourselves." And a committee of this same convention called the militia "all men, able to bear arms."

These words from the Maryland Convention echo the Virginia Ratifying Convention in which George Mason (a long-time friend of George Washington) argued that "the militia is the whole people, except for a few public officials."

Curran is retailing the Handgun Control, Inc. myth that the Second Amendment applies only to a state's ability to maintain a militia and does not protect a God-given right of individuals to keep and bear arms. As recently as 1991, the Supreme Court in *U.S. v. Verdugo-Urquidez* held that throughout the Bill of Rights where the term "the people" is used, it refers to an individual right—as in the first, second, fourth, ninth, and tenth amendments.

Another thing Curran denounces as a "myth," as "hype," as "false propaganda," is that handguns are needed for self-defense. He says, "Study after study shows that guns are rarely used successfully in self-defense."

Rarely used? His own report quotes a U.S. Justice Department survey estimating that there are, on average, 108,000 defensive uses of gun annually—which is 9,000 times a month, 2,077 times a week, 296 times a day. This isn't "rare" by any definition.

And there are even higher and more reliable estimates. For example, Gary Kleck and Marc Gertz estimate that 2.5 million Americans use a gun in self-defense each year. Curran, however, says this figure is "wildly over-estimated."

But, the late Marvin E. Wolfgang, a liberal icon who called himself "as strong a gun-control advocate as can be found among criminologists," said in *The Journal Of Criminal Law & Criminology* (Vol. 86, No. 1) that Kleck/ Gertz's research is "an almost clear-cut case of methodologically sound research in support of something I have theoretically opposed for years, namely, the use of a gun in defense against a criminal perpetrator." Wolfgang, who had done research on guns and violence for over 25 years, added that he had to admit "my admiration for the care and caution expressed" by Kleck/Gertz in their research.

There was a time in colonial Maryland when—depending on who was in power—Protestants passed laws to disarm Catholics, and vice-versa. And, of course, in Maryland, a slave state that remained with the Union, slaves were prohibited from carrying guns without "a license from his said master" before the War Between the States, and free blacks were completely forbidden possession of either firearms or ammunition.

Now, Attorney General J. Joseph Curran, Jr. would make all the law-abiding citizens of Maryland "slaves" by seeking to deny them their Constitutional right to keep and bear arms and use handguns to defend themselves against criminals. But, this must not succeed. We hope that all the good, decent, law-abiding citizens of Maryland will rise up and say to Curran and his report what King Charles I said when Parliament demanded control of the militia: "By God, not for an hour!"

Not only do the people of Maryland need to make their opposition known to Curran's tyrannical views, but the citizens of all states should let their attorney general know that they want a quick goodbye said to *Farewell to Arms.*

William Jefferson Clinton

It's true that in any given month—as our most anti-Second Amendment President in history—Mr. Clinton could have been given this dubious achievement award.

But, we have chosen him this month because of his exceptionally idiotic interview on the NBC *Today* show (3/2/2000) in which he was unusually absurd and, at times, incoherent.

In fact, Mr. Clinton's replies in this preposterous interview reminded me of something said in Lewis Carroll's *Alice In Wonderland* where Alice says it is no use trying, that one cannot believe impossible things. To which the Queen replies that this requires practice and "sometimes I've believed as many as six impossible things before breakfast."

So it is with Mr. Clinton. Whether it was his relationship with Monica Lewinsky or his arguments for "gun control," he is an expert at asking us to believe impossible things. And he did this with a vengeance in his *Today* interview.

Let us count some of the ways he asked us to believe the impossible:

Trigger Locks For Handguns

When asked about the tragic death of the little 6-year-old girl in Michigan who was shot by another 6-year-old, Mr. Clinton repeatedly chanted his "trigger lock" mantra, implying that such a device would have saved this young child. He said, at one point, "If we had passed the child trigger lock provision and we had applied it to all new guns, then at least those guns would not be used by 6-year-olds to kill other 6-year-olds."

A few days later, he said, again, "I'm not at all sure that even a callous, irresponsible drug dealer with a 6-year-old in the house wouldn't leave a child trigger lock on a gun." *The Washington Post* (9 March 2000).

Mr. Clinton even went so far as to say on the *Today* show: "And then when all those kids were killed at Columbine I thought, surely, we can...have child safety locks....We need the public to be aroused on this."

And it should be noted that then Vice President Al Gore, also on the *Today* show (3/8/2000), has declared, "I can't understand why anyone would not be in favor of mandatory child safety trigger locks—not voluntary but mandatory child safety locks—after that horrible tragedy in Michigan."

But, what I don't understand is why anybody would believe that trigger locks would have in any way prevented either the tragic shooting in Michigan or the slaughter at Columbine. I mean, the kid who killed the little girl in Michigan got his handgun from under a blanket in the crack house where he lived among drug-using criminals who would not have had trigger locks on their guns even if they were mandatory (sorry, Al).

And the murderers at Columbine were not children; they were young adults hell-bent on mass murder and would in no way have been deterred by trigger locks.

Get real please, Mr. Clinton and Mr. Gore.

Guns and Cars

I am really getting sick of this phony analogy and will explore it in some detail in a future column. In any event, Clinton says, "Ultimately, what we ought to do is license handgun owners the way we license people who drive cars."

But, of course, if this were done, would Clinton then favor letting all who have licensed guns take their weapons where licensed car drivers can take their cars—to work, church, to school? No way! And this is why the gun-car analogy is phony, a total fraud.

When it is noted that one opponent of gun licensing says that criminals are not going to stand in line to get their photos taken (like car drivers do), Mr. Clinton says, incoherently, "Well, you could say that about people with automobile licenses, too."

Huh? What, exactly, does this mean? In fact, it is undoubtedly true that all kinds of criminals have driver's licenses with their photos on it.

The president says, referring to the man who stole the gun that was used to kill the little 6-year-old girl in Michigan, that if handguns were licensed, "he could never get a license." Maybe, maybe not. But, the real-life point is this: Such a criminal would never apply for a gun license!

Finally, denouncing those who oppose the licensing of handguns like car drivers are licensed, Mr. Clinton says: "They're saying guns are special, guns are different than cars....That's their argument and I just disagree with them." OK. So, at long last, the President gets one right.

Yes! In fact, he is exactly correct! We, along with our Founding Fathers, do say guns are special! You bet. And their specialness—our God-given right to keep and bear them—is guaranteed and legally protected by the Second Amendment to our Constitution.

However, our Constitution is evidently so irrelevant that neither Mr. Clinton nor his interviewer, Katy Couric, mention it in this lengthy interview. At one point, all Couric wants to know is if it would be "practically possible" to "check every gun owner in America to see if he or she is carrying a license?"

To which Mr. Clinton replies: "Well, none of these things will happen instantaneously, overnight. But, yet, they will begin to make a difference." Well, yes. Such checks would "make a difference." They would turn our country into a police state!

But, forget about practicality. What about the constitutionality of such checks—their obvious violation of the Second and Fourth Amendments? Silence. About this, the President and Couric say nothing. Zip. Zilch.

In conclusion, Clinton referring to what he has proposed in this interview, says: "We need to...just systematically go do them. None of them interfere with the right of any lawful citizen to hunt or engage in sport shooting." But, again, what about the U.S. Constitution?

The Second Amendment does not recognize and legally protect just the right to hunt and sport shoot. It recognizes and legally protects the right to keep and bear arms. Thus, what Mr. Clinton proposes does interfere with the Constitutional rights of our citizens. And this is why he is this month's "Anti-Gun Nut"—a very dangerous man.

Maryland State Senator Barbara Hoffman

At the heart of what makes an individual an anti-gun nut is his or her absolute, hysterical, irrational fear of guns that are seen—always and in every way—as evil and of no good use under any circumstances.

Usually accompanying such fanaticism is, of course, an utter and total disregard of the Second Amendment. All of these characteristics lead us to this month's anti-gun nut, Maryland State Senator Barbara Hoffman, a Democrat.

In response to the raffling off of a 9mm handgun by Carroll County (Maryland) Republicans, Hoffman introduced Senate Bill 341 which would prohibit a person from operating a raffle in which a handgun is offered as a prize. In a statement regarding her bill, Hoffman said:

> There have been very few occasions in my life when I have been at a loss for words; yet this time I am, perhaps because the issue is so clear to me as it is to many others....A handgun is not an appropriate prize for a raffle. It trivializes the tragedies of thousands of Americans....As such, it is an appropriate response of government to take action.
>
> We do not allow alcoholic beverages to be advertised or used or sold everywhere, although it is a legal product. The same is true for cigarettes. The same theory should be true for a handgun, a legal product but one whose primary purpose is to do harm.

Well, now. Too bad Hoffman wasn't, literally, at a loss for words because what she says here is absurd. In no way do handguns, necessarily, "trivialize" anything. Indeed, raffling off a handgun could more likely be said to honor the hundreds of thousands of Americans—some estimates say millions of Americans—who use handguns every year in self-defense.

And Hoffman's comparison of handguns to alcohol and cigarettes is equally ludicrous because there is no Constitutional right to drink or smoke. There is, however, a Constitutional right for individuals to keep and bear arms.

But, as an anti-gun nut, Hoffman could not care less about self-defense or Constitutional rights, as was made clear when we confronted her at the Maryland State Capital in Annapolis. Here's the way our brief interview with her went when we attempted to discuss her bill, the Constitution, and self-defense:

Q: What about the U.S. Constitutional Second Amendment

protection for the right of individuals to keep and bear arms?

A: Why, I don't think it has anything to do with it. I mean, this bill has nothing to do with the Second Amendment. We regulate a whole lot of legal products. And saying that a group can't use a handgun as a raffle prize doesn't say anything about whatever your interpretation is of the Second Amendment.

Q: But [the Second Amendment would apply] to those people keeping the arms (to raffle them and to those winning the handguns).

A: No, no, no, no.

Q: Don't law-abiding citizens have the right to keep arms and sell (raffle them off) to other law-abiding citizens?

A: Only if they follow the law. And if we say by law that you can't raffle a handgun, then they can't.

Q: You say that such a raffle trivializes the tragedy of thousands of Americans.

A: Yes.

Q: What about the hundreds of thousands of Americans—some research says millions of Americans—who every year use handguns in self-defense? Guns aren't used just to harm people. Do you care about the lives saved by people using handguns in self-defense?

A: Sure. And they can go buy their guns in a gun store.

Q: But who are you to tell them where they should buy their guns?

A: I'm a legislator, sir. If we pass a law that you can't raffle a gun, you can't raffle a gun.

Q: Really? So, there's no appeal from your law? Nobody can contest it in a court?

A: What do you mean contest it in a court? If you want to buy a gun legally, then you certainly have lots of places to buy the gun.

Q: In fact, the analogy you use—you say guns should be treated like alcohol and cigarettes, which are legal to buy!

A: Yes, but not everywhere to every person.

Q: But your bill [would prohibit anyone from buying a gun from a raffle].

A: I'm finished.

Q: You're finished all right.

A: But, not the way you think though.

Q: Your bill's going nowhere. It's insane.

A: You know what? Let me tell you something. That bill probably won't pass here.

Q: You don't care about the Constitution of the United States.

A: You know what I care about? I care about the thousands of children who have been killed by people with handguns who don't take care of them.

Q: But not the hundreds of thousands of lives saved by handguns.

A: I don't believe that for one minute.

Q: That's because you don't do any research on it. You're ignorant.

A: And you, sir, are rude.

Q: Better than ignorant.

To make a long story short, Hoffman's bill, as predicted, was killed in a committee and never saw the light of day, thank God. But, there's a fascinating footnote to this tale which proves that handguns—even those won at raffles—are not necessarily always put to a bad or harmful use, as Hoffman seems to believe. As Maryland Republican State Senator Timothy Ferguson told us:

> Someone called me from Allegheny County. He told me that some years ago he had won a handgun at a sporting event raffle held at a carnival. He said he subsequently used this handgun to save himself from being a victim of a violent crime on his property. He obviously believed he couldn't be here today if he had not had that handgun.

Ferguson says this man did not want to be identified by name "because he didn't want to be ostracized in this anti-gun climate where there is this sinking feeling among Second Amendment supporters that you will be treated as a second-class citizen if you believe in gun ownership."

Maryland Alderman Wants Federal Law Banning Toy Guns

When I first read the story in the *Washington Times* newspaper I thought it was a joke, a spoof. I double-checked the date of the paper. No, it was April 20th, not April 1st. The headline read: "Buyback Of Toy Water Pistols Sought."

The story told how Cynthia A. Carter, a Democrat alderman in the city of Annapolis, Maryland, wants police to buy back cap guns, water pistols, and other toy weapons to curb violent behavior in children. She's quoted as saying, "Children can't distinguish between a real gun and or a play gun, nor do they understand the difference between life and death." She wants people to weigh the possibilities, asking, "What good does a toy gun do and what harm does it do?"

Still not sure that this story was for real, we contacted Alderman Carter, interviewed her and here's the way it went.

Q: So, what's wrong with kids playing with toy guns, cap guns, and water pistols?

A: Well, if you follow me, when they were making toys guns which, first of all, should never have been, to take something that could be so detrimental, something so deadly, and turn it into a toy, and capitalize on it at the cost of children and the risk of their lives, and just bodily harm.

So, they got away with it over the years. But, with time change, like with the seatbelts and the metal detectors at school and other precautionary measures taken to protect the children, I think we better look at what we have here—to do the same thing. Times have changed.

I don't know if you've ever seen some of those video games. There is some pretty nasty stuff on there—shooting and killing and destroying each other. Children need at this point in time, with things being as they are, to be taught to respect, to care, and to love.

And when they get older and if they decide they want to get a gun and do hunting or collect them as a hobby or whatever. But the same laws they have restricting children from tobacco, driving and alcohol need to be put on any form of a gun....

Q: You think police should buy back these violent video games, too?

A: Absolutely! Absolutely! If we could get some of those things—
these kids get together in these rooms, turn on these videos
and freak out. I can't stand to look at them. Can you imagine
what's going through these young minds? But, we had better
take note and check ourselves.

Q: Should it be illegal to make these toy guns?

A: Absolutely!

Q: Really?

A: Absolutely! And if I had my way it would be.

Q: Making toy guns should be a crime?

A: Yes.

Q: And what should be the punishment?

A: The same as it would be if you made a real gun.

Q: But, it is not illegal to manufacture most guns. What specific
punishment would you support for those who make toy guns?

A: I'm sure the federal government could find a fine—I guess the
same fine that there would be if a kid was sold a real gun.

Q: So, there should be a federal law against selling toy guns?

A: Absolutely. Absolutely.

Q: You seem to think that all guns and all uses of guns are bad.

A: Understand what I am saying. What it's doing mentally to the
children. What you do with a gun when you become of age—
some fathers think it is right to take these boys out and show
them how to kill an animal. These children cannot distinguish
a difference—their minds absorb—and, again, and my backup
on the whole thing is that if you train up a child in the way he
should go, when he gets older he will not stray from it.

Q: Right. That's from the Old Testament book of Proverbs.

A: Exactly, Proverbs 22:6.

Q: So, if you train up a child to know the difference between a toy
gun and a real gun then—

A: You can't.

Q: Sure you can.

A: No, you can't. The idea that it is a very destructive piece of equipment that was made to look like, and to be played with to kill, is the whole direction this whole thing has gone.

Q: But is all killing bad?

A: Yes. If you teach a child to kill—

Q: What about self-defense?

A: There is a difference. A child does not have the ability, to my knowledge—and I'm talking about little children—to kill somebody to defend themselves.

Q: But, I'm alluding to that Proverb you quoted. It's true. So, if you trained up a child, with toy guns, to teach them to respect real guns, and use them for self-defense, when necessary, then—

A: No.

Q: Sure you could.

A: You know, there's one thing about anything that happens in this world. There's no correct way of doing it. I want to initiate something that needs to be initiated, and that right now is to let children know that guns are not toys. And we start by eliminating them as toys.

Q: But toy guns are toys.

A: We're adults and we know. But we should know better by now that we need to stop manufacturing them and giving them to kids and stop letting it be a toy.

Q: But what's wrong with training kids to know about and respect real guns and to know how to use them in self-defense?

A: We can teach the children about a lot of things. But to teach them about using a firearm to kill, they have to first learn to respect life before they can learn the rest of it. We as parents are supposed to protect these children. They should not have to have a firearm to protect themselves or to get a meal (?).

Q: No, I'm not talking about kids having real guns. I'm talking about training them, when they are kids, to learn to use a real gun later, possibly in self-defense—which, incidentally, shows a respect for human life!

A: No. I don't agree with that. We have other things to teach our kids. We need to teach them to respect life.

Q: It's not either/or. You can do both. You can demonstrate a respect for human life by using a gun to defend your life or somebody else's life.

A: This is something the Lord (?) has laid on my heart. I find it necessary, just like we need to put prayer back in school. This is what I want to do for my community. The kids cannot watch TV all day long. They cannot watch certain movies and things on there. They cannot do those videos. We need to put a book in their hands, or they should learn to ride horseback, go to the arts, dancing. This is what we need to do. But there are not too many parents in the homes taking care of kids nowadays.

Q: We're not going to disagree on that. Are you aware that hundreds of thousands of people in this country—some studies says millions—of Americans use guns in self-defense every year?

A: Should a five or six-year-old kid be put to that? I'm not talking about someone who is 19, 20, or 21. I'm talking about the youth. We gotta start somewhere.

Q: I'm sorry. I'm not getting my point across. I'm saying that one valid reason for allowing kids to have toy guns is to show them how to use real guns responsibly when they grow up for, among other things, self-defense.

A: Then take them to a whorehouse and show them how to have sex! You might as well do the whole nine yards.

Q: Really? So, you think teaching kids how to responsibly use firearms is like teaching them to fornicate?

A: No, baby. Self-defense didn't mainly start in the home. That is where most children are harmed where they are molested by those who are supposed to love and care for them. We gotta teach these kids that that is not the thing to play with.

Q: I'm not talking about teaching kids to play with real guns!

A: Not every child can distinguish between a real and a toy. Their minds are not developed that way. We are the parents, the caretakers. And we must direct these children the right way.

Amazing, no?—and truly lunatic—which is why Cynthia A. Carter is our "Anti-Gun Nut of the Month."

The Episcopal Church

Considering the fact that the Episcopal Church in America has lost hundreds of thousands of members during the past two decades, you'd think that these folks would be doing everything possible to protect and preserve this endangered species of Christians.

Thus, specifically, you would think that, maybe, this church would enthusiastically endorse the right of self-defense, specifically the right of private individuals—in this case Episcopalians—to own firearms for self-defense. But, if this is what you think, you would be sadly mistaken.

Meeting recently in their 73rd General Convention in Chicago, Episcopalians passed a resolution that calls upon all members "to work intentionally in their several communities, legislatures and institutions toward the removal of handguns and assault weapons from our homes, other residential communities and vehicles."

But, why? Since there are many law-abiding Americans who use guns in self-defense every year (many, many more than there are Episcopalians), why seek to deny these persons the capability to use guns to defend themselves, their families, friends, and/or property?

In an attempt to get an answer to this question and others, we spoke with Helen Moore, interim dean of the Cathedral of St. James, the Episcopal Church in which this anti-gun, anti-self-defense resolution originated. We also spoke with Duncan Moore, a member of Interim Dean Moore's church, who served on the Peace and Social Justice Commission which drafted this resolution. First, Interim Dean Moore:

Q: About a dozen studies and polls show that as many as three million Americans annually use guns in self-defense, including handguns. So, why do you want this protection removed, which is what would happen if your resolution was obeyed?

A: Well, we're asking people to prayerfully consider this.

Q: But, why? Why, since so many Americans use guns for self-defense and to defend others and property?

A: Because of so many statistics—that I don't have with me— about how many teen suicides come from homes where guns are available, and much more domestic violence.

Q: But, the studies and polls I just mentioned show that

hundreds of thousands more Americans use guns in self-defense in every year than use guns to commit suicide and/or commit domestic violence.

A: I think, probably, that we don't see it that way.

Q: But, have you looked at the studies/polls on guns and self-defense?

A: Yes, we looked at all of that and we still felt that [our resolution] was very important as an expression of our Christian faith and Christian witness to ask people to *think* about the presence of firearms.

Q: Well, but your resolution actually calls on people to *remove* certain guns from their homes and elsewhere.

A: Right. Right...What we were looking at as far as the data is concerned was how the presence and ready availability of firearms in the home showed a considerable increase in teen suicides and domestic violence. We want people to *think* about that.

Q: But, again, even if what you say here is true, the data show that there are hundreds of thousands more good uses of guns, in self-defense, annually, than there are bad uses of guns.

A: Well, I think we didn't, necessarily, see that—that the good uses outweigh the bad.

Q: A lot more kids die in the home by falling, from poisoning, suffocating, and drowning in water buckets, than die from guns every year. So, why single out only guns in your resolution?

A: I think, part of it is—you know, there's no perfect answer to any of this. And I don't think we were trying to achieve anything like that....

Q: You don't see anything un-Christian about self-defense do you?

A: No, I don't. But as Christians we are supposed to work against violence by any means.

Q: Should all handguns be banned?

A: Not necessarily.

Next we spoke to Duncan Moore, a man Interim Dean Moore said could probably give us "some more helpful information."

Q: Why remove guns from the home when a dozen studies and polls show that as many as three million Americans annually use guns in self-defense, including handguns?

A: Well, I haven't seen those studies. The studies I've seen... show that the presence of a gun in the home vastly increases the likelihood that a member of the household will be injured by that gun.

Q: So, you're unaware of the self-defense data I just mentioned?

A: I know that many people make this argument. But, I don't subscribe....

Q: I'm not talking about arguments. I'm talking about studies and polls. In fact, a Gallup Poll in May of this year showed that 14.3 million adult Americans say they have used a gun in self-defense. Are you aware of any of this data?

A: I'm aware that some people allege that such studies exist.

Q: So, have you checked out these allegations to see if they are true?

A: No, I've been reading the medical literature which is fairly straightforward on the risks involved in keeping a gun in the household.

Q: But, I'm talking about *self-defense!* I'm talking about the risk posed to *criminals* by armed homeowners who have guns to protect themselves, family, and property. Do you care about this?

A: No, I don't believe that's true. It's a bogus argument. I subscribe to the argument that guns are not Christian. *That* is the crux of my argument.

Q: And where in Scripture do you see support for your view?

A: Jesus doesn't talk about self-defense. Jesus talks about caring for other people. And if we care deeply for other people, we should remove the weapons that cause other people harm.

Q: But, wouldn't caring for other people include protecting yourself, family, and friends by, when necessary, using guns against criminals in your home?

At this point, Moore says this conversation is not being conducted "properly" because he is being "proselytized." He hangs up the phone.

Well, now. In a way that Interim Dean Moore certainly did not intend, Duncan Moore has, indeed, given us "some more helpful information." And what he has helped us to see is that he could not care less about "caring for other people" because he does not care about the right of self-defense with firearms.

Moore also helps us to see that he is truly a know-nothing ignoramus by charging, falsely, that it is not true that millions of us, every year, defend ourselves with guns, as a huge body of data proves. And this is why Moore and every Episcopalian who voted for his wretched resolution are our "Anti-Gun Nuts" this month.

Targeting Water Pistols

This month's "Anti-Gun Nut of the Month" award is a first. It is not, as usual, an individual "Anti-Gun Nut" award. Instead, the dubious achievement of receiving this award has been accomplished by a group (and they know who they are): All those who rallied for the mutilation of a water fountain sculpture in Santa Fe, New Mexico.

And why did this sculpture have to be mutilated and changed? Why, because it showed a young person with—a water pistol!

Twenty years ago, Linda Lee Strong, a local artist, sculpted a bronze fountain for a city park. It shows (or showed, I should say) two of her children having a water fight. A little girl holds a hose. A little boy aims a water pistol at her.

On the NBC *Today* show (8/3/2000), Strong said the message she sought to convey was: "Joyfulness, joyfulness and fun." But, then, after the murders at Columbine High School, many in our country went absolutely, well, nuts against guns, any kind of guns, for any reason—indeed, nuts against any thing that might even resemble guns, particularly handguns.

So, post-Columbine, sculptor Strong began to hear "complaints." Letters to a local newspaper complained. Calls to City Hall complained. The Santa Fe Arts Commission wanted the sculpture changed. The fountain was vandalized. Someone wrote "no guns" on the boy's legs.

And what was being complained about was that since there was a drought in the West, the water in the fountain was turned off on a number of occasions. And, since, on these occasions, there was no water coming from the water pistol, this made the water pistol look like, in the words of *Today* co-host Matt Lauer, "An ordinary pistol!" In any event, to keep a long and unbelievably stupid story short, Strong—who says that originally she "sloughed off" these complaints—caved-in. She agreed to saw off her boy's hand and replace it with a garden hose. Ah, yes. We all know how the west was won— with a garden hose, right?

Defending her cave-in to the "Anti-Gun Nuts," Strong has said many silly and ridiculous things. On the *Today* show, she said that though it took several months and cost $1,700 to sculpt a garden hose, and this was "a pain in the neck," still: "Everything changes....Life changes, life evolves. And the fountain can evolve as well." She's even admitted, "I capitulated." And she has said, "We all need to take responsibility for the violence that's in the world out there, and this is the way I can do my part."

Well, now. As if all this isn't weird enough, things—if you can imagine this—got even weirder when we interviewed Linda Lee Strong. She didn't sound like your typical "Anti-Gun Nut." And she seemed, at times, to regret her cave-in, though she readily admitted she did cave-in to this "political correctness carried to wretched excess," as the *Boston Herald* editorially referred to this ludicrous anti-gun flap.

For openers, Strong—who says she's been a practicing Buddhist for "about 12 years"—tells us: "You know, I was raised with guns and have about 20 in the house and most are loaded. Why have an empty gun?"

Q: So, you're not an "Anti-Gun Nut"?

A: No.

Q: You believe in the Second Amendment?

A: Yes.

Q: Then why not refuse to change your sculpture? Whatever happened to standing up for what you believe in regardless of the consequences?

A: Well, you've got a good point....But, I'm not giving up any of my guns.

Q: So, if somebody breaks into your house, you will not confront them with a garden hose?

A: Right.

Attempting, at this point, to try and make the proverbial silk purse out of a sow's ear, Strong notes that even though she did cave in, this is not "all negative" since she's gotten a lot of publicity and this has allowed her, as an artist, to re-introduce herself to her community and the world.

Q: But, this is weird. You're not disagreeing that you *did* cave in to the hysteria of the Anti-Gun Nuts.

A: No, I agree.

Q: But, if you now admit—as you seem to—that you did all this against your better judgment, but your cave-in has helped your career, you are corrupt!

A: No reply.

Q: But, again, you said you are not an Anti-Gun Nut.

A: No, I am not.

Q: OK. Then let me end here by trying to give you a verbal backbone transplant. That can be sawed off can be put back on, right?

A: That's true.

Q: So, recant! Say that you've reconsidered. Say that you were bullied by the 'Anti-Gun Nuts' and went against your best judgment. Say that you've decided that the water pistol should be restored to your sculpture. And if they say no, then tell them you want your entire sculpture removed from that park!

A: I just might. Thank you for calling. I really appreciate your point of view.

Well, maybe she does, maybe she doesn't. We shall see.

FBI Law Enforcement Bulletin

Comedian Jeff Foxworthy has made a good living with his routines and book titled *You Might Be A Redneck If...*. He lists a series of things which, if true, mean you might, well, be a redneck. Much of what he says is hilarious and, for the most part, good clean fun.

Following in the footsteps of Foxworthy—though unwittingly I'm sure—the FBI Law Enforcement Bulletin has given us its version of what this Southern comic has done. You might call what the Feds have done in this publication "You Might Be a Member of an Extremist Group If...." The difference here, however, is that Foxworthy's humor is good-natured. The article in this "bulletin" is definitely not funny and, arguably, slanders and smears a lot of decent, law-abiding, God-fearing Americans.

The piece in question is titled, "Vehicle Stops Involving Extremist Group Members." It appeared in the December 1999 issue of the FBI *Law Enforcement Bulletin*. Its author is identified as James Kobolt, director of the Institute for Public Safety at Lake Superior State University in Sault Sainte Marie, Michigan. The objectionable portions of this egregious article are as follows:

"Members of extremist groups may reveal their affiliations in a number of ways....Specifically, extremists' vehicles may sport bumper stickers with anti-government or pro-gun sentiments.... The occupants of the vehicle may show other signs of extremist group involvement. Drivers who hold anti-government beliefs may...present handmade [driver's] licenses, a copy of the Constitution, a Bible, or political literature...."

Well, now. So, how do you measure up? Do you pass or flunk the FBI test? Have you ever sported an "anti-government" or "pro-gun" bumper sticker? Have you ever showed a law enforcement officer a copy of the Constitution, a Bible, or "political literature" (whatever this means)? If you say "yes," then you might—"may"—be a member of an "extremist group."

But, this is pernicious nonsense. Evidently, for the publishers of the FBI *Law Enforcement Bulletin,* extremist rhetoric in pursuit of alleged extremists is OK. When we interviewed John Ott, editor of the Bulletin, to register a vigorous complaint regarding the previously quoted outrageous assertions, here's the way it went:

For openers, Ott readily agrees that the overwhelming majority of those with such bumper stickers are law-abiding citizens. He says the purpose of the Bulletin is "a forum for discussion" and "this is why when we edit the articles we make very sure that they use the words 'may' and 'possible' that these are signs of extremist activity and not literal or clear signs of actual extremist activity."

Q: But these "extremists" may also be wearing Levis or Mohawk haircuts or be associated with a hundred other things. So, why single out pro-gun and/or anti-government sentiments on bumper stickers, or showing a cop a copy of the Constitution or a Bible?

A: We're discussing officer safety during legitimate traffic stops in response to actual traffic violations. Any other traffic stops are clearly illegal.

Q: But, why single out only what is mentioned as ways you "may" encounter an "extremist"?

A: Because they have occurred, and there have been incidents where this has happened. It's just a possibility.

Q: But, as I say, there are, presumably, many other things associated with such extremists. So, why mention only what you mention?

A: Those were just two examples.

Q: But, why mention only these two?

A: Because he was talking about right-wing supremacists, militia, primarily.

Q: And showing a copy of the Constitution and/or Bible also makes one an extremist?

A: A lot of the extremist groups believe some Millennial ideas. It's a possibility. That's all. It's a possibility. It's a suggestion for officers to be aware.

Q: But, if we agree that the overwhelming majority of folks with pro-gun, anti-government bumper stickers—and who show a copy of the Constitution and/or the Bible—are law-abiding citizens and not extremists, how does it help a law enforcement officer to say that these things "may" indicate an extremist? "May" also means "may not."

"Well," says Ott, "most officers know their area and groups in it. They have only a limited number of pages in the Bulletin. This is "a discussion. And I emphasize...that contributors' opinions and statements are not considered an endorsement by the FBI whatsoever."

Q: I'm sorry you consider one an extremist who is anti-government.

A: Not at all.

Q: Not at all?

A: No, that article does not say that. These are all "maybes" and "possibles." Things that officers should be aware of.

Q: Our country was founded by folks who were anti-government, or at least anti-a-certain-government.

A: Fine. I have no problem with that. I don't agree with all of what was in the article. But it opens a forum for discussion and gives some information for officers to look at. We didn't ask for this article. He simply submitted it. It wasn't written by an FBI employee.

Q: But, it was approved by an FBI employee.

A: No.

Q: You're not an FBI employee?

A: I am and approved it for publication. And it was approved by our Behavioral Science Unit.

Q: Oh, my goodness! So, the shrinks said it was OK! So, where's this forum for discussion you keep mentioning? I see no letters-to-the-editor section. Also, the article uses the word "extremist" as pejorative. But is being "extreme" always bad, every time, about everything?

A: It's a term that has been used in law enforcement and in other areas to describe the group of people we are talking about. And we didn't want to say rightwing conservatives.

Q: But, you did say that in this conversation.

A: I know. But we're more concerned with extremists, people who are involved in extreme activities. And that's obvious and that's why we used the term.

Q: Right. Like people with pro-gun, anti-government bumper stickers.

A: No. That's not what we're talking about. That's not even the gist of the article.

Q: But the article specifically mentions these kinds of bumper stickers! And I still don't see how a cop is helped by being told that such bumper stickers may or may not indicate extremists.

A: These are just clues that such people may have some views that may effect the process of the arrest. That's all. It's one tiny clue.

He says we're picking on "some small parts of the article." Ott notes that he's a conservative and carries a Bible in his car. Ott says that what we're complaining about is only "a small portion" of the article "and the editing of it and the wording of it may be unfortunate..."

Q: May be! There's that weasel word again.

A: And I can guarantee you that I may be more careful about editing these types of articles in the future because I am much more aware of the concerns of people like yourself because we've received about nine complaints like yours.

Well, let's hope Mr. Ott will be more careful in the future. If you'd like to contact him, the address is: FBI Law Enforcement Bulletin, c/o Federal Bureau Of Investigation, 935 Pennsylvania Avenue, NW, Washington, D.C. 20535-0001.

Actor Martin Sheen: No Right of Self-Defense

This month's "Anti-Gun Nut" is actor Martin Sheen.

In a television commercial for Handgun Control, Inc., a grim-faced Sheen, with an American flag behind him, asks, among other things, if the next President of our country should be a person who has "signed a bill that allows hidden handguns in churches, hospitals, and amusement parks."

Sounds pretty scary, huh? *Hidden* handguns.

But, the truth is that making it legal to carry concealed weapons in these places is not as crazy as Sheen and his anti-Second Amendment, gun-grabbing friends at Handgun Control, Inc. would like us to believe.

Consider the following examples:

Churches

In September of 1999, Larry Gene Ashbrook walked into the Wedgewood Baptist Church in Ft. Worth, Texas, with two guns. He murdered seven people, injured seven others, and then killed himself. Two video tapes showed Ashbrook calmly firing his guns. The acting police chief of Ft. Worth, Ralph Mendoza, says these tapes show this cold-blooded murderer committing his massacre in a "methodical manner," standing there where he "fired shot after shot after shot," pacing back and forth.

But, of course, Ashbrook was able to carry out his slaughter at a leisurely pace. Why? Because none of his victims, or anybody else in the church at that time, were armed. Thus, they were sitting ducks and never had a chance. Had even one person had a weapon and known how to use it, he or she could have shot Ashbrook and saved many lives.

And there are many other examples where a person with a "hidden" handgun in a church could have saved lives.

A *Washington Post* story (15 July 2000) reports how in 1993, the Reverend Michael R. Duesterhaus, a Roman Catholic priest at Holy Spirit Catholic Church in Annandale, Virginia, woke up at 3 A.M. to the sound of someone breaking into his study. The priest took out a 9mm pistol, flipped on a light, and ordered the intruder to freeze and lie on the floor. The intruder stopped and then reached for his belt. Deusterhaus fired. The man paused, apparently wounded, then ran into the hall. The priest pursued him and fired again, at his feet. The priest fired a third time, deliberately wide of his target. The man ran out the side door escaping with a small amount of cash. The *Post* says this incident "contrasts sharply" with the June, 2000, "brutal slaying" of Monsignor Thomas Wells at the Mother Seaton Catholic Church in Germantown, Maryland, who died after being repeatedly stabbed. The difference between these two events is that Monsignor Wells was unarmed.

In March of 1999, in Gonzales, Louisiana, Shon Miller, Jr. entered the New St. John Fellowship Church, fired two rounds into the ceiling and 17 more shots, murdering his son, his wife, a deacon, and injuring four others. You guessed it. None of Miller's victims or anyone around them were armed.

In Columbia, Tennessee, on New Year's Eve of 1999, two men were shot in the parking lot of the First Freewill Baptist Church. One died, one did not. Jamie Edward Thompson was charged in these shootings. Again, no victim was armed.

In Trotwood, Ohio, at the Christ Temple Apostolic Faith Church, in September of 1998, Pastor Andrew Lofton was fatally shot. Once again, only the murderer was armed.

In Salmon, Idaho, in March of 1997, the Rev. Wilfred Keele, retired pastor of the Faith Bible Church, was shot to death in his church as he and his wife visited with members of the congregation after the morning service. And yes, once again, nobody was armed but the killer.

Hospitals

A *Washington Post* story (2 October 2000) reports that in Ventura, California, at the Community Memorial Hospital, "a man stabbed three staff members in a hospital waiting room, then was shot and killed by police." None of those attacked were armed.

In April of 2000, in Waterville, Maine, a man with a .357 magnum abducted his estranged wife at gunpoint inside a local hospital. He fired a bullet into the floor outside the door of a dialysis unit. Nobody in this hospital was armed but the man with the .357 magnum.

In March of 1999, at the Mt. Zion Medical Center in San Francisco, three nurses risked their lives when they dashed to the waiting room to rescue a bleeding man who had just been shot in the hospital lobby by his son. When they lifted the victim on to a gurney, the gunman stood waving a gun in one hand and an ammunition clip in the other. The man died. None of these nurses were armed.

Amusement Parks

The Bergen, New Jersey *Record* newspaper (12 October 1993) reports that metal detectors at the Six Flags Great Adventure amusement park netted 62 guns confiscated, twice as many as in past years. Also seized were knives, brass knuckles, throwing stars, and nunchakus.

And the *Los Angeles Times* (12 June 1990) reports that Nathan Nicholas Tripp was found not guilty by reason of insanity in the 1988 killings of two Universal Studios guards. These guards were murdered, shot to death, when they turned Tripp away from this amusement park gate. Oh, and these guards were *unarmed*.

So, yes, Mr. Sheen, the answer to your question, sir, is that we should definitely elect a President who, among other things, favors the right of our citizens to carry concealed weapons in churches, hospitals, and amusement parks. If this is allowed, a lot of lives can be saved and crime will be reduced.

As John Lott documents in his excellent book *More Guns, Less Crime*, laws that allow concealed handguns have reduced the murder rate by 8.5 percent, rape by 5 percent, and severe assault by 7 percent. And had such laws prevailed throughout the country, there would have been 1,600 fewer murders, 4,200 fewer rapes, and 60,000 fewer assaults.

U.S. Senator Jack Reed:
Enemy of the Second Amendment

Associate U.S. Supreme Court Justice Louis Brandeis once said, "The greatest dangers to liberty lurk in insidious encroachment by men of zeal, well-meaning but without understanding."

Well, amen! How true. And a current example that proves, with a vengeance, what Brandeis feared, is a bill (S. 2099) introduced by U.S. Senator Jack Reed (D-RI) which would, among other things, tax and register our handguns.

His legislation would treat handguns much like machine guns. The law would (1) require the registration of handguns in the National Firearms Registration and Transfer record; (2) provide for the sharing of registration information with federal, state, and local law enforcement agencies; (3) provide for the imposition of the five dollar transfer tax on handguns and a $50 tax on the making of each handgun.

To be sure, Reed is well-meaning and zealous. But, in an interview with the Rhode Island Democrat, it becomes obvious that when it comes to "gun control" and the Second Amendment to our Constitution, he is without understanding. And this is why he is so dangerous to our liberties. Following are some excerpts from the interview with Sen. Reed:

Q: What evidence would you cite that any gun control law has ever worked?

A: Well, I think some evidence is the original federal laws that regulate the registration of machine guns, sawed-off shotguns, and silencers. There's not a proliferation of those weapons on our streets, not anything compared to the handguns that are awash in the United States.

And there is no evidence that these weapons have been confiscated arbitrarily. In fact, there are legitimate bona fide gun owners that have these weapons and fire them regularly, as they are registered. So, that's an example of one that works. The Brady background check is—

Q: OK. But, let's stop on this one. Is there a study you can refer me to that shows the registration law you just mentioned actually reduced crime?

A: Uhhh, I think...we'll certainly look for a study. But I would guess this is more on the order of observation and what's going around. I mean, frankly, it is the rare exception when someone has an automatic weapon, a machine-gun, really.

Q: But, do you know of any evidence that this registration law you mention has reduced machine-gun crime? I didn't know there was a lot of this.

A: Well, back in 1930 was when the law was passed. This law has been on the books for 60 years. I don't think most people realize that. They assume that there's never been any registration of weapons at the federal level, that this is a bold and novel approach when in fact Congress more than 60 years ago...simply said, This is a threat to the public safety and we're going to stop it.

Q: You don't think Al Capone really obeyed that law do you?

A: Uhhh, well, you know, if he didn't he would have gone to jail on that as well as tax evasion.

Note: Several months after this interview, Reed's office failed to produce any evidence that the anti-machine gun law he mentions had any impact on the crime rate.

Q: Brady. You were going to mention the Brady Law.

A: I think the Brady Bill has shown a reduction in...I don't know if you can make the correlation to a reduction in crime [which has been reduced] because of difficult measures. But, what Brady has uncovered is a number of felons who were trying to purchase weapons...and they have been prevented from doing that. In that sense, it's been successful.

Q: I press you on this gun control laws issue because my pre-supposition is that behind all such laws is the desire to reduce crime, reduce the illegal use of guns, right?

A: The idea is to reduce violent gun crime.

Q: Yeah, that's what I mean.

A: Yeah, yeah.

Q: The *Journal of the American Medical Association* has recently published a detailed study which shows there is no evidence the Brady Law has had any effect on gun crime, on homicides. Are you familiar with this study?

A: I'll become familiar with it. We've seen a decline in violent crime....

Q: Which started before Brady, actually.

A: Yeah. And I would be the first to say that crime is not a single factor phenomenon. It's a whole bunch of things. But, again, in trying to be not as analytical and scientific, but just in terms of human behavior, the ease of obtaining weapons is such that there's a higher likelihood that something before, you know, a scuffle between kids could escalate now to a shoot-out.

A lot of this is anecdotal. But, up in Rhode Island, about a year ago, two kids out rough-housing—

Q: How old? What are you calling a kid?

A: Sixteen or 17. They were rough-housing. Somebody's pride was injured...somebody in the crowd, because of the ease of getting handguns, a kid pulls a gun out and shoots, seriously injuring one individual. And then [the shooter] takes his own life.

Q: I think anecdotes are important. They are real life. But, what law would have stopped this?

A: Well, I, you know...

Q: I don't think any law would have stopped that.

A: Well, no, I think...if there is a registration law—if someone gets a gun without registering it—they're a criminal by definition.

Q: But, criminals are not going to commit crimes with guns registered in their own names.

A: Well, but the point is, and one of the points of this legislation (S. 2099) is that this will allow law enforcement officials to better be able to trace weapons used by criminals in crime.

And I think the prototypical person that we all want to see exercise their rights as Americans to...and one right is to own weapons—are homeowners, people who are recreational shooters or hunters, those people will register their weapons, et cetera.

But, frankly, if a police officer comes across a crime scene, and there is a weapon, he now has a much faster and better way to trace that weapon. Oh, and by the way, if he observes someone who is involved in some type of criminal activity or probable cause to suspect, and the weapon is not registered, that person is guilty of another crime.

Q: But, if we agree, as we did earlier, that gun control laws are supposed to stop crime, your supposed benefits of registration come after a crime is committed. So what? So what if you find out who a gun is registered to? I know of no evidence that registration has prevented crime. Do you?

A: The point is to have a system in which police can trace weapons more quickly, that criminals...this raises the barrier for them to get weapons. And then you have to make an assessment whether that's high enough to deter all gun crime. Frankly, it would be naive to say that. But, I—

Q: But, when has a registration law ever reduced violent gun crime?

A: Well, I would say the law we have on the books now on registration has significantly limited access by criminals and other people to machine guns, silencers, and sawed-off shotguns without effecting the rights of law-abiding Americans to own these weapons. This might be the only correlation you can safely make.

Here's the scenario (re: S. 2099): This law passes and some law-abiding American registers their handgun at home. There's a domestic dispute and someone uses the weapon to hurt someone else.

You would ask, "Has this law stopped crime?" And I'd agree the gun-crime was not stopped. But what it might have stopped...or at least impeded...is someone stealing that gun and selling it to somebody else and no one knowing any the wiser about it. Or someone breaking in and taking the gun, et cetera. So, I mean, you know...

Q: But, why would your registration law stop a thief from breaking in and stealing a gun since the gun would not be registered in the name of the thief? Why would a thief care about this?

A: I think they'd care just like someone who goes in and steals a car that is registered. There's a record of who owns that car, and they ain't the one who owns it.

Q: But, why would a criminal care if the gun he steals is registered to someone else?

A: [The gun] would be less easily disposable if there is a registration system.

Q: But would a criminal really commit a crime with a gun registered in his own name?

A: Uh, but that might be another disincentive to committing the crime. I mean, you have this theory that hardened criminals are going to get weapons any way they can.

Q: Sure.

A: Kill anybody they can, etc. And they'll never take into consideration what the law is.

Q: Right. And that's why they are criminals! Because they don't care what the law says!

A: No, they do in fact consider how to get around the laws, how to break them without getting caught. And frankly [registration] is another way, like giving the police authority to register automobiles and more of an ability to trace stolen vehicles and a sense that people don't just casually borrow cars because, you know, it could have been theirs. No one knows.

Q: Your car-gun registration analogy is interesting. But, I wonder if registration has actually deterred car theft since within hours after many cars are stolen they are chopped up and sold for parts and/or they are on a boat being shipped to Brazil.

A: But, I think your premise is that no gun control laws have ever had any effect on crime or the level of violence in the country.

Q: Exactly. But, the burden of proof is on those who argue that gun control laws have been effective.

A: The burden of proof is on those who say we should do nothing when 30,000 Americans die annually by gunfire... and in every other industrial society in the world where they have much more stringent gun control laws you do not have this phenomenon of gun violence.

Q: Do you agree that under the Second Amendment individuals have the right to keep and bear arms?

A: In what, I mean...subject to regulation, yeah. Frankly, I think there's a very strong argument that the Amendment as originally constituted had to do about the arming of militias. But, at this point in time, I think practice and custom and the history of the country suggests that access to weapons by individuals is something that would be constitutionally protected. The question is: "How can we regulate that access?"

Q: What would you say to someone who would say that what you are advocating [in S. 2099] are the kinds of infringement the Second Amendment prohibits? Aren't registration of and taxing of guns an infringement on the constitutional right to keep and bear arms?

A: I would say no, not at all. In fact, history suggests that we do it all the time. We've been—

Q: Well, there's no doubt Congress has been violating our constitutional rights for a long time!

A: I would suspect also that the courts have looked at this question and consistently upheld these firearms laws, particularly the registration law.

See what I mean? Sen. Jack Reed is without understanding. He has no evidence that any "gun control" laws have ever worked. He's obviously not familiar with the most detailed study which shows that Brady has been a flop. Nor is he familiar with the rise in violent crime in England following its gun ban.

He's introducing a law which clearly "infringes" on our rights under the Second Amendment. But, he denies that taxing and registering are infringements! The Senator is precisely the kind of person Associate Justice Brandeis warned us about.

Ohio Court Crushes Cincinnati Anti-Gun Nuts

Have you heard about the first appellate court ruling which has shot full of holes and blown to bits the arguments of anti-gun nuts who were trying to blame gun makers and firearms associations for—well, just about anything they could imagine?

Probably not. The national news media have scrupulously avoided any detailed attention to this important case.

In Ohio, the city of Cincinnati sued for millions of dollars seeking reimbursement for police, medical, and other municipal services provided as a result of alleged negligence in the design and safety of gun features. A lower trial court dismissed this suit. And the Ohio First District Court of Appeals (OFDCA) has now agreed.

So, what, exactly, were the anti-gun nuts claiming? They were claiming just about anything that could be imagined: (1) strict product liability for the defective condition of firearms; (2) strict product liability for failure to warn of the risks of firearms; (3) negligence; (4) negligent failure to warn; (5) unfair and deceptive advertising practices; (6) public nuisance; (7) fraud; (8) negligent representation; and (9) unjust enrichment.

The OFDCA was buying none of this. Accusing the city of Cincinnati of using "a shotgun approach," Judge Ralph Winkler said that the city had "nowhere in its 43-page complaint...set forth facts that, if proved, would provide a basis for recovery....The city has made broad assertions without alleging a direct injury caused by a particular firearm model or its manufacturer."

In his scathing ruling, Judge Winkler noted that if the city of Cincinnati was allowed to recover for its municipal services it would "open a Pandora's box." He says, "The city could sue the manufacturers of matches for arson, or automobile manufacturers for traffic accidents, or breweries for drunken driving.

"Guns are dangerous. When someone pulls the trigger, whether intentionally or by accident, a properly functioning gun is going to discharge, and someone may be killed. The risks of guns are open and obvious.

"We hold that the trial court properly dismissed the city's complaint. The city's claims are too remote and seek derivatively what should be claimed only by citizens directly injured by firearms. The city cannot recover municipal costs. We overrule its assignment of error and affirm the judgment of the trial court."

Now, let's look at some of the particular claims and how they were demolished by the OFDCA:

First, it was ruled that the city of Cincinnati was not even a proper plaintiff in this case! Why? Because, as a corporate entity, it could "prove no harm to itself in the form of death, physical injury, or emotional distress." Moreover, there wasn't even an allegation of any physical damage to the city's property. Thus, any product liability claims failed as a matter of law.

Next, nowhere in its 43-page complaint did the city identify even a single defective condition in a particular model of gun at the time it left its particular manufacturer. In fact, out of the complaint's 162 counts, the city's sole assertion naming a single manufacturer and its gun implicated none of the defendants, because the harm was caused by the intentional act of a criminal, not by the gun manufacturer. Thus, "rather than targeting a specific manufacturer, product, and defect, the city makes generic claims against all the manufacturers in an effort to gloss over the fatal omissions in its complaint."

Regarding the claim that gun manufacturers failed to warn about the dangerousness of their product, the OFDCA dismissed this objection not only because the city failed to identify injuries caused by specific gunmakers, but also "because the manufacturers have no duty to give warnings about the obvious dangers of handguns." At this point, Section 10.37, 147 of the Ohio Products Liability Manual is quoted:

> A manufacturer has no duty to warn of an obvious danger. Knives are sharp, bowling balls are heavy, bullets cause puncture wounds in the flesh. The law has long recognized that obvious dangers are an excluded class. As the colorful Seventh Circuit Judge Richard Posner once wrote in an Indiana federal case, if you 'go to the zoo and put your hand through the lion's cage, and the lion bites your hand off...you do not have an action against the zoo.'

As for negligence claims—that gun makers and trade associations may be held liable for foreseeable injury inflicted as a result of the criminal or careless acts of third persons—the OFDCA said foreseeabilty alone is not enough to create liability. In fact, generally, under Ohio law, "there is no duty to prevent a third person from causing harm to another in the absence of a special relationship between the parties." And no such relationships were cited by the city of Cincinnati. It is added that on this basis, "courts have uniformly rejected attempts by plaintiffs to hold gun manufacturers and distributors liable for the criminal misuse of their products."

A "public nuisance?" No way. The OFDCA points out that the Supreme

Court of Ohio has refused to extend the law of public nuisance to the design and construction of products. Also, since selling guns is not illegal, generally speaking, "an activity that is authorized by law cannot be a public nuisance or an absolute nuisance."

"Unjust enrichment." This claim alleged that the sale of handguns resulted in an increase in the city's expenditures for medical care and law enforcement. But, said the OFDCA, the city "has not, and cannot, allege that its expenditures have conferred a benefit upon any of the [gun] manufacturers. The city has not, and cannot, allege that the [gun] manufacturers have been aware of any so-called benefit [as the "unjust enrichment" law requires— L.P.]. The beneficiaries of the city's expenditures are its own residents, not the [gun] manufacturers." Thus, this claim fails.

The OFDCA also points out that the city's claims are barred by "the doctrine of remoteness." This doctrine bars recovery for indirect harm suffered as a result of injuries directly sustained by another person. There must be a *direct* relation between the alleged injury and the defendant's conduct. A U.S. Supreme Court ruling (*Holmes v. Securities Investor Protection Corp.*, 1992) is cited in which it is said: "[A] plaintiff who complain[s] of harm flowing merely from the misfortunes visited upon a third by the defendant's act [is] generally said to stand at too remote a distance to recover."

In its wonderful common sense ruling against the city of Cincinnati, the OFDCA refers to the city's complaints as suffering from "infirmities." But, to refer to the city's pathetic and embarrassingly ignorant arguments this way is to make a gross understatement. It's like saying that on its maiden voyage, the *Titanic* took on a little water.

Commenting editorially on this excellent judicial opinion, the *Cincinnati Enquirer* newspaper declared, in part: "Gun makers should not be held responsible for people who misuse their legal product any more than Ford and General Motors should be sued for homicidal drivers. The lawsuit is a thinly disguised attempt to achieve though litigation what cannot be done through legislation: Put gun makers out of business—at least in this country....The city should drop any plans for an appeal and spare taxpayers more silly and wasteful litigation."

Amen!

And Thomas Fennell of the Dallas, Texas, office of Jones, Day, Reavis & Pogue—who represented the Colt Manufacturing Co. Inc., and was part of the defense team in this case—says he expects the OFDCA decision "to be a guiding light, not just in Ohio, but in other states." I hope he's right.

America Online Needs To Be Turned Offline

Let me fully disclose my feelings about America Online. I do not like the company. I do not like their politics, and I do not like their service.

When I had America Online I frequently found it impossible to download big programs. They would take so long that the little dialog box would pop up and tell me when I wasn't looking that I had not been using the computer, and would I like to stay connected? By the time I looked at the screen again I was offline.

I concluded that America Online would be better named America Offline. So, I turned the provider off permanently.

Now I am urging you to do the same, even if you like the quality of their service. By patronizing AOL you are aiding and abetting the enemy.

Please let me explain.

Reports are frequently received at Gun Owners of America that AOL filters out pro-Second Amendment web sites.

Now, AOL has decided to escalate their war against our firearms freedoms. The Ogden, Utah, office has fired three men pretty much because they are gun owners.

Luke Hansen, Paul Carlson, and Jason Melling were well aware of the anti-self-defense prohibition on guns in the workplace at AOL where they worked. They respected this dangerous workplace requirement.

However, one day they were in the parking lot which is leased but not owned by AOL. On their own time, they were seen transferring firearms from their trunks to Hansen's trunk for an expedition to the shooting range.

Because of that, they were fired. The three are in court, but more should be done to support these three freedom fighters.

Sarah Thompson, a medical doctor and director of the Utah Gun Owners Alliance, has called for a boycott of AOL. I agree.

I would urge that you do two things.

Contact the folks at *keepandbeararms.com* on the web and sign up for their internet access service. If all you want is e-mail, that is free. The *keepandbeararms.com* internet service is competitively priced with AOL and is for unlimited service.

Then, call to cancel your AOL service so that you can tell an AOL represen-tative why they are losing your business. Be polite, but be firm. You could also call the AOL national representative in Northern Virginia who is covering this issue, Nicholas Graham, and tell him what you have done. His number is 1-703-265-1746.

You might ask him if an identical rule to his policy would have stopped the killing of the seven people in the Wakefield, Massachusetts dot-com office.

This is a "two-fer," folks; you're helping a great group at *keepandbeararms.com* (where you ought to be checking every day for firearms related news, anyway), and no longer will you be enriching a rabidly anti-gun company.

Environmentalists Target Gun Rights

If anti-gun zealots in government are frustrated that they have not yet been able to completely infringe on our right to keep and bear arms, the United States Forest Service (USFS) has found a politically correct issue to use against gun owners.

In Azusa, California, there is a shooting range in the city's mountain suburb. The Burro Canyon Shooting Park opened with a bang in November, 1993, on a 76-acre allotment near the Angeles National Forest. Since the shooting park is on land unconstitutionally owned and administered by the United States government, Burro Canyon operates with a permit from the USFS, itself an unconstitutional agency desperately in need of elimination.

About a year ago, the USFS discovered that the railroad ties in use at the range had to be removed because the creosote in them was disturbing the pristine environment of Burro Canyon. This creosote is apparently different from that in the telephone poles all over other federally protected land. The railroad ties went, but trouble was just starting. Through an alleged irregularity in the deeding of the 76 acres for the shooting park, in spite of the USFS's earlier approval, the Rangers managed to whack the shooting park down to four acres.

Then the shooting park was told to be sure that all that horrible human activity that occurs there would not endanger any exotic plants. You see, the natural habitat must not be disturbed. By the way, the Burro Canyon Shooting Park sits on top of a landfill. By October of 2000 the USFS discovered that shotgun shells are an environmental threat, and the shooting park was not picking them all up.

Next the USFS decided that there was too much picnicking going on, so the picnic tables had to go. Oops—haven't you gotten rid of all those metal plates the cops used for their long-range practice? "Why, you're not in compliance. Those plates are polluting the pristine canyon."

Finally, after months of a death-by-a-thousand-cuts, the Burro Canyon Shooting Park closed on January 2, 2001. The anti-gun nuts in the bureaucracy have managed to squelch constitutional freedom under the guise of protecting the environment.

Doesn't this make you want to go hug a tree?

There is a happy ending to this story. Months later, Gun Owners of California working with Representative John Doolittle were able to get the forest service to do an about-face. Doolittle's position on the appropriations committee in the House of Representatives helped the forest service see the error of their ways. Score one for accountability.

Stewart Udall: "Thinking" Person?

Among those who have enthusiastically praised Emory History Professor Michael A. Bellesiles' book, *Arming America: The Origins of a National Gun Culture* (Knopf, 2000), is former Secretary of the Interior Stewart Udall.

In a promotional blurb distributed by Bellesiles's publisher, Udall says: "Thinking people who deplore Americans' addiction to gun violence have been waiting a long time for this information. Michael Bellesiles has uncovered dramatic historical truths that shatter the 'Ten Commandments' hokum peddled by the National Rifle Association and its ersatz Moses."

Pretty tough stuff, huh? And snidely arrogant, too. Did you catch the part about "thinking people?" I guess he means people like himself. But, how much of a "thinking person" is Udall? He's not much of one, as was revealed when we interviewed him.

For openers, Udall reiterates his polemical endorsement of the Bellesiles book saying it has in it "a lot of scholarship." He adds: "I don't throw off blurbs lightly. I think this is a very fine book and very much needed."

Q: How do you know this book is accurate?

A: Because of my own research and writing.

Q: Are you aware that the Bellesiles book is being criticized and refuted by a growing number of academics and scholars with expertise in the field of gun history and the Second Amendment?

A: No, I am not.

Foundational to the Bellesiles book and his conclusions is his assertion that he has examined some 11,000 probate records.

Q: How many probate records have you examined?

A: I haven't done that kind of research.

One of Udall's complaints is that American movies have misrepresented the kinds of guns that were used in the Old West. He says the Bellesiles book corrects the record.

Q: What would be an example of this kind of misrepresentation? Which movie gives this kind of false impression?

A: All of them.

Q: *All* of them?! Like which one?

A: I'm not a moviegoer, so don't try to make me an expert on movies.

Q: Are you aware that as many as 2,500,000 Americans annually use guns in self-defense?

A: You're getting far afield as far as I'm concerned.

Q: But, you've denounced gun violence as if all gun violence is bad. Some gun violence is good because it is in self-defense. Are you a pacifist?

A: No, I was a soldier in the big war.

Q: Should the private ownership of guns be banned?

A: I'm not involved in all of that big political quarrel in this country. I think we have too many guns and they produce too much violence.

Q: So, what's the solution to all this gun violence?

A: I don't own guns. I've never had a gun in my house. I'm 81. I've been around. I grew up in the country where guns were used for hunting, and I hunted. So, I'm not anti-gun. I just think there are too G-D—many of them. Are you trying to discredit me for writing a blurb for a friend?

Well, now. Stewart Udall gives us far too much credit here. He impeaches his own credibility by admitting that he has double-checked none of Bellesiles's most important research and that he is unaware of any of the compelling criticisms of the Bellesiles book.

As for Udall's assertion that he is not "anti-gun," he speaks here with a forked-tongue. The truth is that by praising *Arming America* he has endorsed what is arguably the most anti-gun book ever written in this country.

A footnote: Like Bellesiles, Udall also has trouble with the facts. At one point in our interview—seeking to demonstrate that there is too much gun violence in America—he said he was in Las Vegas recently and there were 17 murders there in January of 2001. How many with guns? Well, he doesn't know but "I suspect most of them." A spokesman for the Las Vegas Police Department tells us that there were 20 murders there in January: 9 by guns; 3 by stabbing; 6 by blunt force trauma; 2 stranglings; 1 unknown.

Reviewer Wink Blinked

One of the ways Michael A. Bellesiles' book, *Arming America*, has acquired credibility is, sad to say, by assigning it to reviewers who didn't have the foggiest idea what they were writing about. A case in point is the March 21, 2001, review by Walter Wink in the ultra-liberal *Christian Century* magazine. Wink is a professor of New Testament at the Auburn Theological Seminary in New York City.

In his review, Wink hails Bellesiles' book as "an historical tour de force" based on "painstaking and compendious research" that "exposes the myths that have elevated the gun to its unique place in American life—and death." He goes on to say, "Turning aside from our enthrallment with guns will require a spirituality of nonviolence, a willingness to turn in our guns....If we do our work well, perhaps Bellesiles' future book can be titled *Disarming America.*"

Curious as to how much Wink really knows about the subject of the Bellesiles book, we interviewed him. Well, no, he says, he is not familiar with any of the scholarly criticisms of *Arming America*. None. Zero. Zip. Zilch. And no, he says, he is not any kind of an expert on guns in America. He says he was assigned the book because he has done "a lot of work on non-violence."

Okay. So, how does Wink know the book is true? How does he know if Bellesiles has accurately used probate records and other sources he cites? Well, he says, he found the book was "internally consistent." Thus, Bellesiles' use of records was "convincing."

> Q: But, in fact, you have no idea, do you, if Bellesiles accurately reports on the more than 11,000 probate records he says he examined?
>
> A: No, you'd have to spend several years [to check this].

When asked if he is serious about everybody having a willingness to turn in his or her guns, Wink says yes, he is. Does he really think criminals would turn in their guns? Wink replies:

> In England it's now a felony to be in possession of a gun. And therefore any who's arrested or stopped even and has a gun is arrested. And that has lowered the gun-death rate considerably and has proven to be a very effective way of disarming a public. Now, this is very hard to do of course.

When told that England's violent crime rate is now higher than America's, Wink says, incredibly: "That is not true. You just made that statement up." But, this statement is true. It is not made up.

The March 23, 2001, issue of the *London Daily Mail* newspaper states that, according to an international crime report, Britain "has a higher crime rate than any other rich nation except Australia." According to this crime report, 3.6 percent of the population of England and Wales were victims of violent crime in 1999; in the U.S. only two percent of the population suffered an assault or robbery. British Home Secretary Jack Straw is quoted as saying, "Levels of victimization are higher here than in most comparable countries for most categories of crime."

As for gun crime, the British December 13, 2000, issue of *The Observer* newspaper reported:

> Gun crime in Britain is soaring to record levels: executions, woundings and related incidents in the past year are set to be the highest ever, an investigation by *The Observer* has revealed....The true figures could be even higher because victims of many of the most violent gun crimes are reluctant to involve the authorities....The use of guns outside the big towns and cities is rising too....The number of illegally held guns is estimated at three million. As handguns can no longer be bought or sold legally, the police believe the vast majority of those coming on to the market have been smuggled from abroad.

So much for Walter Wink's absurd, idiotic, and dangerous view that gun control in England has been a "very effective way" of lowering the gun-death rate and of "disarming a public." As always, everywhere, every time, in England, gun control has disarmed only law-abiding citizens, leaving them helpless against criminals who will always get guns.

In our interview, when Wink was asked if he knew that millions of Americans use guns in self-defense every year, he said yes, he knows this.

Q: So, why should these Americans have to turn in their guns?

A: One thing is being in possession of a gun raises the possibility of your getting killed.

Q: Says who?

A: The information on that I can't recall right now...

Q: So, whom should we give our guns to?

A: The local police.

Q: So you're for banning private ownership of all guns?

A: I...let's see, I, I prefer the English method.

When told that that was a distinction without a difference, Wink hung up the phone. When faced with the facts, Wink blinked.

Section Twelve

⊰—◆—○—◆—⊱

Michael A. Bellesiles: Discredited Anti-Gun Scholar

Overview of *Arming America:*
The Origins of a National Gun Culture

It is a little early to be saying who will be the anti-gun nut of this century. But, for now, a superlative designation is the least that is warranted. Michael A. Bellesiles, professor of history at Emory University, is the author of the 603-page book, *Arming America: The Origins of a National Gun Culture* (Alfred A. Knopf, 2000).

Now, to be sure, Professor Bellesiles denies that he is an anti-gun nut. In fact, when I debated him on KQED Radio in San Francisco (11/14/2000), he said, presumably with a straight face, that he has been a "gun enthusiast" for 35 years during which he has fired guns in many different countries. And, he says, he has always enjoyed skeet shooting.

But, what Emerson said in another context must be said to Professor Bellesiles: "Do not say things. What you are stands over you the while, and thunders so that I cannot hear what you say to the contrary." In other words, what matters is not what he *says*, but what he has *written*. And what he has written is a sustained, snide, sneering, condescending, grossly irresponsible, rhetorically reckless, vicious, anti-American, anti-gun screed which a growing number of firearms and Second Amendment scholars are blowing full of holes the size of the Grand Canyon.

In this section, I will touch on several issues. I will address the snotty tone of the professor's book and some ways in which he—unwittingly I'm sure—reveals his true anti-gun, anti-Second Amendment colors. I will examine some of the devastating falsehoods he presents, and I will show refutations for those falsehoods. Finally, I will explore the shocking lack of concern for factual accuracy shown by his publisher.

Edmund Burke, in his "Second Speech on Conciliation With America" (1775), said the following regarding America: "I do not know the method of drawing up an indictment against a whole people." Professor Bellesiles, however, has no problem at all doing this. He repeatedly smears his fellow countrymen as gun-crazy. He writes, "Guns are central to the identity of Americans, to their self-perception as a rugged and violent people, as well as their perception of others" (p. 8). He says guns are "absolutely fundamental" to the way we understand ourselves, that the gun is "central" to the American identity (p. 9). He says the gun in America "leads a charmed life of perfect freedom" (p. 9).

Now, it's true that millions of us own guns, but, to portray all Americans as being guilty of an obsession concerning firearms that borders on idolatry, is to lie. And to say that there is "perfect freedom" for the gun in America is—well, another lie since there are some 20,000 laws restricting firearms in our nation.

Professor Bellesiles excels at the cheap shot, the low blow. Alluding to shootings in Jonesboro, Arkansas, in 1998, and the fact that one shooter got a shotgun for a gift when he was six-years-old, he asks, "How did we acquire a culture in which Santa Claus gives a six-year-old boy a shotgun for... Christmas?" (p. 4). Cheap shot. Low blow. Millions of young people have been, and should have been, given firearms and taught how to use them responsibly. Thus, his rhetorical question is absurd and reveals nothing other than his own anti-gun bias.

Professor Bellesiles laments the fact that "since the United States does not register guns, no one knows how many there are or who actually buys them" (p.4). The implication here is obvious: He thinks guns *should* be registered— a dangerous and anti-Second Amendment idea.

In a truly bizarre complaint, Professor Bellesiles criticizes American gun magazines because "they never have an unkind thing to say about American-made guns—all guns are thought to be above average" (p.6). It seems not to have occurred to him—an expert at saying unkind things about guns—that this is because American-made guns *are* above average. Professor Bellesiles notes, critically it seems, that one gun magazine even had the gall to feature "the best means of carrying concealed weapons" (p.6). So what? Scores of states have made this legal, and studies have shown that where concealed weapons are allowed, crime has gone down.

Professor Bellesiles also notes, with alarm, that some gun magazine ads show "diminutive pistols made especially for the ladies" (p.6). But, again, so what?! Don't women have the right to defend themselves?

Professor Bellesiles criticizes one individual for saying, correctly, that our country must avoid "England's Orwellian nightmare" of gun control (p.7). Well, amen! Is he unaware that the banning of all privately owned guns in England has resulted in a violent crime rate in that country that is now higher than in our country?

Snidely, and with drooling sarcasm (p.8), Professor Bellesiles ridicules one gun ad that boasts for its gun: "Just for fun. 10 shots in 2 seconds." He replies, "What could be more fun than that?" Well, the answer is: *Nothing*— particularly if you are, say, a female trying to stop a rapist or possible murderer and you need to stop this thug quickly.

Professor Bellesiles dishonestly notes that some legislatures have even encouraged gun use, such as in Louisiana where a law was passed granting citizens "the right to shoot to kill anyone attempting to steal their car" (p.9). But, this is a blatant distortion of this law which allows the use of deadly force regarding *car jacking*—not merely stealing a car.

Professor Bellesiles is upset that Congress has forbidden the Centers for Disease Control from using any funds for injury prevention and control to advocate or promote gun control (p.9). But, why should the CDC be allowed to do something that is in no way a part of its legal mandate? For that matter, what is the constitutional mandate for the CDC?

Critique of Bellesiles's Probate Records Analysis

Not surprisingly, the publisher of Professor Michael A. Bellesiles's book, Alfred A. Knopf, effusively praises *Arming America: The Origins of a National Gun Culture* as a book that will "completely transform America's gun debate." To convince us this is so, a press release accompanying the book features quotes from various individuals. These comments include the following:

"A myth-busting tour de force...deeply researched, brilliantly argued...good history...an authoritative account...sensible analysis...a superb piece of historical work...a classic work of significant scholarship...an eye-opener."

But, a growing number of gun and Second Amendment scholars and other academics qualified to critique Bellesiles's book are blowing holes in it the size of the Grand Canyon. The most documented-in-detail, devastating demolition to date we have seen is an as yet unpublished 57-page paper by James Lindgren and Justin Lee Heather of Northwestern University titled "Counting Guns In Early America." Lindgren is a professor of law and director of the Demography of Diversity project. He has a law degree from the University of Chicago, a B.A. from Yale, and he's currently a Ph. D. student in sociology concentrating on social statistics. Heather has an A.B. from Dartmouth and is expected to get his law degree from N.U. in June of 2001.

To put it charitably, Lindgren and Heather cast serious doubts on Bellesiles's assertion that he examined, among other things, 11,000 probate inventories to reach his conclusion that gun ownership was the exception in early America. In an abstract of their paper, they say that to determine gun ownership from probate inventories they examined three databases in detail: Alice Hanson Jones's national sample of 919 inventories (1774); 149 inventories from Providence, Rhode Island (1679-1726); and the Gunston Hall Plantation's sample of 325 inventories from Maryland and Virginia (1740-1810). They also discuss a sample of 59 probate inventories from Essex County, Massachusetts (1636-1650) and Anna Hawley's study of 221 Surry County, Virginia, estates (1690-1715).

Lindgren and Heather report: "Guns are found in 50-73% of the male estates in each of the five databases and in 6-38% of the female estates in each of the first four databases. *Gun ownership is particularly high compared to other common items* (emphasis mine). For example, in 813 itemized male inventories from the 1774 Jones national database, guns are listed in 54% of estates, compared to only 30% of estates listing any cash, 14% listing swords or edge weapons, 25% listing Bibles, 62% listing any book, and 79% listing any clothes.

"The picture of gun ownership that emerges from these analyses directly contradicts the assertions of Michael Bellesiles....Contrary to [his] claims, there were high numbers of guns, guns were much more common than swords or other edge weapons, women in 1774 owned guns at rates (18%) higher than Bellesiles claimed men did in 1765-90 (14.7%), and 83-91% of gun-owning estates listed at least one gun that was not old or broken."

Lindgren and Heather say they replicated all the portions of Bellesiles' study where he both counted guns in probate inventories and cited his sources. They conclude that Bellesiles appears to have "substantially misrecorded or misremembered" the 17th and 18th century probate data he presents.

In the body of their paper, Lindgren and Heather say Bellesiles claims to have used many sets of probate data, "but in his book he cites only two sets that he apparently used —and so far he has not supplied citations for others." Nearly everything he says about the Providence estates "is mistaken."

Lindgren and Heather say:

> Without data, without counts, without sources, Bellesiles has not done a 'study' of probate records in any conventional sense. Our efforts to get Bellesiles to release his totals for any groups of counties for any period, to release his criteria for what a record is, and to release his list of counties for each period has yielded no direct answers to our specific questions. Instead, he sent several friendly responses, some quite lengthy, describing how he kept his tallies on yellow pads, how the yellow sheets got flooded and are now in his attic still wet, and what were his general criteria for deciding which counties are frontier counties.

Lindgren and Heather note that the American Historical Association's "Statement on Standards of Professional Conduct" (revised May, 1999 edition) says, "Historians should carefully document their findings and thereafter be prepared to make available to others their sources, evidence, and data...."

Lindgren and Heather say that Bellesiles "is virtually alone among historians who work with probate records in thinking that they are more or less complete....For example, 23% of the inventories in the leading colonial database of 919 inventories include no clothes of any kind. Unless at their deaths 23% of the wealth holding males and females in colonial America were *nudists every day all day long*, inventories do not scrupulously record 'every item in an estate'" (emphasis in original).

Lindgren and Heather say: "Whenever Bellesiles writes about guns in probate records, he makes an incredibly large number of misstatements. These misstatements go, not only to trivialities, but to the heart of the matter—the frequency and condition of guns and the sorts of people who owned them."

In an interview, Lindgren calls attention to page 445 of Bellesiles' book, a table that says the national average percentage of probate inventories listing firearms for one period is 14.7%. He says: "Does this look at all plausible? This mean of 14.7%—you can't even get there if there's more than 200 cases in the South and you know there are thousands. Why aren't there any numbers on these tables? Why doesn't the chart match the data above it? 14.7% of what?! What are the cell sizes here? What are the sample sizes? He has not been willing to release sample sizes. He just goes and attacks everyone who asks him a question instead of answering the question."

"[Bellesiles writes about there being] three rifles on the frontier in 1,200 records. This is just *fantastically* implausible and it's been shown to be false. The idea that no women owned guns in 11,000 records he looked at is a *ludicrous* statement. I mean, this is just nuts!"

Well, amen! And that's why we are confidently naming the "Nutty Professor" Michael A. Bellesiles as our "Anti-Gun Nut of the Century."

Next, I will report more convincing and compelling critiques of *Arming America: The Origins Of A National Gun Culture*—a book which, whatever else it may be, is not deeply researched, brilliantly argued, good history, authoritative, sensible, or significant scholarship. But, the book is an eye-opener. It has opened our eyes to the author's anti-gun, anti-Second Amendment agenda.

Second Amendment Scholars
Shoot Down Bellesiles

Alfred A. Knopf, the publisher of Emory University's history professor Michael A. Bellesiles's book *Arming America: The Origins of a National Gun Culture*, says that Bellesiles's work has received a "vast outpouring of... acclaim." But, this book is also receiving a growing number of compelling criticisms by gun scholars, Second Amendment scholars, and others knowledgeable in this field. These critics include the following individuals:

• **Joyce Lee Malcolm,** professor of history at Bentley College and author of *To Keep And Bear Arms: The Origins of an Anglo-American Right* (Harvard University Press, 1996). In an article in *Reason* magazine (January, 2001), Prof. Malcolm says that what Bellesiles is about is something other than writing a mere history. She points out that his book has been "enthusiastically embraced by gun control advocates as an aid in their effort to persuade Americans (and their courts) that they do not have, and never have had, a Constitutional right to be armed."

But, this is not true. Prof. Malcolm says scholars from various fields have delved into this question "and found overwhelming contemporary evidence that the Founders inherited and meant to guarantee an individual right, and none to support the notion that a collective right was intended. This body of work has persuaded such eminent Constitutional scholars as Lawrence Tribe and Leonard Levy that the Second Amendment protects an individual right."

Prof. Malcolm says Bellesiles's so-called "myth busting" findings "are not supported by his sources. Moreover, he presents a skewed selection of records, dismisses contradictory information, and even alters the language of quotations and statutes." She provides numerous specific examples to back up her charges.

Prof. Malcolm concludes: "Point after point meant to illustrate a nearly gun-free early America is, upon examination, unsupported by the copious sources Bellesiles cites. He sidesteps counter-evidence. He ignores or dismisses statements by John Adams, Patrick Henry, Noah Webster, Richard Henry Lee, Thomas Jefferson, James Madison and others to the effect that their countrymen were well-armed."

• **Clayton E. Cramer,** author of, among other books, *For The Defense of Themselves and The State: The Original Intent & Judicial Interpretation of the Right to Keep and Bear Arms* (Praeger, 1994), and *Concealed Weapon Laws of*

Antebellum America," Cramer, who has an M.A. in history from Sonoma State University, says that because the claims of Bellesiles "are so contrary to traditional historical understanding...they deserve a careful evaluation." And Cramer does evaluate these claims in documented detail.

For example, regarding the alleged scarcity of firearms in early America, Cramer says he read more than two dozen published travel accounts and memoirs of the early Republic. What he discovered was that "twenty-four mentioned firearms and hunting as unsurprising and common parts of American life....*None* claimed or even implied that either privately owned firearms or hunting were rare, unusual, or stigmatized. Marksmanship, according to many of the accounts, was highly prized, and high competence with firearms was widespread. Furthermore, these accounts make it appear that this was true for all regions of the United States."

Cramer also provides evidence that Bellesiles is mistaken concerning the production rate of guns in early America. And, he adds, Bellesiles' gunpowder production data "suggests that [his] claims about gun scarcity require considerably more evidence."

Cramer concludes: "To believe that firearms in America were rare, and hunting confined largely to market hunters requires more than a rewriting of American history textbooks; it requires a rewrite of dozens of contemporary accounts as well"—many of which Cramer quotes in detail.

• **Stephen P. Halbrook,** a Second Amendment lawyer and author of *That Every Man Be Armed: The Evolution of a Constitutional Right* published by The Independent Institute. In a column in the *Washington Times* newspaper (5 November 2000), he disputes Bellesiles's statement that before the War Between the States, "the majority of American men did not care about guns. They were indifferent to owning guns, and they had no apparent interest in learning how to use them." Says Halbrook, "Just as Josef Stalin doctored photographs to change history, artists of the early Republic must have inserted muskets over the Colonial mantels that never held a firearm."

He adds, regarding the premise of the Bellesiles book: "[It] seems to be that not many people kept or bore arms and thus recognition of a right to do so in the Constitution is not important today. One could just as well argue that not many people had books back then either and thus the right to a free press should not be taken too seriously."

Halbrook concludes by addressing Bellesiles's claim that our Founders had no concept of a personal right to have arms. He says: "Jefferson refutes this attempt at de-construction. Jefferson proposed for the Virginia Constitution of 1776, 'No freeman shall ever be de-barred the use of arms.' This thinking would find its way into the federal Bill of Rights, which to this day guarantees the right to keep and bear arms."

• **R.L. Wilson,** a distinguished author of more than 30 books on American firearms history. In an article in *Brill's Content* magazine titled "Loaded Words" (February 2001), Michael Korda, Editor-In-Chief of Random House, says that Wilson wrote him a letter in which he said that Bellesiles's book is "an example of gross bias against gun culture" and "a shocking deceit." Wilson has also said that *Arming America* will likely prove to be "the most outrageous example of dishonesty perpetrated to date by the zealots who have the 'gun culture' in their sights." He says that sometimes the introduction to this book "reads like a fund-raising letter from an advocacy group against gun ownership."

Korda deplores the fact that Bellesiles's book has "attracted positive attention from those who tend to see firearms as the devil's right hand and perhaps the deepest flaw in American political reality since slavery....That most reviews accepted [Bellesiles's] claims may merely point to the media's inherent bias against guns and its willingness to accept scholarship, however debatable, regarding anything that deflates the conventional wisdom surrounding firearms."

Korda says that Bellesiles's claims that there were few capable gunsmiths or gun makers in colonial America, that guns were rare, hard to come by, and ineffective, are, and have been for years, contradicted by far more observers of American culture than he quotes in his book. For example, he cites a compilation by the previously mentioned Clayton Cramer which shows 118 gunsmiths and gun makers in New York and New England alone during the early colonial period.

Noting that our 17th, 18th, and 19th century militias were not "just a bunch of clowns"—as caricatured by Bellesiles—Korda says: "It was the militia's troops that did so much damage to the British regulars on their way back to Boston from Lexington and Concord, whence the British had gone to seize militia military supplies. This would suggest that a substantial number of the militia not only were armed but knew how to shoot. At Bunker Hill, the militia stood up to the British bravely, inflicted heavy losses on them, and gave way only when they ran out of ammunition and the British infantry advanced with fixed bayonets."

Other key battles in the War for Independence, which were also won by militia, were the defeat of Gen. Burgoyne in New York and the battle of Kings

Mountain in Tennessee.

As to the meaning of the Second Amendment, Korda says:

> The founding fathers, if they knew nothing else, knew how
> to write clear English, and if they had wanted to ban the
> private ownership of firearms, or to limit ownership of
> firearms to those who served in the militia, no doubt they
> would have found a clear way of saying so. That they did
> not is, self-evidently, because the idea did not occur to
> them. They drew up the Bill of Rights to safeguard, protect,
> and defend the liberties of Americans, not to limit and
> circumscribe them, and nothing in 18th century American
> experience (or the Revolutionary War) would have led them
> to believe that it was a bad idea for a citizen to keep a gun at
> home, or a good idea to let government decide on whether
> or not he could do so.

Korda notes that nearly all the newspapers that reviewed *Arming America*
relied on reviewers "with little or no expertise in the specialized field of the
history of American firearm manufacturing and, for the most part, with a
bias against the private ownership of guns." An editor's note at the end of
Korda's article says that Bellesiles did not reply to an invitation to respond to
his piece.

When Bellesiles's book has been reviewed by someone who has some
expertise regarding his topic, the comments have been very critical. For
example, writing in the *Washington Post* (29 October 2000), John Whiteclay
Chambers II—a history professor at Rutgers University and editor-in-chief
of *The Oxford Companion To Military History*—says that despite Bellesiles's
determination to overthrow the traditional image of the gun in early
America, his "provocative thesis remains unproven. His conclusions
frequently overreach the evidence."

Detailing the problems of relying on probate records as heavily as Bellesiles
has, Chambers adds:

> The author also overstates both the originality and the
> conclusions he draws from militia records....Extensive
> research is undermined by errors of fact, omission and judg-
> ment. His argument that before the 1830s few Americans
> hunted game with guns defies belief....Bellesiles fails to
> prove the emergence of the modern gun culture in the
> [post-Civil War] era....[His book] is also digressive and

repetitive. Unfortunately, Bellesiles takes a rather narrow view of the subject...and he has not proven his thesis of limited ownership of guns and general unfamiliarity with them even among white adult males in the colonial and early national periods.

Contradictions Plague Bellesiles's Scholarship and Views

Surprisingly, and strangely—for a man who insists he is a "gun enthusiast"—Prof. Michael A. Bellesiles says nothing explicit about his own position on the Second Amendment in his 603-page book, *Arming America: The Origins of a National Gun Culture* (Knopf, 2000). He also writes nothing at all—zip, zero, zilch—about the importance of guns in self-defense. This, too, is bizarre considering that studies show that as many as three million Americans annually defend themselves, family, and/or property with guns.

In an interview published by *WorldNetDaily.com* (7 January 2001), Bentley College history professor Joyce Lee Malcolm, author of *To Keep and Bear Arms: The Origins of an Anglo-American Right* (Harvard University Press, 1996), says, "As someone who did a lot of work on the origins of the Second Amendment and the English experience with firearms, with their rights, I can certainly tell you that [Bellesiles] was happy to ignore any evidence that didn't fit in with his thesis."

OK. So, what *is* Bellesiles' thesis regarding the Second Amendment? Well, as I say, he does not say, explicitly, in his book. But, he has said things in various interviews which I believe show clearly that he does *not* believe the Second Amendment protects the right of private persons to keep and bear arms.

For example, in an interview on National Public Radio's "Fresh Air" program (9/26/2000), Bellesiles was asked this question: "So the idea of a well-regulated militia and people having arms for that would be the equivalent now of people having arms who are in the National Guard?"

Bellesiles: "Yes. That's exactly correct...."

He is also asked this question: "Do you think that the gun lobby in America has been drawing upon false history to justify its desire to prevent any further regulation of guns?"

Bellesiles: "If I may restate that, I think they have been drawing upon a mythologized past to justify their position in terms of opposing any gun regulation today. I think that is correct...." In other words, it is a myth—in this case meaning something that is false—to think that the Second Amendment constitutionally protects against any infringement of any right of private individuals to keep and bear arms.

Incidentally, though this program was called "Fresh Air," on the subject of guns it was the same old, tired, *stale*, anti-gun, hot air.

In another interview, on KQED Radio in San Francisco (11/14/2000), when a caller asks Bellesiles directly if he believes the Second Amendment protects an individual right or a right only of the government to keep and bear arms, he replies:

> Well, my personal reading of the context of the Second Amendment...is that it is an individual right collectively defined. In other words, it was understood that those members of the community who were reliable citizens should be enrolled in the militia. And they were included under the protections of the Second Amendment. But, again, let me emphasize that the Second Amendment is simply a limitation on federal authority. And the Supreme Court has continuously read it that way, that it *in no way* interferes with the states passing regulating legislation.

At this point, the caller presses Bellesiles, saying, "So, you don't agree that the 10th and 14th Amendments give the right to keep and bear arms to the citizens of the various states?" He replies: "Oh, my opinion doesn't matter. What matters is what the Supreme Court has decided. And so far the Supreme Court has not incorporated the Second Amendment. If they decide to do so, I will understand their logic."

When the caller, still not satisfied, asks Bellesiles to clear up his own view on the Second Amendment, he replies, in part, that he's never taken a position "on current gun policy." But, why not? If Bellesiles is, as he said on this program, a "gun enthusiast" and a gun owner for 35 years, why has he taken no position on "current gun policy?" Why has he been silent regarding those who want to, among other things, pass laws gutting the Second Amendment and banning the private ownership of all guns?

This makes no sense. I mean, here's a guy who says he spent more than 10 years researching and writing a 603-page book about the history of guns in America. And he has never taken a position "on current gun policy"?

This is weird. And what he says is dishonest. What Bellesiles means is that he has taken no *explicit* position on current gun policy. But, his entire book is, implicitly, an attack on guns. He's a "gun enthusiast," all right. He's enthusiastically *against* guns!

Finally, an example of Bellesiles's intellectual dishonesty is his distorted characterization of the work of gun scholar John Lott. When asked in this KQED interview about Lott's scholarship, Bellesiles notes, dismissively, that he's a person with a "very simple argument" summarized in his book title

More Guns, Less Crime. Bellesiles adds, sneeringly, that if this were true it would, of course, mean that we are "the most crime-free society in the world."

At this point, as a guest who was on this program with him, I told Bellesiles that Lott's thesis stands up very well. I told him that in the parts of our country where there are the most guns we, in fact, *do* have the lowest crime rates. Conversely, the murder rates are highest in the cities which have the strictest gun-control laws where people are not able to protect themselves—cities such as Washington, D.C., Chicago, Los Angeles.

Furthermore, in England, which *bans* the private ownership of guns, the violent crime rate is *higher* than in the United States.

A footnote: Ironically, Bellesiles's own book mentions two examples which prove that where there are "more guns" there is "less crime," and that a well-armed citizenry is a good idea. On page 435, he reports on the great Oklahoma land rush of 1889 where there were 15,000 men from around the world, "armed to the teeth, each fighting desperately for the best claim." And yet, there was "not a single killing, gunshot wound, or fist fight" that took place.

Also, on pages 443-44, Bellesiles notes that in Northfield, Minnesota, on September 7, 1876, the Jesse James gang robbed a bank and shot a teller. Then the gang came under fire from the "good people of Northfield" who ran home, got their rifles, and shot all eight gang members, killing two of them.

Contemporary Early American Accounts
Refute Bellesiles

In a glowing, sycophantic review of Professor Michael A. Bellesiles's book, *Arming America,* in the *New York Times Book Review* (9/10/2000), Gary Wills hails this wretched work saying that it "has dispersed the darkness that covered the gun's early history in America." But this is hogwash.

If ever there were a book that sheds more dark than light on a subject, it is what this "nutty professor" has written. Almost any book you browse in, at random, contains information blatantly at odds with Bellesiles's assertion that before the War Between the States—as Wills paraphrases him in his review—"the average American had little reason to go to the expense and trouble of acquiring, mastering and maintaining a tool of such doubtful utility as a gun." Below are just a few examples of what I'm talking about:

• **Edward Winslow** (1595-1655) was a founder of the Plymouth colony in Massachusetts. He wrote, "How The Pilgrim Fathers Lived." In this work, referring to a ship which might be friend or foe, he writes, "Whereupon every man, yea boy, that could handle a gun, were ready, with full resolution that, if she were an enemy, we would stand in our just defense, not fearing them." To those in the colony, he advises, "Bring every man a musket or fowling-piece. Let your piece be long in the barrel, and fear not the weight of it, for most of our shooting is from stands." It seems unlikely that these things would be said if guns were scarce.

• The great American historian **George Bancroft** (1800-1891), in his *History of the United States,* says of Patrick Henry that when he was a boy, "it had been his delight to wander alone with the gun or angling rod." In the late 1770s, he says: "Every county in Virginia glowed with zeal to embody its militia; marksmen, armed with rifles, chose the costume of the painted hunting-shirt and moccasins. They pledged themselves to each other to keep a good firelock, ammunition, bullet-moulds, powder-horn, and bag for balls....The Americans were...good marksmen....The British officers, from their own weakness and from fear of the American marksmen, dared not order a sally [during one battle—L.P.]....[The American's] skill as marksmen, never went out of mind [for the British—L.P.]." Concerning the American volunteers of New Hampshire and Massachusetts, Bancroft says they were *"skilled from childhood in the use of the gun,"* they *"had grown up with arms in their hands,"* and were *"the keenest marksmen"* (emphasis mine).

• In his "History of the American Nation" (1911), **William Jackman** says that the settlement of Oregon involved a thousand immigrants—men, their wives and children—"their only weapon the trusty rifle...to protect from savage violence and to procure sustenance from the wandering droves of buffalo and deer."

• In his writings, **Thomas Jefferson** says this regarding why we suffered far fewer losses at Lexington than the British: "This difference is ascribed to our taking aim when we fire; *every soldier in our army having been intimate with his gun from infancy*" (emphasis mine).

• In his *Autobiography*, **Benjamin Franklin** (1706-1790) says, "Just before we left Bethlehem, eleven farmers, who had been driven from their plantations by the Indians, came to me requesting a supply of firearms, that they might go back and fetch their cattle. I gave them each a gun with suitable ammunition."

• American historian **Reuben Gold Thwaites** (1853-1913), writing about the Lewis and Clark expedition, tells how a buffalo invaded their camp at one point causing an uproar, "the men rushing out with guns in hand...."

• In one account, the American Indian chief **Black Hawk** (1767-1838) tells how when he and other Indians arrived near the encampment of some whites, "a number of them rushed out to meet us, bringing their guns with them."

• American historian **Henry Adams** (1838-1918) writing about how the success of the Americans in our War for Independence impressed the Europeans, notes, "Critics said constantly that *every American had learned from his childhood the use of the rifle*" (emphasis mine).

• Irish historian and essayist **William Edward Hartpole Lecky** (1838-1903) says about the battles of Lexington, Concord, and Bunker Hill, "*The New England yeoman were accustomed to firearms from their childhood*" (emphasis mine).

• The English historian **Sir Edward Shepherd Creasy** (1812-1878) says, regarding the American militia's defeat of General Burgoyne at Saratoga, that the Americans were "resolute recruits, accustomed to the use of firearms...."

• In his "Messages and Presidential Papers," **James K. Polk** (1795-1849) says, about our "citizen soldiers" in our war with Mexico, "They are armed, *and have been accustomed from their youth up to handle and use firearms,* and a large proportion of them...are expert marksmen" (emphasis mine).

• In a new book titled *The Historical Atlas of the American Revolution*

(Rutledge, 2000), by Louisiana State University history professor **Charles Royster** (consulting editor) and **Ian Barnes,** head of politics and international studies at the University of Derby, the authors report how—during our War for Independence—American anger and determination was expressed in a dispatch by a British Naval officer to London: "The Enthusiastic Zeal with which those people have behaved must convince every reasonable man what a difficult and unpleasant task General Gage has before him, even Weamin (women) had firelocks. One was seen to fire a Blunderbuss between her Father, and Husband, and from their Windows." In this book, a caption beneath a picture of an American firing a rifle reads: "The American militia were normally expert marksmen and were often backwoodsmen experienced in Indian fighting. Some, known as minutemen, because they guaranteed to take up arms at a moment's notice, fought the Redcoats on the Lexington-Boston road."

• Speaking of the Minutemen, "nutty professor" Bellesiles ridicules these brave patriots. He sneeringly writes about how artists and politicians "crafted the mythical image of the heroic Minuteman, winning American independence with his every-ready musket" (p. 442). **Robert A. Gross,** a teacher at the College of William and Mary and the author of *The Minutemen and Their World* (Hill & Wang, 1976), says the Minutemen *were* heroic. Gross goes on to say, "What we can miss is the ordinary courage of human beings in everyday situations....[The Minutemen] did what they were asked to do....They are people who risked their lives and followed military discipline and routed the British."

Commenting on some of what Bellesiles alleges, Gross adds that whether guns in early America were or were not easily available or scarce and limited "doesn't in any way determine whether you think people have a Constitutional right to bear them." He says he did an independent study with a student recently regarding the Second Amendment and the English Bill of Rights and the way this tradition was passed to Colonial Americans. His conclusion is as follows:

> I think the argument would be that in the view of those who wrote the English Declaration of Rights in 1689 that access to arms was crucial as a means of resisting tyranny. It doesn't mean that everybody has to have them. It only means the government can't stop people from getting access at a moment when they need them.

• And, finally, for now, speaking of the American militia during our War for Independence, Bellesiles, as Michael Korda noted in a previously quoted piece, portrays them as "a bunch of clowns." But, in their book, *For The Common Defense: A Military History of the United States of America* (Free Press, 1984), Allan R. Millett and Peter Maslowski present a very different picture. Millett, when this book was published, was a History Professor at Ohio State University; Maslowski was a history professor at the University of Nebraska-Lincoln. They write, concerning the establishment of our early colonies:

> The most important response to the dangerous military realities was the creation of a militia system in each colony ....Militiamen had to provide and maintain their own weapons....Militia laws emphasized the importance of a well-armed citizenry in numerous ways....Colonies also required that even men exempted from attending musters should be completely armed and equipped.

Regarding the militia system the authors continue: "During the Indian wars from 1622 to 1676, colonists gained confidence in, and glorified, this system, believing that citizen-soldiers defending their homes were far superior to an army of mercenaries....The militia had its deficiencies, but it proved adequate, since the Indians were vanquished, not the whites."

Millett and Maslowski quote the high-ranking British officer Lord Loudon as saying: "The Militia are the real Inhabitants; Stout able men, and for a Brush, much better than their Provincial Troops, whom they hire whenever they can get them, and at any price." The authors add: "Almost all other British officers confused the expeditionary forces with the actual militia, thus misjudging the militia's military potential in defense of its own terrain."

Noting that the continental army complemented rather than supplanted the state militias, and at every critical juncture these forces acted in concert, Millett and Maslowski quote the British General Lord Cornwallis as saying this about the militia's battlefield contribution: "I will not say much in praise of the militia of the Southern Colonies, but the list of British officers and soldiers killed and wounded by them...proves but too fatally they are not wholly contemptible."

In my next section on the book *Arming America*, I will report on the shocking indifference to truth shown by Bellesiles's publisher Alfred A. Knopf—they show an utter lack of concern as to whether Bellesiles's material is true or false.

Bellesiles's Reviewer Not Interested in Whether Bellesiles Is Right

One of those individuals who is a true-believer in Professor Michael A. Bellesiles's book, *Arming America,* is Robert C. Ritchie, director of research at The Huntington Library in San Marino, California. In a press release distributed by Bellesiles's publisher, Alfred A. Knopf, Ritchie is quoted as saying: "At long last a superb book that systematically dismantles one of our most cherished and dangerous national myths. Bellesiles has made a major contribution to a significant public policy debate."

Curious as to how much Ritchie really knows about the book he so enthusiastically endorses, we contacted him and asked a few questions. To put it mildly, he was not pleased with our inquiries.

For openers, Ritchie said yes, he did read the book. OK, so how does he know it is accurate? Says Ritchie, "Well, you never know. You have to take a certain amount of it for granted, particularly in areas you don't know that well."

Is the subject of the Bellesiles book an area he knows well? Ritchie replies: "I know a fair amount about the early American period, yeah. But in terms of tracking out the footnotes, the way they have been tracked out in this one area of colonial probate records—that's the only stuff I've seen. That's been questioned."

This probate record "stuff" is, of course, a key part of the Bellesiles book upon which many of his conclusions rest. Did Ritchie not have the same capability as some others who have checked out, in detail, some of the probate record databases Bellesiles says he examined? And could he not have done this *prior* to his endorsement of *Arming America*? He replies, "Yeah." But, he did not do this.

Would Ritchie not agree that whether the Bellesiles book is "superb" or a "major contribution to a significant public policy debate" is directly related to whether or not it is accurate? Does it matter to him if the book is true or false?

Ritchie replies, "Yes, it does."

And yes, Ritchie says he is aware of many of the detailed criticisms of the Bellesiles book, including the 57-page paper by James Lindgren and Justin Lee Heather of Northwestern University.

OK. So, have any of these critiques caused Ritchie to re-think his endorsement of the Bellesiles book or investigate what any of these critics say? He replies, "I just look at the stuff on the e-mail."

Concerning the devastating demolition of the Bellesiles book by Lindgren and Heather, Ritchie says "There are problems with that, too." Such as? Ritchie responds, "I mean, the whole area of probate is technical. I don't think anybody has sorted all of it out yet. Michael (Bellesiles) has at least agreed to share some of his data with everyone and set up a website." And where can this website be seen? Ritchie says, "He's setting it up as far as I know now. I don't know for sure."

When told that Lindgren and Heather say that Bellesiles told them that he only has tallies on yellow pads, Ritchie says, "Obviously, you have an ax to grind in this." We say that the only ax we have to grind is to try and find out if what Bellesiles says is true.

He replies, "The whole thing here is that it [the truth of the Bellesiles book] can't be really established the way you want to establish about probates. *I think there is a problem with Michael's probate materials*" (emphasis ours).

OK, we ask, then why did you enthusiastically endorse his book if you admit there are problems with his materials? Ritchie replies, "Because the probate records I've seen for the 17th century go right along with what Michael says." And which database is this? Ignoring the question, Ritchie—who is a director of research!—says, "If I was to go and do research on every book I read and give a blurb on, I'd spend nothing else but my time doing that. [The Bellesiles book] seemed to me, from what I knew, to be correct."

We repeat our question: So, what probate records did you check and find out Bellesiles reported correctly? Ritchie says he read "17th century probate records from New York." But, no, he can't tell us which specific records because to do this, "I would have to go to my files."

OK, so did Ritchie check these New York records *prior* to his endorsement of the Bellesiles book? He replies, incredibly, "No. Why would I do that?"

Astonished by his question, we tell Ritchie one reason he might have done this is because he might have wanted to determine that the Bellesiles book was true *before* endorsing it. He says that from his knowledge, "I don't remember there being a lot of guns recorded in the probates for New York in the 17th century."

We ask: So, if they are not recorded, that means, to you, that they didn't exist?

"Yeah," Ritchie responds.

Again flabbergasted, we remind him, but, you have said the probate records are incomplete! To which he replies, "I know!"

When we start to ask Ritchie how then he can say what he said based solely on probate records, he interrupts to say that our conversation is "going nowhere." He says "thank you" and hangs up the phone.

But, of course, our little chat with Robert C. Ritchie *did* go somewhere—not where he wanted it to go, to be sure. But it did go somewhere. And what it reveals is that at least one official endorser of the Bellesiles book was no more careful with his endorsement than the "nutty professor" was in writing his book.

Bellesiles Publisher Unconcerned About Truth

"Pilate saith unto him, What is truth?"—John 18:38.

Have you ever wondered how a book publisher knows if what one of their authors writes is true, is accurate? Are any alleged facts checked? Or, for that matter, do book publishers even care if what they publish is true?

Well, we wondered this about Professor Michael A. Bellesiles's book, *Arming America: The Origins of a National Gun Culture* (Alfred A. Knopf, 2000). This is, after all, a 603-page book with hundreds of footnotes and sources cited. So, we spoke with some of the folks at Knopf to try and get an answer to some of these questions, and what we learned was shocking.

The first person we talked to was Gabrielle Brooks, promotion director at Knopf. She is listed as a contact on a press release promoting the Bellesiles book. We asked her what fact-checking was done by anyone at Knopf on the book. Who did the checking? What, exactly, was checked? And what was learned when you checked his facts? For days, our call was not returned. Then we were told to e-mail our questions. We did, and Brooks told us, by e-mail, "Fact checking was done by the author."

Somewhat taken aback by this reply—astonished, really—we then tried to speak with Sonny Mehta, editor-in-chief of Knopf. But, we got no further than a woman who identified herself only as "Janet," an assistant to Mehta. She explained, regarding the Bellesiles book, "We just trust the author that his facts are accurate. That's generally what publishers do. We're not going to hire people to pour over his documents." So, nobody at Knopf checked *any* of Bellesiles's facts? No. "Janet" refers us to Knopf's production editor, Kathy Hourigan.

Hourigan reiterates what "Janet" said. She tells us, "Unlike magazine publishers, we don't hire fact-checkers to check every fact. We rely on the authors. We sign up and take on authors who are reputable and whose work we trust...." So, nobody at Knopf checked *any* of Bellesiles's facts? "No," says Hourigan, "that's what I'm saying." When we ask if this is not rather scary, she says, "No."

Do the people at Knopf *care* if they've published a book that is not accurate? Hourigan says, "Absolutely. But, we don't believe that is the case with this [Bellesiles] book." But, how do you know unless you check his facts? She says that his editor, Jane Garrett, is "a very, very renowned editor."

But, we say, being "renowned" doesn't mean, necessarily, that you know if what Bellesiles has written is true. To which Hourigan replies, "That's the whole point with an editor taking on books that the editor trusts. We don't take on books from people we don't trust or have a question about the scholarship and the research. We take on writers that we do trust...."

But, how is it known that an author is trustworthy unless his facts are checked?

Hourigan replies, "No, no, that's not what I'm saying. I'm saying we— because the people who are—Jane [Garrett] as an editor has read a lot of books in this field—and she has worked for many, many, many years with writers. And she knows a reputable writer." She adds, "We as book publishers could never afford to publish books if we were fact-checking every fact of a writer that took 10 years to write a book. How could we possibly fact-check the book? We can't afford to do that. No book publisher does that." When asked what makes an author "reputable," she refers us to Bellesiles's editor, Jane Garrett.

Garrett does not speak with us, but her editorial assistant Alexis Gargaglino does. She says what the others say, "The author is responsible for the fact-checking. He [Bellesiles] had outside readers who are academics and scholars." And yes, she says, Garrett is aware of all the criticism of the Bellesiles book. OK, so is Garrett concerned about this criticism? "No, not at all," says Gargaglino.

So, there you have it. Alfred A. Knopf has published a viciously anti-gun book on one of the most controversial subjects imaginable, yet *nobody* at Knopf bothered to check even one of Bellesiles's facts. And Alexis Gargaglino adds insult to injury by saying—arrogantly and ignorantly—that they care "not at all" about any of the scholarly, documented-in-detail criticisms of *Arming America.*

Production editor Kathy Hourigan *says* that Knopf cares—"absolutely"—if they've published a book that is inaccurate. But, alas, their policy of not checking any facts themselves and relying only on the author shows that they do *not* care if this book is accurate. As for her question, "How could we possibly fact-check the [Bellesiles] book?" the answer is obvious: by checking his facts!

Joyce Lee Malcolm Exposes Bellesiles's Errors

Yet one more nail has been hammered into the coffin of Emory History Professor Michael A. Bellesiles's book, *Arming America,* which is rapidly being buried under a mountain of well-documented and compelling criticisms by scholars with expertise in this subject area.

The latest stake to be driven through the heart of this wretched book is an article in the *University of Texas Law Review* by Bentley history professor Joyce Lee Malcolm who, among other things, is the author of *To Keep And Bear Arms: The Origins of an Anglo-American Right* (Harvard University Press, 1996). In addition, Prof. Malcolm is a Senior Fellow, MIT Security Studies Program. She has a Ph.D. from Brandeis University and a B.A. from Barnard College. And she is a Fellow of the British Royal Historical Society. In her article, Prof. Malcolm says:

> Few historians have made such extravagant claims for their monographs nor had them accepted so uncritically as has Michael Bellesiles....In virtually every aspect of his argument, Bellesiles's claims are not supported by his sources and are at odds with those he has chosen to ignore or dismiss. This is not the occasional, unintentional error of fact or difference in emphasis. He has presented a skewed and distorted selection of the records, misquoted contemporary statements and statutes, provided inaccurate information, and erroneous accounts of the particular probate collections he specifically cites.

Prof. Malcolm concludes: "[Bellesiles's] rash and unsupported statements on one issue after another, and his lack of any specifics about his 11,170 probate inventories ought to have alerted both scholars and his publisher that something was amiss. The blame for one of the most erroneous history books to be published in many years lies with its author. He has not busted a myth, he has tried mightily to create one."

Now, some specifics. Here are some of the blanks Prof. Malcolm says Bellesiles has fired in his vicious, anti-gun diatribe:

- Bellesiles says the English "preferred to maintain tight control of guns." Prof. Malcolm points out the "awkward fact" that the English Bill of Rights of 1689 guaranteed that Protestant Englishmen (then some 90 percent of the population) "may have arms for their defence."

- Bellesiles wants us to believe that all militia muskets were stored in government arsenals. Prof. Malcolm says that C.G. Cruickshank, Bellesiles's source for this assertion, explains: "The reaction to this proposition was almost unanimous. It simply would not work....The scheme had no hope of success unless the individual providing the gun were allowed to keep it in his possession and use it when he felt like it." Cruickshank found commissioners of musters paid little attention to this proposal to keep county firearms under lock and key "as virtually all considered the whole scheme to be impracticable."

- Prof. Malcolm notes that Bellesiles asserts, without supporting evidence, that English militia were allowed to train only with pikes, not guns—a statement that "is both false and senseless."

- Was the use of guns rare apart from warfare, as Bellesiles says? Prof. Malcolm says: "On the contrary, firearms seem to have been popular with the common people from the 1540s....Eighteenth-century legal experts leave no doubt that ordinary Englishmen had a right to be armed." For example, in 1780 London's chief legal counsel found the "right of his majesty's Protestant subjects, to have arms for their own defence, and to use them for lawful purposes, is most clear and undeniable." By the early nineteenth century this had been extended from Protestants to all Englishmen as a guidebook for constables explained, "Every man has by law a right to carry ordinary weapons for the defence of his person and property, and (if necessary) to kill those who offer violence to either."

- Prof. Malcolm says that Bellesiles's notion that Americans regarded violence as "the monopoly of the state" simply "does not square with their obligation throughout the sixteenth, seventeenth and eighteenth centuries to defend themselves, their families and their neighbours."

- Did the early muzzleloader, as Bellesiles says, really take up to three minutes to load? Prof. Malcolm says that John Miller, an expert on black powder weapons, says that the colonial soldier was expected to be able to fire three shots per minute. And Robert O'Connell, the author of a book about the history of war and weapons published by Oxford University Press, says a colonial marksman could fire and reload a Brown Bess rifle five times a minute.

- Is it true, as Bellesiles says, that colonial legislatures only "occasionally" encouraged "private ownership of firearms by white male settlers" but realized this was a fruitless effort? Nope. Prof. Malcolm says these laws were not occasional but typical. They did not encourage ownership of firearms, they *mandated* it (emphasis mine). For example, the Plymouth colony ordered not only every militia member, but every householder to provide a musket or other serviceable firearm "for himselfe and each under him able to beare armes." Virginia did the same, although blacks were excepted from this requirement.

- Were *all* militia weapons subject to storage in government storehouses, as Bellesiles maintains? Says Prof. Malcolm, "Not only would this have been impractical if firearms were to be used for individual defense, but laws such as Connecticut's militia act of 1741 specifically ordered every householder to 'always be provided with and have in continual readiness, a well-fixed firelock...or other good fire-arms.'" Similar laws existed in Georgia, Massachusetts, and Virginia.

- Regarding Bellesiles's assertion that "no gun ever belonged unqualifiedly to an individual," that guns might be "privately-owned, but they were state-controlled," Prof. Malcolm says, "Guns were only taken by the state in an emergency, and then generally through purchase or loan. In May of 1775, when a committee of the Massachusetts Provincial Congress reported that 'a few' residents enlisted in its service were 'destitute of firearms, bayonets and other accoutrements,' the Congress resolved that the officials of these men's towns supply them from town stock or 'apply to such inhabitants...as, in their opinions, can best spare their arms or accoutrements, and to borrow or purchase the same.'" Prof. Malcolm explains, "Carts, horses, even houses and land can be requisitioned during wartime. This does not mean they are not privately owned."

- Contrary to Bellesiles's saying that hunting for food was

rare before the Civil War, Prof. Malcolm says that his review of contemporary travel accounts "omit dozens of other travelers who write of the widespread ownership of firearms." For example, the famed French observer Alexis de Tocqueville, in his *Journey To America*, describes a typical "peasant's cabin" in Kentucky or Tennessee as containing "a fairly clean bed, some chairs, a good gun."

- In a section titled "Misquotes, Misleading Accounts And Skewed Evidence," Prof. Malcolm notes Bellesiles has quoted George Washington as saying this about the state of the Virginia militia during an emergency call-up in 1776: "Many of them [are] unarmed, and all without ammunition or provision." But, Washington was *not* talking about the entire Virginia militia. He was, instead, referring to what he called "the odd behaviour of the few Militia that were marched hither from Fairfax, Culpepper, and Prince William counties, many of them unarmed."

- Bellesiles says of the Militia Act of 1792—the new nation's first militia act—that "Congress took upon itself the responsibility of providing [their] guns." Prof. Malcolm says, "In fact, the law actually states that 'every citizen so enrolled and notified, shall within six months thereafter, provide himself with a good musket or firelock' and other accoutrements."

- Prof. Malcolm says Bellesiles also "provides misleading figures on the numbers of firearms in circulation by using a series of federal and Massachusetts censuses of militia firearms as if they were complete surveys of all civilian guns. ....Unpalatable evidence, such as contemporary comments about a well-armed public or good marksmanship are dismissed by Bellesiles as either empty boasting or wishful thinking."

- Prof. Malcolm reports historian Harold Gill as having studied 572 colonial Virginia probate records and learned that 78.72 percent of men's estates and 25.45 percent of women's estates included firearms—percentages significantly higher than those alleged by Bellesiles. Gill examined inventories from York and Louisa counties and from his file of room inventories throughout Virginia. Prof. Malcolm says that since Gill's tally does not take into account the age of the decedent, his tally may be an undercount.

- Bellesiles devotes only one-and-a-half pages of his 450-page book to the drafting and intent of the Second Amendment. In a note, he mentions Roger Sherman's version of the Bill of Rights "which played a key role in the congressional debates, addresses only the militia, with no reference to a right to bear arms." Prof. Malcolm says: "In fact Roger Sherman's version was submitted only to his two fellow committee members, *played no role in Congress' discussion*, and only came to light 200 years later....*The committee's complete rejection of Sherman's version for what became the Second Amendment makes clear its intention to guarantee a right to individuals*" (emphasis mine).

- Prof. Malcolm adds: "If Bellesiles had reported the progress through Congress of what would become the Second Amendment, readers would have learned that a House committee eliminated the stipulation that the militia be 'well-armed' and the Senate rejected the proposal to add 'for the common defence' after 'to keep and bear arms.' *The emphasis was not on how well-armed the militia should be, but on the right of the people to be armed, and to be armed not for the collective, but for personal security*" (emphasis mine).

- Finally, Prof. Malcolm dismisses the notion that even if there were few guns in America before the Civil War that this means the Second Amendment could not have intended any individual right to have them. She says, "If this logic is applied to other rights it would mean if few Americans attended church the First Amendment did not intend freedom of conscience, or if there were few printing presses, freedom of the press was not actually guaranteed. This is a tortured and unconvincing argument."

Bellesiles Honored by Columbia University Even as His Scholarship Unravels

Despite the fact Michael A. Bellesiles's scholarship is being shredded and called into serious question—to put it mildly—this has not stopped Columbia University from awarding him its annual 2001 Bancroft Prize for his book, *Arming America: The Origins of a National Gun Culture* (Alfred Knopf, 2000). This prestigious prize, worth $4,000, is given for "distinguished works in American history and diplomacy."

But, Bellesiles' book is not deserving of such an award. An article in the *Wall Street Journal* (9 April 2001) by Kimberley A. Strassel, an assistant editorial features editor for the paper, says there is a problem with *Arming America*: "A growing number of respected scholars, from across the political spectrum, are saying that Mr. Bellesiles's research and conclusions are wrong. They've charged that [it] is riddled with errors so enormous as to seriously undermine his work. They argue he has incorrectly tabulated probate records, failed to include facts that strongly argue the opposite case, and misquoted and miscited sources."

In this piece, Gerald Rosenberg, a professor of political science at the University of Chicago, says, "From what I've seen, the evidence is so overwhelming that it is incumbent upon Bellesiles as a serious scholar to respond. He has to admit error, or somehow show how his work is right." When we interviewed Rosenberg, he said he's critical of Bellesiles's book even though he (Rosenberg) is "an avid gun control freak" who "wishes Bellesiles was right."

In the *Journal* article, Eric Monkkonen, a professor of history and public policy at UCLA, says of Bellesiles's book, "It didn't feel quite right, especially these dramatic changes he found, between a non-gun-owning country to a gun-owning one. Dramatic changes are more exciting than slow ones, but rare."

In a separate interview, Monkkonen, who says he read Bellesiles's book "carefully," tells us, "To me, the criticism of his use and errors on the probate records sounds accurate and that's certainly making me re-evaluate the book." Monkkonen says he is "a left-winger" who is pro-gun-control. And, like Rosenberg, he adds that he "would like for [Bellesiles's book] to be right, actually, but it doesn't look right."

In any event, on April 19, 2001, we caught up with Prof. Bellesiles at Columbia University when he was there to get his Bancroft Prize. We interviewed him. In this section I will comment briefly on some of what he said. More detailed comments on some of what he said will be addressed in several other sections. A complete text of this slightly edited interview is available on our website at *http://gunowners.org/optb.htm* in the Bellesiles section.

For openers, we asked Bellesiles if he has answered *specifically* any of his critics such as Northwestern University Law Professor James Lindgren, Bentley College History Professor Joyce Lee Malcolm, or Clayton Cramer. Yes, he said, his replies were on his website. But, they are *not*. He does not reply, specifically, by name, to any of the critics mentioned, on his website.

In fact, at one point, Bellesiles says, angrily, that he does not, for example, consider Malcolm to be a serious critic because she said that his book said America was "gun-free" prior to the Civil War and "that's nonsense." He says he *never* said this adding, "So, I can't take her seriously." When pressed as to whether he was saying Malcolm used the exact words "gun-free," Bellesiles says yes, that's what she said in her review of his book in *Reason* magazine.

But, wrong again! Bellesiles—who seems to have trouble reading a simple text—is mistaken. Malcolm does *not* say what he says she said. In her *Reason* review (January, 2000), she says Bellesiles's book says guns were "rare" before the Civil War, that he claims America was "nearly gun-free."

But, what if Malcolm *had* used the words "gun-free?" So, what? Would this one misquote be a reason for dismissing as a serious critic a distinguished scholar like Malcolm who, among other things, is the author of *To Keep And Bear Arms: The Origins of an Anglo-American Right* (Harvard University Press, 1994)? I think not.

Interestingly, the publication, *American National Biography* (Oxford, 1999), says of Frederic Bancroft (1860-1945)—the man whom the Bancroft Prize is named after—that he was "vitriolic and intolerant of those who disagreed with him." Hmmmmm. "Vitriolic and intolerant," eh? Sounds a lot like Bellesiles's attack on Malcolm.

Finally, a disturbing footnote. When we attempted to find out why Bellesiles's book was chosen for this year's Bancroft Prize, who the judges were that made this award, and whether they checked out any of his work, we were told this was not possible because these jurors are anonymous and their names cannot be revealed.

We were similarly stonewalled by the History Book Club which offers Bellesiles' book as one of its selections. In a letter signed by Deborah L.

Sinclaire, editorial director of the club, she says, in part, that they offer no book "unless it has been read and evaluated by one or several of our board of historian-advisors. They judge a book's importance, accuracy, and reliability."

Wonderful, we thought. So, we spoke with Sinclaire and asked for the names of the historian-advisors who checked out Bellesiles's book. No way, she said. "We keep this information confidential. This is a confidential list."

One name we do know, however, because he wrote a History Book Club byline review of the Bellesiles book when it first came out, *before* critics began to demolish *Arming America*. This man's name is Sanford Levinson, a law professor at the University of Texas. In his review, he, among other things, praised the Bellesiles book as "revisionist history at its best."

But, in an interview, Levinson has, well, revised his review. He tells us it wouldn't surprise him if Bellesiles's book is found to have some "fairly major problems." He says that if he reviewed the book today his review "might be a little less enthusiastic because I assumed the data more uncontroversial than they turn out to be. If I was reviewing the book now, I would say there's a real debate about this." Indeed. And Bellesiles is losing it—big time.

Interview with Bellesiles at Columbia University

(The following slightly edited exclusive interview with Michael A. Bellesiles was conducted on April 19, 2001, at Columbia University in New York City.)

Q: Have you answered specifically any of your critics like James Lindgren, Joyce Lee Malcolm, Clayton Cramer?

A: It's on my website.

Q: You've responded specifically to what they have written?

A: Yes. And I will be continuing to do so all summer. And I'm learning how to scan in illustrations so—in order to scan in the actual document—so it will be visible on the website.

Q: What is the address of your website?

A: If you go to the history department at Emory and just click on my name it'll go right there. I don't remember it off the top of my head.

Q: Is there anything written by Lindgren, Malcolm, or Cramer that you've found to be wrong or mistaken?

A: Actually so much of what, to me, obviously from my perspective, so much of what's been going on is raising up other evidence, which is certainly worth discussion—but when someone comes up with one body of evidence it doesn't contradict someone else's body of evidence. Right? So, for instance, Lindgren is using Alice Hanson Jones' collection. And he's right about what this collection has. It's a different set of numbers. And in fact what I'm trying to do now on my website is—I've become suspicious of all these sample sets that take just a year or two because so many factors are dependent on the year or two chosen. So, Hanson Jones is at the very beginning of the Revolution when arms are being handed out by the various provincial governments. The sample set I used for that period was from 1765 and 1766. That was the period when arms had been turned in. So my figures were probably relatively low. Hanson Jones's were relatively high. So what I'm doing now is taking a 20-30 year period in all these counties so that we can see if there is any variation over those years.

Q: But some of the criticism (like Lindgren's) has been that he looked at some of what you say you looked at, and it does not say what you have said it says—that women *did* own guns and the percentage of gun ownership was much higher than you said.

A: Oh, certainly. I didn't say that women didn't own guns. There was a misunderstanding. And I'd like to clear this up. In my sample set I was trying to exclude the women because I thought the women would largely bias the sample because almost every collection I looked at—every total inventory file I looked at for women did not have a gun. There were only a few. So if I included those I thought it would lower the figure and bias it in the direction of my argument. So I was looking at those men because I thought those were the most likely to have guns.

Q: So you never said or implied that women didn't own guns?

A: I don't think I did. If I did, it was a grammatical error.

Q: Cramer says you took a George Washington quote about the Virginia militia and did not use it correctly. Is that right?

A: I just don't remember.

Q: Have you discovered anything that in retrospect you were wrong about or misstated?

A: There were several errors which I have corrected in the footnotes. I found four transpositions of numbers, which I've corrected. I found three misspellings.

Q: But nothing major?

A: One major is the message I sent to all the historical list serves I could is that I quoted the 1803 Militia Act and a paragraph from the 1792 Militia Act. And when I was rewriting the manuscript I did take out the sentence where I said, "And then 11 years later Congress revised the Act in this way." So that was in error. This is being corrected in the revised edition.

Q: In an interview on a San Francisco radio station you expressed surprise that so many people view your book as anti-gun. But your book is an unrelieved trashing of our being a gun-loving, gun-centered, gun-crazy culture.

A: I don't think so.

Q: How we're obsessed with guns and—

A: No, no, no. Well, if I gave that impression—

Q: Two or three times you spoke about how central and important the gun is to America.

A: I believe that's true.

Q: But where's your data to support what you say? Less than half of all Americans even own guns.

A: Yeah, I understand that.

Q: You speak about Americans almost as if there is something psychopathic about our relationship to guns.

A: Oh, I see what you're saying. Yeah. I will dwell on that because that might be a misperception that I created.

Q: Why isn't there more in your book about the Second Amendment?

A: Because I'm personally opposed to gun control laws. I don't want to see any extension of gun control laws.

Q: Really? You're opposed to the Brady Bill?

A: Yeah. For many reasons. One is that I think we haven't been honest about what we hoped they would accomplish. But more importantly I think because enforcement of gun control laws in our history has been incredibly selective. It's tended to be very bigoted. That's my next book.

Q: But you're not against gun control laws because they violate the right of private individuals to keep and bear arms. Do you think the Second Amendment protects the right of private persons to keep and bear arms or only the State?

A: I still haven't made up my mind yet. I wrote an article for *The Legal History Review* and I thought, at the conclusion of my article, I was trying to carve a different terrain, that the Second Amendment was about creating an individual right collectively defined. In other words, the law is going to determine who does and does not get to enjoy that right. That's true of every right....I'm trying to work this out.

(NOTE: Not true. Some rights are unalienable, from God. In the 1876 *Cruikshank* case, the Supreme Court stated that the Second Amendment was not created by the U.S. government; it preceded it. Also, the Second Amendment says there shall be no infringement of this right!)

Q: Why do you think your book has been so loved by the pro-gun control people if you're against gun control?

A: I don't know. I really don't.

Q: Do they know you're against gun control?

A: Yeah. I generally made my opinion clear to them when they want me to speak *for* them. I won't come and speak *for* gun control.

Q: Have any gun control groups asked you to speak?

A: They have. And [I've said] I will speak about historical issues. I will not speak about modern policy mostly because I'm not into that. I *love* history. I love the past.

Q: But you've also said you've been a gun owner for more than 30 years and that you've fired guns in many foreign countries. Presumably you're a citizen of the United States.

A: That's correct.

Q: So, why wouldn't you have some passion about your right to keep and bear arms?

A: I just don't have a passion—I'm sorry—in that way. I mean, for me shooting guns is enjoyable. It is.

Regarding whether the Second Amendment protects the right of private individuals or only the State to keep and bear arms, he says:

> As a historian, I would refer back to the Supreme Court decisions and state court decisions and I think—this is the way I've read it so far—is that in the last 20 years we've gotten into a situation where it is not at all clear what the judiciary thinks about our right to bear arms.

He says "no, of course not," he is not prepared to automatically genuflect in a knee-jerk way to any Supreme Court or state court decisions on this issue (except that he does!).

He adds, regarding why he says so little in his book about the Second Amendment, and why he doesn't say he's against gun control: "Let me give you an example. I'm personally opposed to abortion. And the Supreme Court has decided pretty strongly that people have a right to abortion. I think this is really wrong. But that doesn't mean that I as a historian should be going around saying that the Supreme Court has made a great historical error. It has made an error based on my personal judgment."

I point out that this is not a good analogy because his book is about guns, not abortion! So, it would have been perfectly appropriate to state clearly his views on the Second Amendment and gun control laws.

Q: Why are you against abortion?

A: Because I am a rather devout Christian, a Catholic. And I find it a violation of my moral standards.

Q: I get the feeling from reading your piece in the Atlanta paper that all the criticism of your book is really getting to you and wearing you down.

A: Oh, yes.

Q: But I wish that in your public writings that you'd concentrate on the serious critics of your book—people like Malcolm, Cramer, Lindgren—and not write about how anti-Semites are after you as if the only critics you have are Internet wackos and people who would have been liked by Goebbels. In other words, you had several hundred words in the Atlanta paper article to address your serious critics and you chose instead to give attention to people who deserve no publicity *at all!* Why don't you take on the heavyweights, the big guys?

A: I haven't seen any heavyweights or big guys.

Q: How about Malcolm?

A: I don't agree with that formulation.

Q: She's not a scholar who knows something about guns and history?

A: I think she's a scholar. But, for instance, she characterized my book as saying that America was a gun-free society prior to the Civil War and that's nonsense. That's not what I said.

Q: Gun-free?

A: That's what she said in her review in *Reason* magazine. I *never* said any such thing. So, I can't take her seriously.

Q: You're saying she used the actual words "gun-free?"

A: That's what she said. And that's not what my book says.

Q: So, who is a serious critic of yours, that you've read what he said and are taking it seriously?

A: People who have offered what I think are very interesting criticisms are Richard Slotkin (in the *Atlantic*) and Jackson Lears (in the *New Republic*). They offer very interesting criticisms, more from the left.

Q: How about your notes? Are they dried out yet? Is that a true story you told Lindgren?

A: Of course it's a true story. In the history building (Bowden Hall at Emory University), the plumbers were in there working on a Sunday and they did not reconnect the main pipes. They turned the water back on and *all* my notes got wet.

Q: For your whole book?

A: Yes. And most of them were useless and have been pulped. They were thrown away.

Q: All were in longhand?

A: Yes. All of it. Pencil on a legal pad. That's the way I work.

A subsequent interview with school officials at Emery make it highly dubious that Bellesiles's work was damaged by water at all. See an upcoming section entitled, *The Dog Ate the Homework.*

Bellesiles: His "Yes" Is Not Yes, and His "No" Is Not No

Before one calls a man a liar, one must be very careful. So, very carefully, we say Michael A. Bellesiles is a liar regarding his views on the Second Amendment. How so? Let us count the ways. In his interview with us at Columbia University on April 4, 2001, we asked Bellesiles if he thinks the Second Amendment protects the right of private persons to keep and bear arms or is this only a right for the State? He replied: "I still haven't made up my mind yet....I'm trying to work this out."

But, Bellesiles is lying. He *has* made up his mind. He is clearly against the so-called Standard Model which views the Second Amendment as primarily empowering individual American citizens to own a gun for self-defense and, if necessary, to counter government tyranny by means of armed popular resistance.

In the January 22, 2001, issue of the *New Republic* magazine, Bellesiles' book, *Arming America*, was reviewed by Jackson Lears who teaches history at Rutgers University. Lears, a critic Bellesiles says he takes seriously, writes: "Indeed, the Second Amendment itself, in Bellesiles' reading, was not meant to sanction individual gun ownership. Quite the contrary: it was designed to 'continue the legal British tradition of controlling the supply of and access to firearms....' The Second Amendment, Bellesiles argues persuasively, must be seen as an effort to refine and to clarify that control, and not as an affirmation of an individual right to bear arms."

In a September 7, 2000, interview with David Bowman published by the Internet publication *Salon.com*, Bellesiles says the Second Amendment was conceived by James Madison in the context of the national crisis of our War for Independence when there were not sufficient firearms, when a majority of Americans didn't know how to use firearms. He adds: "It would be a very different story if we were to rewrite the Second Amendment today from the perspective of a gun enthusiast. It would probably be exactly what they claim it is: That the individual's right to own firearms will not be infringed under any circumstances. But that's not what the Second Amendment says."

In a September 26, 2000, interview on National Public Radio's "Fresh Air" program, Bellesiles was asked, "So the idea of a well-regulated militia and people having arms for that would be the equivalent now of people having arms who are in the National Guard." He replies, "Yes, that's exactly correct...." He's also asked, in this disgustingly soft-ball interview (our tax dollars at work!), "Do you think that the gun lobby in America has been drawing upon false history to justify its desire to prevent any further regulation of guns?" He replies, in part, "If I may restate that, I think they have been drawing upon a mythologized past to justify their position in terms of opposing any gun regulation today. I think that is correct."

The Volume 76, Number One, 2000 issue of the *Chicago-Kent Law Review* was devoted to numerous articles trashing the Standard Model of the Second Amendment. This symposium was edited by the appropriately named Carl T. Bogus. One article in this publication is by Bellesiles and is titled "The Second Amendment In Action." In his piece Bellesiles says the Standard Model "usually takes a non-historical perspective, preferring to hunt for supportive quotations while subjecting well-known statements to excruciating linguistic deconstruction rather than undertaking the hard and time-consuming task of archival research." This "postmodernist perspective," he says, "is, of course, blasphemy to a historian....The Second Amendment confirmed [a] commitment to organize and arm a militia."

In the U.S. Court Of Appeals for the Fifth Circuit, there was a case (No. 99-10331) called *United States of America v. Timothy Joe Emerson.* In this case there was a brief filed for an anti-gun group of law professors and historians in support of the government's anti-individual right interpretation of the Second Amendment. Bellesiles was one of those signing this brief.

In an interview, Brooklyn Law School Professor David Yassky, who organized the signers of this brief, told us that he was reluctant to characterize Bellesiles' position on the Second Amendment. But, he says, "It's safe to say he rejects the Standard Model." Well, the Standard Model is the scholarly name for the individual right to keep and bear arms view of the Second Amendment.

In the Fall 1998 issue of the *Law And History Review,* in an article titled "Gun Laws In Early America: The Regulation Of Firearms Ownership, 1607-1794," Bellesiles calls advocates of the Standard Model "master rhetoricians" who do things like "stringing together...carefully selected quotes." He says it is his contention "that the early American legislatures shared the British perception that gun ownership should be precisely constrained by law.... The bottom line was state control."

Michael A. Bellesiles is absolutely correct about one thing in this article. He says that the discussions of this subject "are far from over." Indeed. And the more discussion there is, and the more his supposed scholarship is examined, the worse the lying Mr. Bellesiles looks.

A final note, for now, regarding the so-called Standard Model. In the

Internet publication *Lingua Franca Features: The Review Of Academic Life Online* (Volume 10, No. 1, February, 2000), there's an article by Chris Mooney titled, "Liberal Legal Scholars Are Supporting The Right To Bear Arms. But Will Historians Shoot Them Down?" In this piece, Mooney says that since 1989, "legal scholars have turned *en masse* to the individual-rights view (of the Second Amendment), filling law reviews with what may be more than a hundred articles defending this position....Today, the Standard Model appears to be on the verge of graduation from the law review to the court-house" with many judges sharing this view.

A TALE OF TWO GEORGES....

Bellesiles Wrong About Audubon

Emory history professor Michael A. Bellesiles, author of *Arming America: The Origins of a National Gun Culture* (Knopf, 2000), is losing it. He's cracking under the growing criticism of his book. More and more, he's sounding like the paranoid Lt. Commander Queeg in *The Caine Mutiny*. A case in point is Bellesiles'address at Columbia University (4/19/2001) when he accepted the prestigious Bancroft Prize in history. When he spoke—like Commander Queeg—you could almost hear the ball-bearings clicking as he denounced his critics as, among other things, rattlesnakes.

Tight-lipped and grim-faced, and citing no source for the anecdote he's about to tell, Bellesiles begins his address by telling this story:

> In 1831, John James Audubon was nominated for member-ship in the American Philosophical Society. Many amateur experts resented Audubon's insistence on field work and realism which threatened to take science out of its cozy libraries into the swamps and forests of America, into the natural archives.
>
> These adversaries drew attention to *one* [emphasis his] of the hundred plates in Audubon's latest book that showed a rattlesnake attacking a nest of mockingbirds in a tree. Rattlesnakes cannot climb trees, they exulted. Clearly, Audubon was fabricating his material and should *not* [emphasis his] be admitted to the Philosophical Society. It is amazing to us that anyone would seek to deny the value of Audubon's work because of a single mistake. But they did.

As Bellesiles tells it, evidence was produced that rattlesnakes *do* climb trees. Thus, the Philosophical Society elected Audubon as a full member. At the end of his address, Bellesiles declared, "As scholars we have a duty, as citizens a responsibility, and as teachers a profound obligation to speak the truth—despite the rattlesnakes."

Okay. So, Bellesiles's not-so-subtle point here is, obviously, that, like Audubon, he too is being savaged, accused of fabricating material, etc., and like Audubon, he will be proven to be correct.

But—speaking of the profound obligation to tell the truth—has Bellesiles told the truth here about what supposedly happened to Audubon?

In an interview, Rob Cox, curator of manuscripts at the American Philosophical Society, tells us that it appears the rattlesnake bit was "probably a minor player at all, if anything" regarding Audubon's admission to the society. He says there is a letter about this matter but it was written *after* Audubon became an APS member in 1831. Cox says he found records of members opposing Audubon's scientific practices. But, "I can't say this had to do with his membership at all." He reiterates that all comments about the rattlesnake bite were "after Audubon was elected" to membership. "So, obviously, this didn't have much to do" with that. Cox adds that he asked Winfield Bell, Librarian Emeritus of the APS, about the rattlesnake bite. And Bell, who was at the society for 50 years, said "he never heard the story before."

In another interview, we spoke with Allan Garrett, assistant administrator of Mill Grove, the Audubon Wildlife Sanctuary and first home of Audubon in America. When asked if he knew of any evidence that Audubon was in any way opposed for membership in the American Philosophical Society because of his rattlesnake/mockingbird drawing, he says: "No. I would have to say no on that. That certainly would not have had anything to do with his denial of admission to the society."

Finally, Rita Tehan, who is in the information research division of the Congressional Research Service at the Library of Congress, says she reviewed six Audubon biographies and none of them mentioned anything about Audubon being denied admission to the American Philosophical Society because he believed rattlesnakes climb trees.

There is, however, at least one way in which Michael A. Bellesiles *is* like John James Audubon. And that similarity is that Audubon, like Bellesiles, also told some whoppers, some tall tales. In *John James Audubon: A Biography* (G.P. Putnam, 1966) by Alexander B. Adams, the author details what Audubon said was the "disgusting" mode of copulation by rattlesnakes. Says Adams of Audubon's erroneous description, "It was enough to send any informed herpetologist, amateur or professional, into guffaws of laughter."

Adams also mentions Audubon's solemn repeating of "one of the oldest folk tales about rattlesnakes, the legend of the tooth in the boot." To keep a long and involved story short, this tale tells how, supposedly, a Pennsylvania farmer was bitten lightly through his boot by a rattlesnake. He died a few hours later. A year after this, his son put on his father's boots. Later, taking them off, the snake tooth stuck in the boot scratched him. He, too, died in a few hours. About two years later, a second son put the boots on. As he did, he was also scratched by the tooth. You guessed it. He also croaked.

Says Adams: "A true story? There was not a grain of truth in it. The poison remaining on one tooth through a piece of leather would be imperceptible; and the poison of a rattlesnake quickly loses all its potency when exposed to the open air....The story is a palpable falsehood, and Audubon should have known it or, what is more likely, actually did know it."

Bellesiles Taking Others Down With Him

One of the many scandals swirling around Emory history professor Michael A. Bellesiles's book, *Arming America*, is the way supposedly reputable academics have praised Bellesiles—and, implicitly, his work—without knowing if what he has written is true. A case in point is Professor Alan Brinkley, chairman of the history department at Columbia University.

In April, Bellesiles was at Columbia University to receive, with two other authors, the prestigious Bancroft Prize in history. In his remarks at this ceremony, Brinkley noted that there were "very high standards" for this prize which Bellesiles, and the other two authors, "maintained and perhaps in some ways exceeded."

Referring to Bellesiles and *Arming America*, Brinkley said it was always "difficult and courageous" to presume to recreate part of the past we can never retrieve. "But, so much more courageous to attempt to retrieve and reinterpret a part of our past that is layered over with so many powerful myths and images that are deeply entrenched in the American mind." Noting that Bellesiles has this kind of courage, Brinkley said that his book "challenges one of our most powerful—both culturally and politically—images of our past."

But, does Professor Brinkley really know what he's talking about here? Did he read Bellesiles's book? More importantly, has he read any of the scholarly criticisms of the book?

In an interview, Brinkley says he read "part of the book" but not "the whole book." And, "oh, yes," he says, "I certainly am aware of the many criticisms of the book. Most of them are not scholarly criticisms, though some are."

When asked if he has read any of the serious scholarly criticisms, Brinkley says, "I've read accounts of them." He has not, however, read the actual criticisms. Has he read any of the scholarly criticisms by James Lindgren, Clayton Cramer, or Joyce Lee Malcolm? Brinkley says no, he has never heard of these people! When Malcolm's name is mentioned, he asks, "Who is she?"—a strange question for a history professor since Malcolm, too, is a history professor (at Bentley College) and one of the leading Second Amendment scholars in America who has been quoted many times in, among other places, the *New York Times*, which one would think Brinkley reads.

When we note that his remarks praising Bellesiles's courage seem to presuppose that what Bellesiles has written is correct, Brinkley says: "No, I don't assume that. I'm not in a position to judge that. It's not a subject in my field of expertise." Still, he says, he stands by what he said about Bellesiles "even though I'm not prepared to say that everything in the book is correct. I just don't know."

Brinkley readily agrees that if Bellesiles's scholarship is shoddy, then, of course, he would not have praised his courage. But, he adds, he's not prepared to say that Bellesiles's scholarship is shoddy.

> Q: Wouldn't it have been wise for you to have, in some way, *prior* to praising Bellesiles, checked his facts to see if what he has written is true?
>
> A: I'm not going to comment on that. I said what I said and I'm not going to comment on it.
>
> Q: But is Bellesiles's so-called "challenge" to our myths, etc., *true?* All kinds of people "challenge" all kinds of things.
>
> A: Look, I've told you my view. I have nothing more to say. I can't answer these questions. You can make whatever you like out of what I said at that event. That's your right.

Brinkley says the suggestion that he should have, in some way, tried to determine the truthfulness of what Bellesiles has written, before praising him, is "unrealistic." Why? Because "we assume that members of the historical profession, when they present a work of scholarship, have exercised professional integrity in doing their work. If someone were to prove that Michael Bellesiles did not do this then I would certainly change my view of the book."

> Q: But, at the time you spoke, praising Prof. Bellesiles, there was already a lot of serious scholarly criticism of his book. Why did you not read any of this criticism?
>
> A: If I had been convinced that his scholarship had been discredited, certainly I would have spoken differently.
>
> Q: So, are you making any effort *now* to see if Bellesiles's scholarship *has* been discredited?
>
> A: Am I now?
>
> Q: Yes.

Brinkley says, incredibly, "no," that he has "no connection" with this book other than introducing Bellesiles, reading part of his book and hearing that there are criticisms of it. "So," he adds, "I am not investigating it."

> Q: But, if you knew there were serious scholarly criticisms of
> the book, *before* your remarks, why did you not get and
> read any of these criticisms? They might have changed your
> mind. This suggestion is not unrealistic, is it?

> A: Well, maybe it's not. But I did not do it.

Pathetic, huh? And outrageous, too, no? I mean, it's one thing to have made
a mistake and not checked *any* of the facts of an author you are praising.
But, to say that even *now* you have no intention of doing this reveals a
shocking indifference to truth. As for the bit about assuming that historians
exercise "professional integrity," I predict that Professor Brinkley will live to
regret such an assumption in the case of Michael A. Bellesiles and his
wretched book trashing guns.

"The Dog Ate the Homework"

It's not exactly the same as the excuse: "The dog ate my homework." But, it's close. And it is certainly one of the more bizarre happenings surrounding Michael A. Bellesiles' book, *Arming America*. I'm alluding here to his claim that all the notes for his book got wet, a flood rendered most of them useless, and they were destroyed.

In our interview with Bellesiles at Columbia University (4/19/2001), he explained, testily: "Of course it's a true story. In the history building (Bowden Hall at Emory University), the plumbers were in there working on a Sunday and they did not reconnect the pipes. They turned the water back on and *all* my notes got wet." *All* the notes for his *entire* book? Yep. He says: "Most of them were useless and have been pulped. They were thrown away." A friend of Bellesiles', Law Professor Paul Finkelman of the University of Tulsa, says, in an email, that Bellesiles had "about 100,000 pages of notes"—which is a lot of notes.

But, as is all too often the case, the way Bellesiles tells things does not appear to be the way events actually occurred. *The Emory Report* (May 8, 2000, Volume 52, No. 32), which is published by the administration of the University, says, in part: "On the evening of Sunday, April 2, a connector on a sprinkler main broke on the building's third floor. Contractors had been working on the plumbing. When the flow of the water was finally cut off about 25 minutes later, standing water was two inches deep in some places, and practically no part of Bowden Hall escaped completely dry."

Now, if a scholar at a university had all of his notes destroyed for a well-known book which took more than 10 years to write—as *Arming America* did—you'd think this would be big news and a lot of folks would know about such a disaster. But, we've been unable to confirm Bellesiles' story. In fact, we've found much evidence to contradict his claim.

For example, the previously mentioned *Emory Report* quotes Janice Mohlhenrich, preservation coordinator for Emory University, as saying of the Bowden Hall Flood, "We were able to look at things that professors thought were irretrievably lost, but we looked at them and said, 'Sure, we can fix this.'" In an interview, when asked about the extent of damage to Bellesiles' materials, Mohlhenrich said: "I don't know. I know that we brought a number of his things over to the preservation lab and dried them out for him."

Q: Did Bellesiles bring a lot of stuff to you?

A: No, not a great deal.

In a story about the flood in the Emory student newspaper *The Wheel,* four professors were mentioned whose offices were in Bowden Hall. Bellesiles is not mentioned.

In an interview, Barney Gimbel, editor of *The Wheel,* who wrote the story about the Bowden Hall flood, was asked, "Are you aware of any professors who had serious and major damage to any of their work?" He replied, "No…. It really wasn't that bad of a flood in all reality." He says he has never heard the story about all of Bellesiles' notes being destroyed. Indeed, he says that, at the time, he called Bellesiles but Bellesiles never returned his call. He adds, regarding Bellesiles: "[He's] not a very friendly person. I can say that because I had a class with him. He's a very snide guy. He's very full of himself. He's a prima donna."

History Professor Patrick Allitt, who also has an office in Bowden Hall, tells us no, he, too, never heard from Bellesiles or anybody else that all of Bellesiles' notes were destroyed.

Dr. Walter Adamson is head of the History Department at Emory. In an interview, he tells us that the only person he remembers as sustaining damage from the flood was Associate Professor Cynthia Patterson who had some photos of Greece destroyed. When asked if he was aware of Bellesiles saying that all of his notes for *Arming America* were destroyed, he says, "No, I'm not aware of any damage that substantial." He adds that 100,000 pages of notes "sounds like more than anybody really accumulates." Dr. Adamson refers us to Rosalyn Page, the History Department's administrative assistant in charge of dealing with insurance claims filed by professors who had materials damaged in the Bowden Hall flood.

In an interview, Page—who says that all insurance claims have come through her—says, "We were very, very fortunate in that all of the contents [damaged] were all replaceable and repairable."

Q: Do you know if any professors suffered any major damage to their works, to their notes?

A: Not that I know of. I assume if that was the case, you know, I would know.

Q: Do you know Professor Bellesiles?

A: Yes, he's in our department.

Q: Did he make any kind of claim as you know?

A: Yes, he had some materials that needed to be replaced.

Q: Was it much damage?

A: No. Like I say, we were very fortunate. Most people didn't have a whole lot of things.

Q: And you are thoroughly familiar with everyone who filed a claim and everybody's damage?

A: Right.

Q: So, you know of no one in the history department who suffered any damage to his work?

A: Right.

Q: And you *would* know if such major damage was suffered by any professor?

A: Right.

Finally, David King is senior vice president of Disaster Services Incorporate, the firm who cleaned up and dried out Bowden Hall. He was first on the scene and went office-to-office to see the flood damage. In an interview, he tells us he'd "be shocked if anything was destroyed, to be honest with you." He agrees with preservation coordinator Mohlhenrich who says that most of what was damaged was saved.

Hmmmmm. "To be honest" with us, eh? Sounds like, from what we've been able to learn, that, once again, Michael A. Bellesiles hasn't been.

Section Thirteen

>⊷⊶⊙⊶⊷<

FREEDOM UNDER ATTACK ABROAD AND AT THE UNITED NATIONS

England: Anti-Gun Poster Child—Not

The anti-self-defense crowd that believes America will be better off when guns are banned wants us to learn from other countries that have much stricter gun control.

I think they have a point. We can learn from other countries. Can we agree starting out that we will apply here the lessons we learn there?

Let's look at England. England has the kind of gun control that former President Clinton, Senator Schumer, and Sarah Brady of Handgun Control, Inc. would like to see here. If they did not want a gun ban for the whole country they would not tolerate the gun ban in Washington, D.C., which is by the Constitution under Congress' legislative control.

For decades, the only gun a Brit could own was one that was registered with the government. When the gun banners decided a couple of years ago to ban them all (with insignificant exceptions), it was no problem to get them all.

But all is not well in the gun banners' island paradise. According to a study done by the Clinton Justice Department and Oxford University in England, the British violent crime rate is now greater than that of the U.S.

British police officials estimate that there are some 3,000,000 illegal firearms, many of them machine guns, in the hands of criminals.

The country's media has labeled the city of Manchester as "Gunchester."

The government's commitment to disarming the people reached a new peak of absurdity when in April an English lawyer lost his court battle to recover his shotgun. It turned out that the authorities thought he was too careless with how he stored it—his octogenarian mother knew where the key was for the safe where the gun was stored.

If a gun ban on an island has not kept criminals from getting their hands on guns, how will submitting Americans to a background check, or imposing a gun-free zone around schools, churches, post offices, and other places keep guns out of criminal hands?

England, I Told You So

The British Home Office, in its "Practical Guide To Crime Prevention," offers what are referred to—presumably with a straight face—as some "sensible precautions."

Regarding how to stay safe at home, the guide says:

> If you wake to hear the sound of an intruder, only you can decide how best to handle the situation. You may want to lie quietly to avoid attracting attention to yourself, in the hope that they will leave. Or you may feel more confident if you switch on the lights and make a lot of noise by moving about. Even if you're on your own, call out loudly to an imaginary companion—most burglars will flee empty-handed rather than risking a confrontation.

> Ring the police as soon as it's safe for you to do so. A telephone extension in your bedroom will make you feel more secure as it allows you to call the police immediately, without alerting the intruder.

This same "guide" suggests the following: "If the worst happens," and one is actually attacked, "You have every right to defend yourself, with reasonable force with items you have with you like an umbrella, hairspray or keys can be used against the attacker. The law however doesn't allow carrying anything that can be described as an offensive weapon."

But, of course, in England, individuals are not legally allowed to decide how best to deal with those who break into their respective homes. For example, private persons cannot legally own handguns for protection—which in the case of repelling a home intruder would be a defensive weapon.

What is suggested in this "guide" is neither "practical" nor "sensible." An umbrella? Hairspray? Keys? Please. This is dangerously absurd. In America, several studies have estimated that from 1,000,000 (the Clinton Justice Department number) to 2.5 million individuals (a Florida State University scholar's number) every year use firearms successfully in self-defense. Proportionately, based on your population, there is no reason to believe that this would not also be true if firearms were as easily available in England as (thank God) they are in our country due to the Second Amendment of our Constitution.

And there appears to be a stronger need than ever for their government to allow law-abiding citizens to arm themselves for self-defense if they so desire. In a recent letter-to-the-editor in the American newspaper *USA Today* (7 February 2000), Jennifer Arney of Shere, Surrey, England, writes, in part: "After living in England for more than two years, I know there are no tragic results that come from the confiscation of guns. I've never felt safer strolling through London, where the only arms bearers are selected Bobbies."

But, to put it charitably, Ms. Arney seems not to have the slightest idea of what's happening in her part of the world. The BBC's *News Online* (January 18, 2000) reported that home office statistics reveal "a huge surge in muggings, amid a worrying rise in violent crime." The number of robberies (most of them muggings) increased by 19 percent in the year to September. And the biggest rise in crime was in London which saw a 22 percent increase—more than one million offenses.

Overall, the violent crime rate in England now exceeds that of the U.S. rate according to a joint Oxford University/U.S. Department of Justice study.

And are the "only arms bearers" in London "selected Bobbies?" Not exactly. In London last year, there were more than 20 fatal shootings allegedly linked to the "Yardies," gangsters who have their roots in Jamaica.

Indeed, according to the January 16 issue of *The Times,* criminals have an estimated 3,000,000 illegal guns in the country. Once again we see that gun control works—against the law-abiding only, not against the criminals.

Last July, Tim Westwood, a BBC hip-hop disk jockey, was shot by a man who opened fire on the car in which he was traveling in South London. And Amnesty International reports that London is a base for another gang, the "Tamil Tigers" of Sri Lanka, who extort money from London's Tamil community and then buy guns and explosives which they give to terrorists. On the night of August 30, 1999, at the Warren Farm Sports Center in Southall, UK, two gangs said to work for the "Tigers" attacked each other with guns and machetes.

In addition, the *Manchester Guardian* has lamented the fact that their city is now called "Gunchester" with police sources quoted as saying that guns had become "almost a fashion accessory" among young criminals on the street. Shootings in the area totaled 41 last year with three people being shot dead during a 10-day period last summer.

One of these victims was Patrick Logan who was murdered by a hooded intruder who broke into his home. I guess he forgot to lie still and/or turn on his lights, yell to a non-existent companion, or call the police immediately.

Or, maybe, he didn't have handy an umbrella, hairspray, or keys.

The British suicidal anti-self-defense lobby is wrong. So-called "gun control" has not and will not make their country safer, and they are seeing the truth of this assertion with a vengeance. According to a U.S. Justice Department victim survey, in 1995—the last year for which complete data was available for both countries—an individual in England is nearly twice as likely to be robbed, assaulted, or have a vehicle stolen, as in America.

There were 20 assaults per 1,000 households in England and Wales but only 8.8 in the U.S. One article in a major British newspaper *(London Sunday Times,* 11 January 1998), calling Britain "the crime capital of the West," has noted that more than one in three British men has a criminal record by the age of 40. The question is asked, "Where have we gone wrong?"

One place they have gone wrong is by denying their citizens the right to defend themselves, their family, friends, and property with firearms. This is immoral and stupid. As Colin Greenwood, the chief inspector of the West Yorkshire Constabulary, has correctly observed, "There is no case...in which [gun] controls can be shown to have restricted the flow of weapons to criminals, or in any way reduced crime."

Shortly before the British government's last assault on lawful gun owners, I debated a member of Parliament on CNN International. I predicted to him that their crime rate would increase if the gun confiscation bill were to pass.

It gives me no pleasure to say, "I told you so." Those of us who favor the God-given right of self-defense and the right of private individuals to keep and bear arms, have argued all along, as the old saying goes, "That when guns are outlawed, only outlaws will have guns." England has proven that with a vengeance.

Switzerland: Guns Down, Crime Up

Switzerland is a low crime, low murder rate place that is under attack from the anti-self-defense crowd among their European neighbors. Switzerland's neighbors are clamoring for Switzerland to toughen up its restrictions on firearms. In the name of economic prosperity, Switzerland has opened its borders to the European Union. That has opened Switzerland up to the movement of many more people across its borders.

Now European governments are hurling at Switzerland the same accusation we hear from many city mayors in the United States. They want to blame their high murder rates on those jurisdictions where guns are much easier to get and to carry. They allege that guns "flow" from the low crime/high gun ownership areas. Of course, their whining should be received with no sympathy. The fact is, even if the guns were "flowing" from places where gun laws are less burdensome, they have no explanation for why crime is low there but high where they rule.

Switzerland has, year after year, turned in one of the world's lowest murder rates even while sending machine guns to every home of every member of their citizen army. And they do not keep their machine guns in safes or encumbered with trigger locks. They keep them at the ready. But Switzerland can now expect its crime rate to begin to increase. Now, you may be thinking, I am contradicting myself. No, unfortunately, Switzerland has fallen to many of the foreign pressures for gun control.

Six years ago, a gun could be purchased in Switzerland without a background check. Half of the population lived in cantons where they could carry a concealed firearm as a matter of right. They needed no concealed carry license or permit. Half of Switzerland was as free as Vermont.

Now Switzerland imposes a background check on all gun purchasers. Naturally, this law is disregarded by the crooks. And now they can only carry a concealed firearm if they convince a bureaucrat that they have a need. Of course, bureaucrats surrounded by armed guards seldom understand why the rest of us who do not have the funds for private bodyguards might choose to protect ourselves with our own gun.

I correctly predicted that if Britain moved to their now virtual total gun ban, that crime would increase. Indeed it did, often carried out by thugs wielding the estimated 3,000,000 illegal guns in that island nation.

Sad to say, I can now predict that Switzerland will see its crime rate increase. Switzerland will be joining that European chorus that has been singing, "Hello gun control, bye-bye safety."

South Africa: Gun Control Hitler Would Have Liked

South Africa is a country in turmoil and transition from a government that oppressed blacks to one that promises to end all discrimination. Now, all South Africans are being oppressed. The government, dominated by the African National Congress, is pushing for passage of a bill that will limit the number of firearms one can own.

At the moment they are proposing to limit South Africans to one handgun for self-defense and one for sport. A sporting rifle and a shotgun might also be allowed. Permits don't have to be issued, but the government "may" do so.

The bill would jail a gun owner who used the sporting gun for self-defense. It would also jail a gun owner who carried a gun without a current permit. It would not change the current $40 fine for driving a car without carrying one's permit. Any firearm offense under the bill would assume the guilt of the accused, requiring proof of innocence. This would reverse the current presumption of innocence and also reverse the burden on the government to prove guilt of the accused.

Why the push for such draconian measures? Perhaps the murder rate is out of control? Not really. It is but two-thirds of Washington, D.C.'s, and unlike Washington, the rate had been heading down for the two years prior to the government's refusal to publish more data.

No doubt the South African wannabe dictators felt that a declining murder rate would not help their propaganda blitz aimed at convincing their people that the country "needs" tighter gun restrictions.

It is interesting to note why the murder rate has been declining in South Africa. Since 1994, blacks have been able to buy guns legally. Of course, prior to taking power the African National Congress bought lots of AK-47s that continue to be readily available through illegal sales. What is different now is that law-abiding blacks are buying legal guns. Blacks could not buy guns in stores before 1994. Gun dealers report that most of their sales recently have been to blacks.

Since most of South Africa's crime has occurred in black townships, it is not surprising that an increase in legal ownership of guns has lowered the murder rate.

Americans should not be surprised that more guns means less crime. We have seen that principle at work for years among our own states. Those states that have made carrying a concealed firearm legal and easy have enjoyed declining murder rates with each year such laws have been on the books. The restrictive states have not enjoyed such declines. And, as I have reported before, we have witnessed the sad experience of England. There, a virtually complete gun ban has resulted in a rise in their violent crime rate that now exceeds that of the U.S. Their authorities complain that criminals possess some 3,000,000 illegal guns. People in England are being robbed, raped, and murdered because of gun control.

Sarah Brady will never believe it, but in truth, guns save lives and gun control kills.

Surprise! Communist Chinese Support U.S. Gun Control

And now—as they used to say on the old "Monty Python" TV show—something completely different. The information office of communist China's state council has issued a report—*U.S. Human Rights Record 2000*—criticizing human rights in America.

That's right. The country where communism has killed an estimated 100 million people, the country whose leader Mao Tse-tung was once listed in the Guinness Book of Records as history's greatest mass murderer, is complaining about human rights in *our* country.

And—surprise!—one of the things the red Chinese don't like about our country is that many of our citizens keep and bear arms. In a section about the ways in which our freedoms are supposedly in jeopardy, it is said: "The United States, the only country where carrying a private weapon is a constitutional right, is a society ridden with violence....The excessive number of privately owned guns has resulted in countless gun-related assaults, resulting in tragedy for many innocent people."

OK. So, what is there to say about this breath-taking hypocrisy on the part of the Chinese communists regarding human rights? Well, the first thing is that, ironically—unlike the liberal gun grabbers in our country—the red Chinese at least acknowledge that private American citizens *do* have a constitutionally-protected right to keep and bear arms.

But, of course, their report says nothing at all about the fact that as many as 2,500,000 of us, annually, use guns in self-defense to protect our lives, the lives of our family and friends, and our property. Why was this information omitted? This report doesn't say. So, we contacted the communist Chinese embassy in Washington, D.C., to ask "why" and other questions. Here's the way our interview went with Yuan Yuan Zhang, press spokesman for the red Chinese government:

Q: Is there a constitutional right to keep and bear arms for private citizens in your country?

A: Certainly not.

Q: Is it illegal in your country for private citizens to keep and bear arms?

A: It is not—one has to get a permit to carry weapons. Of

course, some people carry weapons because of their official duties, such as policemen or soldiers.

At this point, Zhang tells how four or five years ago in suburban Peking some private people had guns to shoot pheasants and rabbits. But, "later on the government asked them to surrender their weapons, actually purchased back their weapons," he says, laughing. *"Purchased back?"* Strange phraseology here since the government never owned these guns.

Q: So, why were these guns confiscated by your government?

A: Well, sometimes you had a weapon in your closet and then someone stole it and that may uhhhh, you know, cause some trouble....Sometimes people just make their own rifles from makeshift shops and turn out some kind of very primitive type of gun.

Q: And what happens if a person does this, if a person has a gun but no government permit?

A: That's a crime. That's a big crime.

Q: Does a big crime mean a fine and jail?

A: Yes! It would be dealt with in accordance with the criminal code.

Zhang explains that his government bans the private ownership of guns to ensure "the social tranquility and safety and security of the population." This is why they "confiscate or buy back" weapons possessed by private persons.

Q: Why does your report make no mention of the fact that as many as 2,500,000 Americans use guns every year in self-defense?

A: I have a sense we are going to have a very long conversation. I have to go. I have a lunch engagement in three minutes.

Q: Are you aware that millions of Americans use guns in self-defense every year?

A: Yes. I am aware of that. I've been in this country for many years. I know people use guns principally to defend themselves. But even very decent citizens who have guns at home may sometimes find that their weapons have been put to, you know, very wrong use—good things in the wrong hands, you know.

Q: And sometimes people in the government who have guns put them to wrong use, too. Did you know that?

A: (After long pause) Of course I know that. Sure.

But, Zhang adds: "We are not challenging the constitutional right in the U.S. We're just presenting the basic facts. Yours is the only country in the world that the Constitution allows its citizens to carry guns."

Q: But, why does your report leave out the basic fact that many, many times more Americans use guns for good things, like self-defense, than use guns for bad things?

A: [Our report] is not intended to be a very, very exhaustive study of gun issues. It is just a short article trying to tell people the human rights situation in the United States. It is not perfect. We may be wrong about this gun-related matter. But we see this as one of the areas in which we think the American peoples' human rights are in jeopardy because of this excessive ownership of guns.

Q: Are you aware that America won its freedom and independence because, among other things, many of our private citizens had guns? Do you know this?

A: Of course I know that. And you know Chairman Mao's famous quotation?

Q: Yes. He said that political power comes out of the barrel of a gun.

A: We needed guns to fight back the Japanese invaders. We have 100 million men in our militias with guns.

Q: But, your point about Chairman Mao's quotation is very interesting. He said what he said when he was a private citizen and not a member of the government, right?

A: Right.

Q: So, under your present laws, Chairman Mao would not have been allowed to have guns!

A: I'm trying to figure out your point.

In their book, *Lethal Laws* (Jews For the Preservation of Firearms Ownership, 1994)—which is about how "gun control" has been the key to genocide in many countries throughout history—authors Jay Simkin, Aaron Zelman, and Alan M. Rice note that just as in Nazi Germany, "gun control" was the key to

Mao Tse-tung's genocide especially during the so-called "Great Leap Forward" (1957-60). At this time, "the government's imposition of policies that promoted massive rural starvation plainly depended on its monopoly of armed force."

Communist China's first "gun control" law was enacted by the Standing Committee of the National People's Congress on October 22, 1957. Article 9 barred the unauthorized making, purchasing, possession, repair, or use of firearms or ammunition "in contravention of safety provisions."

On September 2, 1983, the Second Meeting of the Standing Committee of the Sixth National People's Congress approved a law titled "On Severely Punishing Criminals Who Gravely Endanger Public Security of the Society." This law stated:

> The following criminals who gravely endanger public security of the society may be punished more heavily than the severest punishment currently stipulated in the Criminal Law, and may be punished by the death penalty.

And who might some of these "criminals" be who deserve death? Among those listed in this law is, "A person who illegally makes, trades, transports, steals or purloins weapons, ammunition or explosives in a particularly serious way or with serious consequences."

But, of course, what *really* endangers the security and freedom of a people is when the only ones who are legally allowed to keep and bear arms are those who work for the State. This way leads to true tyranny. We must hope and pray this never happens in America.

Gun Registration in Canada and California

Canada has had handgun registration and owner licensing since 1934. According to Deputy Prime Minister Herb Gray, it has never helped solve a single firearms crime. Is solving crime not what registration is supposed to be all about? Not to be deterred by the facts, the Canadian government has extended this "crime fighting" tool to include all guns and their owners.

The rifle and shotgun registration and licensing scheme was estimated to cost $65 million (Canadian). Gary Mauser, a scholar at the Fraser Institute in Vancouver, British Columbia, has put the cost at the end of 2000 at $600 million and climbing. The gun registry bureaucracy has bloated to some 1,700 at a time when the Mounties have faced flat budgets and a decline in the number of officers. It is the Mounties and the provincial governments that have to bear the financial burden for the program. Dr. Mauser estimates the final cost will soar to between $1 billion to $1.5 billion.

The good news is that a surprisingly large number of Canadians are not complying with the government's desire to control them and their guns. In Alberta, perhaps the most freedom-loving province in Canada, it is estimated that non-compliance is running at about 60%. Estimates of non-compliance nationally put the number of Canadian scofflaws around 3,000,000. The non-compliance rate is so large (about 12% of the population) that the government has scaled down its initial estimate of gun owners to minimize the apparent scope of this passive resistance to the government's tyranny.

One reason for the reluctance to trust the government (other than the genocidal record of gun control in Germany, Russia, China, Cambodia, Uganda, Armenia, Ruwanda, etc.) is that under a conservative government, certain registered guns were confiscated in 1991. Implementation of the current law will result in confiscation of many, if not most, handguns in Canada.

Californians seem to be equally skeptical of the good faith of their government officials. Attorney General Bill Lockyer estimates that the number of unregistered semi-automatics (the so-called "assault weapons") is far higher than the 10,000 that were registered. The skepticism was confirmed when it was leaked out to Gun Owners of California that plans were being developed to confiscate unregistered guns that could be located from firearms dealers' records. The resulting publicity at least temporarily inhibited the government from proceeding.

Under a proposal in the California legislature (AB 35: June, 2001) registration fees for the state's estimated 13.5 million gun owners would be $25 per handgun, not to exceed $125 per licensee. In other words, the costs range from $270 million to $1.7 billion.

Quite apart from constitutional objections, it seems that despotism can be objected to on grounds of cost. And for a scheme that totally fails to achieve its purported objective of solving crimes!

They're Gonna GATT Your Guns

GATT represents a transfer of sovereignty from the United States to the World Trade Organization (WTO). According to Representative Newt Gingrich who testified earlier last year before the Ways and Means Committee, "The World Trade Organization is a de facto transfer of authority from the U.S. to Geneva, Switzerland."

William Holder, the deputy general counsel of the International Monetary Fund told a WTO conference at the American University on November 19, 1994, that, "The WTO is de jure world government."

Article 16, paragraph 4 of the WTO charter (which is part of the GATT legislation) states that each government "shall ensure the conformity of its laws, regulations and administrative procedures with its obligations...." This is the language that lays out what Gingrich and Holder were talking about. To understand the significance and the broad reach of this language, we need to see how the commerce clause of our U.S. Constitution has been distorted into a way of justifying government intervention into anything the planners in Washington want to regulate. Then we will be able to understand the danger of the WTO charter's language.

When the commerce clause was included in the U.S. Constitution, it was intended to keep states from interfering with trade between states. In other words, Virginia could not prohibit Maryland timber from being sold in Virginia nor could Maryland put a tariff on Virginia tobacco being sold in Maryland.

In the wake of the Roosevelt revolution, the commerce clause was expanded to govern everything because everything has been in commerce. It has been this distorted view of the commerce clause that provided the rationale for forcing gun dealers to get a federal license. Similarly, the same view of the commerce clause justified requiring all sales of new guns to go through dealers. It should be perfectly obvious that this view goes way beyond prohibiting trade restrictions between states. The commerce clause has justified increasingly restrictive federal gun controls. Of course, a lot of other unconstitutional federal action has been justified by the commerce clause, but that is not the point here.

Guns are clearly protected in the United States Constitution, yet the federal government is shamelessly in the business of infringing upon the right to keep and bear arms without a constitutional amendment. Before the days of the distortion of the commerce clause, the prohibition of alcoholic beverages

—which are not even protected in the Constitution—required a constitutional amendment.

So it is with alarm that we should view the language of GATT and the presumption in the GATT treaty that everything can be regulated because everything enters commerce. The recent GATT vote (cast by members of Congress who had not read the 26,000 pages of text) was the equivalent of the constitutional convention of 1787—only nobody called it that and its significance was never brought into focus.

The U.S. will have only one vote and no veto in the WTO. Any two other governments could gang up on the U.S. to object to its policy of "allowing" widespread civilian firearms ownership (something already under discussion in the U.N). They could raise environmental objections. This may seem silly, but then, what are we to say of the federal government's inclusion of virtual desert lands up to 50 miles from the Rio Grande river as a wetlands and then subject the private uses of that land to tree-hugging extremism?

The European Union used to be called the European Common Market. It was a European version of the World Trade Organization. Now the socialist governors in the European capital of Brussels presume to call themselves the European Union. Increasingly they are succeeding in the sublimation of the sovereignty of member nations to the Brussels government.

At least our U.S. Constitution has a commerce clause with a very restrictive original intent. There is no such limitation built into GATT and the WTO. If the linkage of banning guns with trade practices does not satisfy the one-world impulse to disarm the planet, then the international commerce clause language in the WTO will be argued as a sufficient justification for the Geneva gnomes where the WTO is headquartered to regulate anything they want. This is the way the socialists in the U.S. have been arguing for the last 60 years.

The U.N. and You

A lot of folks in the U.N. want the cop to be the one patrolling your neighborhood. They want the U.N. to be your Big Brother.

A couple of years ago, the U.N. sent an African diplomat into the U.S. to evaluate our human rights violations. What were the charges? Why, the U.S. executes convicted murderers!

The Australians got their nose pushed in the same foul brew when the U.N.'s Human Rights Commission wanted to get involved in Australia's treatment of its aborigine population. At the moment, Australia is wisely denying permission for the international busybodies to even visit their country.

The Labor Day confab at the U.N., attended by most of the world's heads of state, underscored how close we've really come to being a one-world government. Ground work for the assemblage has been underway for some time. One of the chief instigators is the Gorbachev State of the World Forum, founded by the last thug to rule the Soviet Union, Mikhail Gorbachev. His tutelage for shaping world government is not what most Americans would like, but he seems to fit in just fine with the U.N. crowd.

The agenda at the Labor Day world leaders' "love in" included ironing out details of what is called Charter 99. The U.N. website tells us that the Charter includes 12 areas for urgent action. Among these areas are the raising of revenue (that translates to paying taxes to the U.N.), ratification of the international criminal court, and a standing army. Those measures would give the U.N. the means to steal sovereignty from every government in the world.

How extraordinary that a president of the U.S., Bill Clinton, having taken an oath under God to uphold the U.S. Constitution, would go to the U.N. and call for a standing army to serve as the U.N.'s strike force. What is even more alarming is that there were no mass demonstrations in front of the Congress demanding that the President be impeached for treason.

There was a bill in this Congress to set up just such a U.N. standing army. It was H.R. 4453 introduced by Representative James McGovern, a Democrat from Massachusetts. Consider what tender mercies the U.N. has. Boutros Boutros-Ghali, a former secretary general of the U.N., was minister of foreign affairs in Egypt during the genocide in Rwanda that slaughtered nearly 1,000,000 Tutsis in a month's time.

Boutros-Ghali authorized the sale of the mortar bombs, rocket launchers, grenades and ammunition used in the genocide. He continued to authorize such sales even during the course of the Rwandan holocaust. Our leaders will be like this if the U.N. is not stopped and if the U.S. does not get out of the U.N.

By the way, the Rwandan government first registered the guns of the Tutsis, then confiscated all of them—even their machetes.

The U.N. v. the U.S. Constitution

The U.N. talks a great deal about human rights. A look at their actions helps translate what sounds good to the American ear into English we understand.

For example, I found during a recent excursion to New York City to address an anti-U.N. rally that getting into the U.N. compound from First Avenue requires leaving the U.S. Bill of Rights on the city sidewalk. My companion had a yellow sticker depicting a Jewish star of David with the message "No to Gun Control" written inside the star. He, and others with whom I spoke, were not allowed to enter until he removed the pro-gun sticker.

A person is on foreign territory when visiting the U.N. every bit as much as while visiting the embassy of a foreign country. We have in this way put the U.N. on an equal footing with real countries.

What most Americans do not realize is how much of the U.S. Constitution has already been supplanted by the U.N. Charter. I am indebted to Dr. Herb Titus, a preeminent constitutional lawyer, and to the Liberty Committee (consisting of a number of conservative representatives) which commissioned his work for the analysis that follows.

The U.N. Charter is not a treaty, in spite of bearing the name of treaty. Actually the U.N. Charter is a constitution. Its ratification as a treaty by the U.S. Senate does not change the nature of the U.N. Charter, which international authorities have defined to be " 'similar' to national constitutional law...."

The charter violates the U.S. Constitution by delegating to the U.N. the power to declare war, a power specifically delegated to the U.S. Congress. However, the Constitution delegates the power to conduct war to the U.S. president. From Korea to the Gulf War, the U.S. has fought wars under the authority of the U.N., not following a Congressional declaration of war.

Consider the implication of the term "police action." Countries fight wars among themselves. Police actions are conducted by a government within its own territory. The implication of a U.N. police action clearly is that the U.N. is the government of the world and all the countries are but subdivisions of the U.N.

The charter unconstitutionally delegates the power to levy taxes. The U.N. has arrogated unto itself the power to assess "dues" which are calculated just like a progressive income tax. If the U.S. does not pay its "dues," after two years it loses its vote in the general assembly of the U.N. The U.S.

Constitution vests the power to levy taxes in the House of Representatives.

The U.N. Charter violates the Tenth Amendment of the United States Constitution. A whole gamut of state powers—health, welfare, education, crime, environment—are nowhere to be found as powers delegated to the federal government. They are reserved to the states. The U.N. Charter claims the power to act in all of these areas through treaties which would override state laws.

For years, Congress has appropriated funds for various U.N. organizations which in effect transfers powers reserved to the states. Consider, since the Congress is prohibited from enacting laws regarding rape, could it get into this arena by relying on the U.N. Charter to do so?

The U.N. in this way could institute a gigantic Interstate Commerce Clause and it could be abused even more than has been the ICC of the U.S. Constitution. U.N. spokesmen are arguing that one's physical security (i.e., freedom from rape) is an international security issue. It is the same totalitarian logic that has stretched the Interstate Commerce Clause beyond what it was ever intended to do. Originally, this provision was intended to prevent the balkanization of the states. Now, it has been stretched to the point that the federal government can regulate anything that affects interstate commerce—even to the point where it regulates inactivity because not doing anything has a negative impact on commerce.

All these operations of the U.N. are those of a government operating under a constitution. Yet the U.S. Constitution was based on "We, the People" and ratified by the people in conventions assembled. The U.N. Charter was approved only by government agents and never submitted to the people of the U.S. for their legislatures or conventions to ratify.

That flaw is fatal and makes the U.N. Charter completely illegitimate.

Gun owners should be particularly concerned because one of the "human rights" in the minds of most of the U.N. bureaucrats and member countries is "freedom from guns." Strictly speaking, they envision a world without privately owned guns where governments have a monopoly. The U.N. website leaves no doubt that this is the preference of the U.N. bureaucracy. As with speech, the U.N. has no regard for the right to keep and bear arms.

These are reasons why the U.S. should get out of the U.N. The best way to do that is to pass Representative Ron Paul's (R-TX) bill, H.R. 1146, to get us out of the U.N.

Section Fourteen

><----><----O----><----><

NO SPEECH,
NO GUNS

President Clinton and the Sedition Act

It's nothing short of shameful whenever people use a tragedy to further their own political agenda. Sadly, that is exactly what is happening in the wake of the Oklahoma City disaster.

Let me say right up front that what happened in Oklahoma was a heart-wrenching tragedy, not only because innocent children were brutally murdered, but because defenseless people of all ages had their lives taken or destroyed.

But let's return to the political agendas of those who seek to exploit this tragedy. Just hours after the bombing, amidst the cries for justice and condolences for the bereaved, a dissonant chord began to ring out. We were being told that the bombing was somehow linked to gun control opponents.

The Clinton administration was among the first to change the subject from terrorism to gun control, alleging that certain patriot or militia groups were involved in the bombing. Militias and other "right-wing fanatical" groups, we're told, are literally obsessed with the Constitution, especially the Second Amendment.

But any group who believes in something strongly can be labeled as fanatics by those who disagree with them. Former President Clinton thinks militias are comprised of a bunch of fanatics, and militiamen may think Clinton is a fanatic. And all that is fine, so long as the discourse flows freely in the vast marketplace of ideas that makes America so diverse.

The danger, however, is that Mr. Clinton has been vilifying militia groups so vehemently that he now wants the groups to stop even talking about their strong opposition to certain government policies. Says the former President: "They (government critics) spread hate. They leave the impression, by their very words, that violence is acceptable."

With that type of thinking, Mr. Clinton seeks to take us back almost 200 years to the Sedition Act of 1798. Yes, even back then there were critics of the government. In truth, this country was founded by people who were highly critical of the government.

In 1798, the way the Federalists tried to deal with critics of their president was to pass the Sedition Act. The act declared that "if any person shall write, print, utter, or publish...any false, scandalous, and malicious writings against the government...with the intent to defame government" they could be imprisoned for two years. This law lapsed under Jefferson a few years later.

A similar law was passed in 1917, in an attempt to quiet critics of the U. S. involvement in the war effort. This law condemned "abusive language about the form of government...[bringing it] into contempt, scorn or disrepute," and such crimes were also punishable by imprisonment. The Supreme Court later ruled that law unconstitutional.

Throughout this century, there have been numerous other instances of the government unjustly taking away peoples liberties, from the detainment of Japanese-Americans during the second World War, to the infiltration of the peaceful civil rights protesters of the sixties. In every instance, the government's actions have been condemned.

When the former President of the United States talks about quieting the harsh critics of the government, that should be cause for concern by people across the political spectrum. If he is allowed to use the tragedy in Oklahoma to further curtail our First and Second Amendment rights, we will have another kind of tragedy: the loss of freedom.

For the record, Mr. Clinton assures us that "Americans will retain fundamental freedoms of speech, assembly, and the right to bear arms." But he has also said that Americans must give up some of their freedoms. This leads one to wonder if the former President even understands the meaning of a "fundamental freedom."

Clinton should observe the lessons of history. In a free country, innocent people should not be condemned and stripped of their rights. His blaming the Oklahoma incident on the speech of militias and other "right-wing" organizations would be tantamount to blaming the bombings by the Weathermen on all Vietnam war protesters, of which he was one.

In the case of the Oklahoma bombing, the perpetrators should be punished to the fullest extent of the law. But as for law-abiding citizens who love freedom, whether from the right or the left, to take away their rights would be to severely attack the principles that have made this country great.

Campaign Finance Reform:
A Threat to Freedom

The McCain-Feingold Bill to regulate campaign financing is one of the most dangerous threats to freedom that has ever been before the U.S. Congress. One wonders what the Congress is thinking when they presume to pass any legislation dealing with speech. The First Amendment is quite clear: "Congress shall make no law...abridging the freedom of speech, or of the press...."

What else but an abridgment can we call a limit on how much a candidate can raise from a person or corporation? These limits are purely political, as a study of their history will reveal. Each party comes up with campaign finance restrictions designed to impair the competitive advantage of their opponents. They are not concerned about corruption.

Rather than toss out the current unconstitutional restrictions on campaign finance, this bill constitutes a return to the infamous Sedition Act passed during the administration of our second president, John Adams.

Under the Sedition Act, newspaper editors were clapped in jail for criticizing federal officials. The Act was so odious that it led to Adams being a one-term president. The Sedition Act was repealed under Jefferson, and the prisoners were set free.

Under McCain-Feingold, it will once again be illegal to criticize federal officials, namely those incumbent members of Congress and of the presidency who are running for re-election. Specifically, a ban on mentioning their names by groups such as Gun Owners of America will go into effect 60 days before an election.

Sixty days is chosen for a purpose. It is from that point to the election that most voters begin to look for information about the candidates. McCain-Feingold makes sure that there will only be two sources for that information: incumbents and the media. The media is specifically exempted from the restrictions of McCain-Feingold which are aimed directly at groups such as GOA.

McCain-Feingold is intended to restrict voters' knowledge of elections to what the media chooses to tell them. And if the incumbents are politically correct, as defined by the media, then the media will describe them as courageous statesmen striving for the good of humanity. If not, the incumbent risks being smeared, or perhaps even worse, ignored.

If you oppose the assault on freedom embodied in so-called "campaign finance reform," you need to contact your Representative in the U.S. House of Representatives.

You had better speak now or forever hold your peace.

Sensible Media Control Measures

I am indebted to James William Barnes for first publishing the following in *Sierra Times* via the Internet. I hope you will get the drift of how the following suggestions are taken from the firearms debate.

Election's have demonstrated the necessity for implementing sensible media control laws. No intelligent person can dispute this position.

Of course, some unprogressive traditionalists, not to mention free speech extremists, will argue that the First Amendment protects the media from restrictions on the basis of free speech guarantees. But the First Amendment was written and ratified by individuals over two hundred years ago who could not have conceived of how our democratic society would evolve, especially with respect to the technology by which news is disseminated in this modern era.

In the state of Florida alone, many voters may have been dissuaded from voting because of the actions of the media extremists who announced erroneous results for Florida before the polls were even closed throughout the state.

Imagine how these possible effects may have been magnified on the citizens of other states where polls were nowhere near being closed. This applies to voters for any candidate since some might feel their vote was futile, while others might feel their vote wasn't required to elect the candidate of their choice.

The harm done by irresponsible free speech media extremists in disenfranchising our fellow citizens is incalculable. Some might suggest that the possible voters were responsible for their own actions or lack thereof. Such an incorrect oversimplification of the extremely complex dynamics of this event can be rejected without comment.

Surely the Founders would not condone the media's propagation of the recent obviously untrue reports as fact, especially on an issue of such supreme importance for our democracy. To make such an assertion desecrates their memory.

While none would suggest restrictions on the free speech rights of responsible media to report factual news, no reasonable person can argue that media being required to wait until polls close throughout the country during a national election constitutes a restriction on freedom of speech.

This cooling off period would prevent erroneous information presented as fact from injuring our society's most sacred democratic process, not to mention preventing the psychological damage done to innocent citizens whose only mistake was believing the "news" media were reporting factual information.

The media present themselves as purveyors of news, which is understood to mean actual facts. After the cooling off period to allow the polls to close, any "results" presented by the media before each state has certified those results should be accompanied by a disclaimer that the information represents the unfounded conjecture of the media outlet, rather than verifiable fact.

Media extremists will violently object to these sensible measures as restrictions on their right of free speech. However, freedom of speech does not allow one to yell "fire" in a crowded theater, because others may be injured in the ensuing panic.

If these restrictions are acceptable in a small theater where only a relatively few of our citizens are present, is the broadcasting of "any additional vote is irrelevant" to our entire country a less grievous crime when the very fabric of our democracy is at stake?

Please contact your congresspersons today and demand the passage of the Sensible Media Control Act of 2001.

Our children will inherit the chaos and, as a result, will suffer irreparable harm to their psyches should we fail to act responsibly now to see that this monumental injustice is not repeated. No right-thinking person can fail to act. No responsible individual can object to these common sense measures. Our very democratic society is at risk.

FEC Commissioner Bradley Smith:
Campaign Finance Laws Unconstitutional

After reading FEC Commissioner Bradley Smith's book, *Unfree Speech: The Folly of Campaign Finance Reform*, I determined to interview the author on my weekly radio show *Live Fire*.

Smith points out that campaign finance laws don't ensnare big-bucks donors attempting to corrupt the political process, but they do ensnare grassroots activists who are not aware of, and don't have the funds to comply with, the speech restrictions in campaign finance laws.

One example Smith reports involves a voter in the congressional district of Representative Nancy Johnson. He was outraged by her vote to impeach President Clinton and set up a web page to urge her defeat. The FEC told him that the cost of his computer and home electric bill had to be calculated. Were those costs to go over $250, he had to file with the Federal Election Commission. Smith provides many other cases of harassment of grassroots activists and hapless, poorly-funded campaigns that fell afoul of the FEC and were fined and threatened with jail.

The history of campaign finance laws is clearly one of Republicans trying to get the advantage over Democrats and vice versa. The picture Smith paints of these laws is one of corruption—campaign finance laws are themselves corruption and abridgments of free speech. The language of the First Amendment is that "Congress shall make no law... abridging the freedom of speech...."

Soft money, Smith argues, is nothing more than money that is free from unconstitutional regulation. Therefore, Senators McCain and Feingold want to limit freedom.

New ideas are kept out of the political arena because of restrictions on the amount of contributions that can be given by one person (or a political action committee). As a result, only those ideas favored by the establishment and the media are well-known enough to raise money on—unless one is independently wealthy.

Steve Forbes is a case in point. He was able to spend millions of dollars of his own money for his presidential campaign during the 2000 presidential primary. Although he did not prevail, his millions forced the issue of tax relief into the debate during that election. Governor (now President) George W. Bush proffered his own tax relief plan in response to Forbes.

In a way, Forbes's campaign was successful on that matter, but had he not been wealthy, he would have had to seek small contributions from lots of people. The time and energy required to raise the money would have consumed more time than would have been available to put forth his tax relief program.

Smith argues forcefully that campaign finance reform drives new and unorthodox ideas out of the public forum. This reform can only favor those in power by shielding them from competition with those with different ideas.

For example, a few individuals were all that were needed to get Ronald Reagan started on his political career. A few large contributions got Reagan off and running to become governor of California. He did not have to spend his time raising money; he spent his time defending his ideas.

The raw hostility to free speech that Smith has uncovered is staggering. He quotes House Minority Leader Richard Gephart (D-MO) arguing that, "What we have here are two important values in conflict: freedom of speech and our desire for healthy campaigns in a healthy democracy. You can't have both."

Presumably a healthy campaign is one that Gephart and his anti-freedom allies are guaranteed to win. And of course, that is the purpose of campaign finance laws: these laws don't protect individual speech; they protect the expression of favored speech.

Smith clears up an important point that is often confused. Namely, "We're not talking about speech. We're talking about money."

The answer is that if you can't pay the huge expenses to get your speech heard on radio, on television and in print, then you might as well go shout in a cave. And if we're not talking about speech, why does McCain-Feingold specifically exempt the mainline media?

If there is any doubt that Commissioner Smith is the best thing that could happen to the Federal Election Commission short of its abolition, consider this: During Smith's nomination contest in the U.S. Senate, then Vice President Al Gore said this, "The last thing we need is an FEC commissioner who publicly questions not only the constitutionality of proposed [campaign finance] reforms, but also the constitutionality of current limitations."

Those opposed to the McCain-Feingold Campaign Finance Bill, better known as the Incumbents' and Media Protection Act, should communicate their opposition to their U.S. Representative in Congress.

Section Fifteen

><><><><

POTPOURRI

Referenda: Dagger In the Heart of Representative Government

Referenda and initiatives give the people a direct voice in their government. Sounds great, doesn't it? What could be fairer than that, right? Wrong. Plebiscites are the way to hand government over to the elite with the deepest pockets. This was one of the chief reasons the Founders set up the United States as a representative republic, not a direct democracy.

Government is supposed to be run by elected representatives, not the people voting on matters directly. When legislators vote against the Constitution or in ways that displease the people, they can be voted out of office. That is accountability.

When the people vote against the Constitution, where are the mechanisms of accountability? Is anyone proposing that we deprive the people their vote when they blow it on a plebiscite? Do we simply accept the notion that the people are always right? Those are heavier questions than most of us want to deal with.

And so it is clear that the Founders got it right when they set us up as a democratic republic.

Let's look at how the people in Oregon recently approved an initiative which prohibits private sales at gun shows.

Overwhelmingly, the paid advertising came from the deep pocket of Andrew McKelvey, the billionaire head of *Monster.com*. Ironically, the media spots were voiced by that great hypocrite and enemy of the Constitution, Senator John McCain (R-AZ). Using tons of soft money, McCain, the Senator who would outlaw soft money, spewed outright lies about the initiative.

Gun Owners of America raised thousands of dollars for the pro-freedom cause against hundreds of thousands of paid advertising supporting the anti-gun position. The Oregon Firearms Federation, which actually ran the pro-gun ads, pointed out that the initiative was much more than a background check. It was a registration scheme to enable the capture of the name, address, and complete description of each firearm by the state police.

Anti-gunners admitted that those illegally trying to buy a gun at a store are never prosecuted, so the conclusion was obvious—the object of registration is to know the identities of the law-abiding citizens who own guns so their firearms can subsequently be confiscated, as in New York City and in California right now.

In 1999, an almost identical measure as the ballot initiative was defeated in the state legislature by the Oregon Firearms Federation—even in the face of the pro-gun groups' support. The initiative was defeated because the politicians feared for their jobs.

When the initiative was before the people, the voters were accountable to no one, and most of them had nowhere near an accurate understanding of the measure.

Down with plebiscites! Long live representative government!

Washington Post–ABC News Poll:
Anti-Gun Nut Propaganda

One of the things that disturbs me, and I suspect millions of other Americans, is how, over and over, in many articles about guns—particularly in the liberal media—there is such little concern about the right of self-defense. In fact, this basic life-and-death right is thought to be so irrelevant that it is often not mentioned at all. A case in point is an article which appeared earlier this year in the *Washington Post.*

The main headline on this piece reads, "Poll Finds Firearms Threats Common." The smaller subhead reads, "45 Percent Say Their Households Have Weapons." The lead paragraph of this story says, "Nearly one in four Americans say they have personally been threatened with a gun, including about one in 10 adults who report that someone had taken a shot at them, according to a new *Washington Post–ABC News* national survey."

A spokesman for Virginians Against Handgun Violence, Michael Rau, is reported to be "startled by the number of people who claimed to have stared down the barrel of a gun." He is quoted as saying that this survey makes it "clear" that "the American public is at great risk."

But, of course, this survey doesn't "clearly" show *anything*—except the rabidly anti-gun position of the *Post* which has editorialized repeatedly for the banning of all handguns. Indeed, this survey is grossly incomplete. It is nothing more than an editorial masquerading as a "news story," the purpose of which is to alarm readers and make them, too, anti-gun.

So, almost one in four Americans say they have personally been threatened with a gun. Well, so what?! Some folks should be threatened with a gun! And many are. Surveys have shown that as many as 2.5 to 3 million Americans annually defend themselves, family, and/or property with a gun—most often by merely brandishing the weapon. And a recent Gallup Poll showed, 18 million adults said they had used a gun in self-defense.

Therefore, until we know whether those Americans threatened with a gun were, or were not, criminals, the nearly one in four statistic is useless, just a number designed to scare people. But, the *Post–ABC News* survey says nothing about this key fact at all. Nothing. Zero. Zip. Zilch.

But, why? Why does this survey completely ignore this vital issue of self-defense? Why does it make no attempt at all to ask whether those who had guns pointed at them were law-abiding citizens defending themselves or criminals who should have been staring down the barrel of a gun?

Curious to know the answer to these questions, we contacted one of the *Post* reporters who wrote this story, Claudia Deane. She, along with another *Post* reporter, Rich Morin, decided the questions to be asked in this survey in consultation with other *Post* reporters and *ABC News*. Here's what Deane told us:

> Q: Why no question about how many people used guns to defend themselves?

> A: You know, someone else called me and said that. And in retrospect, yeah, that would have been a good idea. We should have put that on there. We were timing it to sort of, you know, be part of the stories about the [Million Mom] March. So, we were curious about people's experiences with gun violence.

Deane agrees it would be "appropriate" to poll on the self-defense issue. But, she says what they did in their story was appropriate and the figures they got were "pretty stunning."

> Q: But, how relevant, how useful is your data really? When you find out that nearly 1 in 4 Americans say they have been personally threatened with a gun, what, exactly, does this mean? How many of these people were criminals and should have had a gun pointed at them? Did you ask about this?

> A: No. There's a limitation to polling. Not a lot of people are going to admit to you—a stranger on the phone—that they are a criminal.

Deane says our questions make a good point and make it well. She agrees there are "good and bad uses" of guns. She says she appreciates our "reasoned argument"—though she insists the "raw data" in their survey "did serve a purpose."

Well, maybe, maybe not. Maybe Deane does appreciate what we say. Maybe, in the future, the *Post* will poll on the issue of self-defense. Maybe the *Post* will, some day, tell us about some of those "good uses" of guns. And, maybe, some day, pigs will sprout wings and fly. But, I'm not holding my breath until the *Post* does any of this because I don't look good in purple.

Meanwhile, some of Deane's answers are most instructive. Note, please, that she admits that her story was timed to coincide with the so-called Million

Mom March, a mob of anti-gun nuts who were coming to Washington, D.C. And in this case, the *Post–ABC News* "raw data" did serve a purpose. It helped fan the flames of anti-gun hysteria—even though a Gallup Poll last May showed that only two percent of Americans said, when asked, that guns were the worst problem facing their communities. Two percent! No wonder the Million Mom March was such a flop, falling well short of the million number when they came to our nation's capitol.

Gun Rights Strengthened by Strong Families

I have frequently said that our freedoms are not likely to stand in isolation. Most gun owners agree that if the Second Amendment falls, the others will follow quickly behind. Perhaps we should give more thought to the reciprocal of that idea. If other freedoms fail, indeed, if key social institutions fail, gun rights will be seriously weakened. This point was made vivid during an interview I conducted on my weekly radio show *Live Fire*. This show can be found in the *Live Fire* archives on the Gun Owners of America web page at *http://www.gunowners.org/radio.htm.*

The interview was with a conservative black pastor in Los Angeles, Reverend Jesse Lee Peterson. Rev. Peterson is staunchly pro-gun. His record in this area includes organizing a pro gun rally in Portland, OR, several years ago and testifying before the Los Angeles County board against their prohibition of gun shows. (The ban was subsequently overturned in court.)

Rev. Peterson explained how the black family has been greatly weakened in the last several decades. Beginning with the War on Poverty, the federal government offered financial assistance, but only to single women (with or without children). The government's message to the man was, "Get out, you're not needed."

The next blow to hammer the black family was the rise of black racism being preached by Louis Farrakhan, Jesse Jackson and others. As Rev. Peterson put it, "They hate whites more than they love blacks." The trouble is, constructive solutions to black problems (such as for the welfare mess) are overlooked because of the negativity of the black racist preachers.

Then enter feminism. Black leaders picked up this ideology with the liberal coalition with which they march in lockstep. Now the black single mom on welfare has been doused with hatred of men. This in turn keeps them trapped in the system that had hammered their families, trapping the welfare moms all the more in the system. Here is where another element of the liberal coalition enters the picture. That element is unthinking acceptance of gun restriction and banning. Many in the black community accept gun control proposals because of uncritical acceptance of the liberal paradigm; the paradigm remains unchallenged because the hatred of whites engendered by the likes of Farrakhan and Jackson who substitute hatred for thinking.

So there you have it. Smash the family, and the new family head—the government—becomes responsible for providing the protection that is the responsibility of any head of family. Only now it is not a man but a bureaucrat.

Get rid of your guns at home, says the new head of the household.

I would strongly encourage everyone to get more familiar with the thinking of Rev. Peterson. In addition to listening to my *Live Fire* interview with him, his book, *From Rage to Responsibility,* is a must read.

Gun Owners: Second Class Citizens

Folks in the media continue to show how little they care about anything in the Constitution other than the First Amendment.

Reporters in Mariposa, California, were recently required to submit to background checks and fingerprinting in order to cover a murder trial in the Mariposa Superior Court.

The court required the background checks for the media but not the general public. While I can appreciate their greater concern about the media, law must apply equally to all. And, of course, there are laws that should not apply to anyone.

The court withdrew the requirement after news organizations and a public interest group, the California First Amendment Coalition, said it violated press freedoms guaranteed by the Constitution.

The coalition had this to say about the policy: It is a "highly intrusive, utterly arbitrary invasion of privacy on professionals whose work is protected from governmentally imposed burdens."

Why would it not be equally correct to condemn the instant background check imposed on firearms owners as a "highly intrusive, utterly arbitrary invasion of privacy on citizens whose right to keep and bear arms is protected from governmentally imposed burdens"?

The First Amendment Coalition was threatening a lawsuit over the violation of civil rights of reporters when the Mariposa court buckled.

I am delighted that the reporters objected because their privacy was being invaded by the court. They might have added that government has no business treating citizens as criminals. Surely that attitude had to chap the reporters and incline them all the more to challenge the background check.

I realize it is asking a lot since the reporters' Second Amendment ox is not being gored (at least they don't think so), but it would certainly be good news indeed if they found it as obnoxious for a gun buyer to submit to a background check as it is for them to do the same to cover a murder trial.

Of course, even a number of gun owners will insist that a background check for gun owners is different from a background check for reporters. After all, we will be asked, how are you going to keep guns from getting in the wrong hands?

The shortest answer is, "We are not going to keep guns from the wrong hands no matter what we do." The English have proven this point. They have a gun ban, and now they have a violent crime rate in excess of that of ours. Their media has dubbed the city of Manchester as "Gunchester."

Anti-gun scholar Jens Ludwig, publishing the results of his study of the Brady Law in the anti-gun *Journal of the American Medical Association*, found that the law had had no impact on lowering crime.

That would make sense. If a gun ban doesn't lower crime—on the contrary—what makes us think a background check of gun buyers will do any better?

So, for those of our friends in the media, we agree that a background check of reporters is useless and obnoxious. Can you see that the same adjectives describe the background check of gun buyers? Let's elevate gun owners to the same level of citizenship enjoyed by reporters.

The Polls Do Not Say Guns Hurt Republicans

Conventional wisdom has it that most Americans want more gun control according to public opinion polls. Thus, any politician that knows what he is doing will either push for gun control if he favors it, or try to avoid the issue if he opposes it.

This conventional wisdom has provided the paradigm for the last six years in Congress. But how strange is this conventional wisdom.

The firearms issue, according to no less a political expert than former President Clinton himself, cost Democrats their control of Congress in the 1994 elections. The power of this issue—in spite of the contrary indication of public opinion polls—should have encouraged the Republicans to showcase Second Amendment votes in order to further reduce Democratic congressional representation in the 1996 elections.

Instead, Republicans did all they could to avoid voting on guns and, in fact, they lost some ground in the 1996 elections. There have been very few pro-Second Amendment votes, such as when Representative Steve Stockman forced a successful vote on repealing the semi-auto ban. The vote had been opposed by the Republican leadership in the House, and in the Senate, the Republican leadership made sure that the matter never saw the light of day.

In the next four years, many Republicans actually voted for gun control, including the Lautenburg gun ban and the Kohl school zone gun ban—two measures that actually were passed into law.

Had the members of Gun Owners of America not been so willing to tirelessly oppose Senator Orrin Hatch's anti-gun Juvenile Justice Bill—with no help from other pro-gun groups in Washington—there would have been still more anti-self-defense legislation enacted by a Republican Congress.

This explains why the pro-gun state of Pennsylvania, which went to George Bush, Sr. in 1988, was not available for George W. in 2000. In fact, it was President Bush's administration that banned the importation of semi-auto firearms. No wonder he lost Pennsylvania in 1992 and lost his bid for reelection.

The firearms issue should have been able to carry Wisconsin, where in 1998 an amendment modeled after the Second Amendment to the U.S. Constitution was approved three to one by the state's voters. Similarly, Michigan, with a Republican senator and governor, should have been able to vote for George W. as well. But W. narrowly lost Wisconsin, as well as Michigan.

Indeed, Senator Spencer Abraham lost his bid for re-election after having voted repeatedly against the Second Amendment.

A close election such as the 2000 presidential contest was tailor-made for the firearms issue to push the Republicans over the top, win the presidency, and enlarge their margin in Congress. Having done nothing to reassure liberty-minded voters of Republican allegiance, Republicans found little allegiance from pro-gun voters.

Corroboration for my argument was provided by the increasing desire on the part of Democrats, led by Vice President Gore, to back away during the campaign from the issue and try to sound pro-gun without actually repudiating his extreme anti-self-defense views.

Response to a White Separatist

*Below is a letter which GOA received in late 1997,
and following it is the reply.*

Dear Mr. Pratt,

This is a second attempt to have my name removed from your mailing list and membership in the GOA.

I will restate my previous reasons for no longer being a member of GOA. Number one and foremost is God cannot bless any individual or organization that violates God's law of race-mixing of which God condemns individuals and destroys nations. Also, your organization like the NRA have not understood the conflict.

The American government has declared war on white Christian America but you have not declared war on your enemies. You are double minded and cannot succeed in your present course of action. Where was GOA or the militia at the freeman stand off in Montana? Where were they at WACO and Ruby Ridge? Where were they in Texas? You and all of the other militias are all talk and no action. The Republicans are as communistic as are the Democrats.

No one is making demands upon the federal government because they have all the political power and the guns and [are] not afraid to murder anyone in this country who opposes them.

I do not know if we can regain our liberties short of the cartridge box but who knows maybe God will drive our enemies from our land in His way and in His timing without bloodshed when we repent and turn from our wicked ways! Your attendance of an integrated church with black pastors is an abomination to God. Your illicit union with a non-white, non-Israelite woman is the sin of fornication/adultery.

Until Israel repents of her sin and puts away the non-European peoples from our midst or God drives them away, God will continue to punish Israel for all of Her fornication and adultery. No political party or an organization like yours can save America from its impending peril unless the minorities are driven from Israel America.

Race-mixing was promoted by the communist civil rights movement to make white people feel guilty to break down racial barriers to integrate with those of other races by promoting racial equality. Anyone who promotes racial equality follows communist ideology. It is the spirit of anti-Christ. You and your organization promote the spirit of anti-Christ by including anyone of any racial or religious affiliation. Such is not the way of God. Integration is a sin! Segregation is a Christian virtue.

Yours for a truly free White, Christian America

Name Withheld

Dear Mr. [name withheld],

Your request has been acted upon and you have been removed from our mailing list.

We are separated by our theologies, and I would argue that yours does not emerge exclusively from the Scriptures. The Christian Identity position you espouse depends upon non-biblical ideas that end up contradicting the Scriptures.

The Bible teaches a six, 24-hour day creation of the world in which there were no humans, and no death, before Adam. There was no human or humanoid existence before Adam and the fall. With Adam came sin and death, even as with Christ came redemption and life (Romans 5:14-19; see also 1 Corinthians 15:22). There is only one human race, from which God made all men. Paul made this point in his sermon to the Athenians when he told them that "He has made from one blood every nation of men to dwell on all the face of the earth..." (Acts 17:26). John begins his gospel by telling us that those who believe do so "not of blood nor of the will of the flesh, nor of the will of man, but of God" (John 1:13). In Paul's letter to the Galatians he tells them that "There is neither Jew nor Greek, there is neither slave nor free, there is neither male nor female; for you are all one in Christ Jesus" (Galatians 3:28).

The cross has taken away the wall of separation having abolished in His flesh the enmity so as to create in Himself one new man from the two, namely the Jews and all the rest of us (see Ephesians 2:15). The church of Jesus Christ is the universal church because the gospel of Christ "is the power of God to salvation for everyone who believes, for the Jew first and also for the Greek" (Romans 1:16).

The church of Jesus Christ is the Israel of God (Galatians 6:16), but this Israel is not racial or ethnic. It never was, even though Old Testament Jews sinfully fell into that belief. Covenant membership was always open to those outside of Israel if they would take the covenant sign upon themselves (circumcision in the Old Testament, see Exodus 12:44; baptism in the new, see Colossians 2:11-12). Non-Israelites were included in the covenant. For example, Moses' second wife was from Cush. Rahab and Ruth were not Israelites, yet they are recorded in the genealogy of Christ. On other occasions non-Israelites were excluded. Is there a contradiction? No. Inclusion was based on conversion. The kingdom is based on faith, not race. Proselytes, those not of Jewish blood, are mentioned throughout the New Testament, e.g., Acts 2:10. The apostle Philip brought the gospel to the Ethiopian eunuch (Acts 8:27-39) who, history records, brought the gospel to Ethiopia and the Sudan.

I have seen the transforming power of the gospel in countries around the world. Communism was defeated in Guatemala because of the gospel. I saw Indians who before coming to Christ displayed all the evidences of the work of the flesh in Galatians 5:19-21. After professing Christ, they became new creations (2 Corinthians 5:17) and their lives reflected that with the fruit of the Spirit listed in Galatians 5:22-23. Thus were many of the men of the self-defense patrols who had been armed in the early 1980's by President Rios Montt, a powerful Christian leader.

Similarly in the Philippines, the Communist insurgency there was over-turned when the people armed and organized themselves in self-defense militias (the Alsa Masa as it was called there). The leadership of this move-ment came primarily from the Christian community, and it was Christian officers in the army who supported these people.

In South Africa, I have seen the same transforming power of the gospel in Zululand. Many Zulus have come to Christ, and they are the ones living in peace and prosperity. Their pagan neighbors are still enslaved in all the works of the flesh that Paul describes in Galatians 5. They live side by side and the contrast is readily apparent.

God is a lot more powerful than His creation, including our race. He uses His Spirit to give us eternal life, and this does not depend on whether our parents were from a particular race. In any case, the races all come from one blood as the Bible clearly teaches. Paul warned the Corinthians: "Do not be unequally yoked together with unbelievers. For what fellowship has righteousness with lawlessness? And what communion has light with darkness?" (2 Corinthians 6:14). The warning is not regarding race. It pertains to mixing spiritual opposites; that is the biblical doctrine of separation. The apostate Jews of the Old Testament and, among others, the Christian Identity adherents of our day, view the Kingdom of God as racially bound.

God does not agree.

May God give you the eyes to see the wonderful transforming power that He offers through His grace that is freely extended to all who will take of it. Consider Jesus' offer to the Samaritan woman. She was not "racially pure," but He offered the living water of life to her, and she accepted. She is in heaven right now along with one of the thieves hanging next to Jesus on the cross.

How interesting it is to consider another significance of the episode with the Samaritan woman. Samaritans were not racially pure, and for that they were despised by the Jews of the day. The Samaritans had lost their racial purity when they were carted away by the Assyrians—something God allowed because of their sinfulness. Well, the same thing happened to the Jews. In 70 A.D. the temple was burned and all the genealogical records of Israel were destroyed with the building.

Can you trace your blood line back to Adam the way Christ could? At least you should be able to trace each of your generations to Abraham if you are of ethnic Israel and are going to depend on racial purity. If you cannot do this, you cannot be sure that the "wrong" blood has not spoiled your blood line. Where does that leave you? Scripture answers this. None of us can be saved—or excluded—by our blood. The only blood that counts is that of Jesus which was shed on the cross. If we depend on anything else than his shed blood to cover us, then we are saying that we are saved by something other than or in addition to grace.

I am enclosing some material on skin color from a book by Dr. Gary Parker entitled *Creation: Facts of Life*. He shows that we all have the same basic skin-color agent, melanin, just different amounts of it. He shows how the races come from the one blood that Paul talked about.

America is not in decline because of so-called "race mixing," but because Christians have not been salt and light. We have not been faithful ambassadors of the Lord Jesus Christ, and the result has been the rise of anti-Christian philosophies. Spiritual purity, not racial purity, is the way to push back the gates of Hell. Christ's triumphant church has been redeemed from all races. I look forward to worshipping God alongside people of all races: "For You were slain, and have redeemed us to God by Your blood out of every tribe and tongue and people and nation, and have made us kings and priests to our God; and we shall reign on the earth" (Revelation 5:9-10). We don't even have to wait until we are in heaven to have this interracial worship service. And from this service will come the church that reigns on earth.

I implore you to come to this true church of Jesus Christ and accept the free offer of grace paid for by His blood and made effective by His resurrection from the dead.

Sincerely,

Larry Pratt
Executive Director

What Does the Bible Say About Gun Control?

The underlying argument for gun control seems to be that the availability of guns causes crime. By extension, the availability of any weapon would have to be viewed as a cause of crime. What does the Bible say about such a view?

Perhaps we should start at the beginning, or at least very close to the beginning —in Genesis 4. In this chapter we read about the first murder. Cain had offered an unacceptable sacrifice, and Cain was upset that God insisted that he do the right thing. In other words, Cain was peeved that he could not do his own thing.

Cain decided to kill his brother rather than get right with God. There were no guns available, although there may well have been a knife. Whether it was a knife or a rock, the Bible does not say. The point is, the evil in Cain's heart was the cause of the murder, not the availability of the murder weapon.

God's response was not to ban rocks or knives, or whatever, but to banish the murderer. Later (see Genesis 9:5-6) God institutes capital punishment, but says not a word about banning weapons.

Did Christ Teach Pacifism?

Many people, Christians included, assume that Christ taught pacifism. They cite Matthew 5:38-39 for their proof. In this verse Christ says, "You have heard that it was said, 'An eye for an eye and a tooth for a tooth.' But I tell you not to resist an evil person. But whoever slaps you on your right cheek, turn the other to him also."

The Sermon on the Mount from which this passage is taken deals with righteous personal conduct. In our passage, Christ is clearing up a confusion that had led people to think that conduct proper for the civil government— that is, taking vengeance—was also proper for an individual.

Even the choice of words Christ uses indicates that He is addressing a confusion or a distortion that was commonplace. Several times in the rest of the Sermon on the Mount Christ uses this same "you have heard it said" figure of speech to straighten out misunderstandings or falsehoods being taught by the religious leaders of the times.

Contrast this to Christ's use of the phrase "it is written" when He appeals to the Scriptures for authority (for example, see Matthew 4 where on three occasions during His temptation by the devil, Christ answers each one of the devil's lies or misquotes from Scripture with the words, "It is written").

To further underscore the point that Christ is correcting the religious leaders on their teaching that "an eye for an eye" applies to private revenge, consider that in the same sermon, Christ strongly condemns false teaching: "Whoever therefore breaks one of the commandments, and teaches men so, shall be called least in the kingdom of heaven..." (Matthew 5:19). Clearly, here, Christ is not teaching something different about self-defense than is taught elsewhere in the Bible. Otherwise, He would be contradicting Himself for He would now be teaching men to break one of the commandments.

The reference to "an eye for an eye" was taken from Exodus 21:24-25 which deals with how the magistrate must deal with a crime. Namely, the punishment must fit the crime. The religious leaders of Christ's day had twisted a passage that applied to the government and misused it as a principle of personal revenge.

The Bible distinguishes clearly between the duties of the civil magistrate (the government) and the duties of an individual. Namely, God has delegated to the civil magistrate the administration of justice. Individuals have the responsibility of protecting their lives from attackers. Christ was referring to this distinction in the Matthew 5 passage. Let us now examine in some detail what the Scriptures say about the roles of government and of individuals.

Both the Old and New Testaments teach individual self-defense, even if it means taking the assailant's life in certain circumstances.

Self-Defense in the Old Testament

Exodus 22:2-3 tells us, "If the thief is found breaking in, and he is struck so that he dies, there shall be no guilt for his bloodshed. If the sun has risen on him, there shall be guilt for his bloodshed. He should make full restitution; if he has nothing, then he shall be sold for his theft."

One conclusion which can be drawn from this is that a threat to our life is to be met with lethal force. After the sun has risen seems to refer to a different judgment than the one permitted at night. At night it is more difficult to discern whether the intruder is a thief or a murderer. Furthermore, the nighttime makes it more difficult to defend oneself and to avoid killing the thief at the same time. During the daytime, it better be clear that one's life was in danger, otherwise, defense becomes vengeance, and that belongs in the hand of the magistrate.

In Proverbs 25:26 we read that, "A righteous man who falters before the wicked is like a murky spring and a polluted well." Certainly, we would be faltering before the wicked if we chose to be unarmed and unable to resist an assailant who might be threatening our life. In other words, we have no right to hand over our life which is a gift from God to the unrighteous. It is a serious mistake to equate a civilized society with one in which the decent people are doormats for the evil to trample.

Trusting God

Another question asked by Christians is, "Doesn't having a gun imply a lack of trust that God will take care of us?" Indeed, God will take care of us. He has also told us that if we love Him, we will keep His commandments (John 14:15).

Those who trust God work for a living, knowing that 1 Timothy 5:8 tells us, "But if anyone does not provide for his own, and especially for those of his household, he has denied the faith and is worse than an unbeliever." For a man not to work, yet expect to eat because he was "trusting God" would actually be to defy God.

King David writes in Psalm 46:1 that, "God is our refuge and strength, a very present help in trouble." This does not conflict with praising the God, "Who trains my hands for war and my fingers for battle" (Psalm 144:1).

The doctrine of Scripture is that we prepare and work, but we trust the outcome to God. Those who trust God should also make adequate provision for their own defense even as we are instructed in the passages cited above. For a man to refuse to provide adequately for his and his family's defense would be to defy God.

There is an additional concern to taking the position that "I don't need to arm myself. God will protect me."

At one point, when Satan was tempting Jesus in the wilderness, he challenged Jesus to throw himself off the top of the temple. Satan reasoned that God's angels would protect him. Jesus responded, "It is written again, 'You shall not tempt the Lord your God'" (Matthew 4:7).

It may seem pious to say that one is trusting in God for protection, and we all must, but it is tempting God if we do not take the measures that He has laid out for us in the Bible.

Role of Government

The Bible records the first murder in Genesis 4 when Cain killed his brother Abel. God's response was not to register rocks or impose a background check on those getting a plough, or whatever it was that Cain used to kill his brother. Instead, God dealt with the criminal. Since the time of Noah the penalty for murder has been death.

We see the refusal to accept this principle that God has given us from the very beginning. Today we see a growing acceptance of the idea that checking the criminal backgrounds of gun buyers will lessen crime but we should seldom execute those who are guilty of murder.

In Matthew 15, and in Mark 7, Christ accused the religious leaders of the day of also opposing the execution of those deserving of death—rebellious teenagers. They had replaced the commandments of God with their own traditions. God has never been interested in controlling the means of violence. He has always made it a point to punish, and where possible, restore (as with restitution and excommunication) the wrongdoer. Control of individuals is to be left to self-government. Punishment of individuals by the civil government is to be carried out when self-government breaks down.

Man's wisdom today has been to declare gun-free school zones which are invaded by gun-toting teenage terrorists whom we refuse to execute. We seem to have learned little from Christ's rebuke of the Pharisees.

Nowhere in the Bible does God make any provision for dealing with the instruments of crime. He always focuses on the consequences for an individual of his actions. Heaven and hell only applies to people, not to things. Responsibility only pertains to people, not to things. If this principle, which was deeply embedded in the common law, still pertained today, lawsuits against gun manufacturers would be thrown out unless the product malfunctioned.

Responsibility rightly includes being liable for monetary damages if a firearm is left in a grossly negligent fashion so that an ignorant child gets the gun and misuses it. The solution is not to require that trigger locks be used on a gun to avoid being subject to such a law suit. Some might argue that this is nothing more than an application of the biblical requirement that a railing be placed around the flat rooftop of a house where people might congregate. But trigger locks are to be used with unloaded guns which would be the same as requiring a railing around a pitched roof where people do not congregate.

Surely in protecting against accidents we cannot end up making ourselves more vulnerable to criminal attack, which is what a trigger lock does if it is in use on the firearm intended for self-protection.

The firearm that is kept for self-defense should be available in an emergency.

Rooftop railings have no correspondence to the need for instant access to a gun. On the other hand, guns that are not intended for immediate use should be kept secured as a reasonable precaution. But to make the owner criminally or monetarily liable for another's misuse violates a basic commandment of Scripture: "The righteousness of the righteous shall be upon himself, and the wickedness of the wicked shall be upon himself" (Ezekiel 18:20b).

Self-Defense Versus Vengeance

Resisting an attack is not to be confused with taking vengeance, which is the exclusive domain of God (Romans 12:19). This has been delegated to the civil magistrate, who, as we read in Romans 13:4, "is God's minister to you for good. But if you do evil, be afraid; for he does not bear the sword in vain; for he is God's minister, an avenger to execute wrath on him who practices evil."

Private vengeance means one would stalk down a criminal after one's life is no longer in danger as opposed to defending oneself during an attack. It is this very point that has been confused by Christian pacifists who would take the passage in the Sermon on the Mount about turning the other cheek (which prohibits private vengeance) into a command to falter before the wicked.

Let us consider also that the Sixth Commandment tells us, "Thou shall not murder." In the chapters following, God gave to Moses many of the situations which require a death penalty. God clearly has not told us never to kill. He has told us not to murder, which means we are not to take an innocent life. Consider also that the civil magistrate is to be a terror to those who practice evil. This passage does not in any way imply that the role of law enforcement is to prevent crimes or to protect individuals from criminals. The magistrate is a minister to serve as "an avenger to execute wrath on him who practices evil" (Romans 13:4).

This point is reflected in the legal doctrine of the United States. Repeatedly, courts have held that the government has no responsibility to provide individual security. One case *(Bowers v. DeVito)* put it this way, "There is no constitutional right to be protected by the state against being murdered."

Self-Defense in the New Testament

The Christian pacifist may try to argue that God has changed His mind from the time that He gave Moses the Ten Commandments on Mount Sinai. Perhaps they would want us to think that Christ canceled out the Ten Commandments in Exodus 20 or the provision for justifiably killing a thief in Exodus 22. But the writer of Hebrews makes it clear that this cannot be, because "Jesus Christ is the same yesterday, today and forever" (Hebrews 13:8). In the Old Testament, the prophet Malachi records God's words this way: "For I am the Lord, I do not change" (Malachi 3:6).

Paul was referring to the unchangeability of God's Word when he wrote to Timothy that, "All Scripture is given by inspiration of God, and is profitable for doctrine, for reproof, for correction, for instruction in righteousness, that the man of God may be complete, thoroughly equipped for every good work" (2 Timothy 3:16-17). Clearly, Paul viewed the Old Testament as useful for training Christians in every area of life.

We must also consider what Christ told His disciples in His last hours with them: "...But now, he who has a money bag, let him take it, and likewise a sack; and he who has no sword, let him sell his garment and buy one" (Luke 22:36). Keep in mind that the sword was the finest offensive weapon available to an individual soldier—the equivalent then of a military rifle today.

The Christian pacifist will likely object at this point that only a few hours later, Christ rebuked Peter who used a sword to cut off the ear of Malchus, a servant of the high priest in the company of a detachment of troops. Let us read what Christ said to Peter in Matthew 26:52-54:

> Put your sword in its place, for all who take the sword will perish by the sword. Or do you think that I cannot now pray to My Father, and He will provide Me with more than twelve legions of angels? How then could the Scriptures be fulfilled, that it must happen thus?

In the companion passage in John 18, Jesus tells Peter to put his sword away and tells him that He has to drink the cup that His Father has given Him. It was not the first time that Christ had to explain to the disciples why He had come to earth. To fulfill the Scriptures, the Son of God had to die for the sin of man since man was incapable of paying for his own sin apart from going to hell. Christ could have saved His life, but then believers would have lost their lives forever in hell. These things only became clear to the disciples after Christ had died and been raised from the dead and the Spirit had come into the world at Pentecost (see John 14:26).

While Christ told Peter to "put his sword in its place," He clearly did not say get rid of it forever. That would have contradicted what he had told the disciples only hours before. Peter's sword was to protect his own mortal life from danger. His sword was not needed to protect the Creator of the universe and the King of kings.

Years after Pentecost, Paul wrote in a letter to Timothy "But if anyone does not provide for his own, and especially for those of his household, he has denied the faith and is worse than an unbeliever" (1 Timothy 5:8). This passage applies to our subject because it would be absurd to buy a house, furnish it with food and facilities for one's family, and then refuse to install locks and provide the means to protect the family and the property. Likewise it would be absurd not to take, if necessary, the life of a night-time thief to protect the members of the family (Exodus 22:2-3).

A related, and even broader, concept is found in the Parable of the Good Samaritan. Christ had referred to the Old Testament summary of all the laws of the Bible into two great commandments: "'You shall love the Lord your God with all your heart, with all your soul, with all your strength, and with all your mind,' and love your neighbor as yourself'" (Luke 10:27). When asked who was a neighbor, Christ related the parable of the good Samaritan (Luke 10:30-37). It was the good Samaritan who took care of the mugging victim; he was a neighbor to the victim. The others who walked by and ignored the victim's plight were not acting as neighbors to him.

In the light of all we have seen the Scriptures teach to this point, can we argue that if we were able to save another's life from an attacker by shooting the attacker with our gun that we should "turn the other cheek" instead? The Bible speaks of no such right. It only speaks of our responsibilities in the face of an attack—as individual creatures made by God, as householders or as neighbors.

National Blessings and Cursings

The Old Testament also tells us a great deal about the positive relationship between righteousness, which exalts a nation, and self-defense. It makes clear that in times of national rebellion against the Lord God, the rulers of the nation will reflect the spiritual degradation of the people and the result is a denial of God's commandments, an arrogance of officialism, disarmament, and oppression.

For example, the people of Israel were oppressed during the time of the rule of the Judges. This occurred every time the people apostatized. Judges 5:8 tells us that, "They chose new gods; then there was war in the gates; not a shield or spear was seen among forty thousand in Israel."

Consider Israel under Saul. The first book of Samuel tells of the turning away of Israel from God. The people did not want to be governed by God; they wanted to be ruled by a king like the pagan, God-hating nations around them. Samuel warned the people about what they were getting into—about the curses that would be upon them if they persisted in raising up a king over themselves and their families. Included in those curses was the raising up of a standing professional army which would take their sons and their daughters for aggressive wars (I Samuel 8:11).

This curse is not unknown in the United States. Saul carried out all the judgments that Samuel had warned the people about. His build-up of a standing army has been repeated in the U.S., and not just in terms of the military, but also the 650,000 full-time police officers from all levels of government.

Saul was the king the Israelites wanted and got. He was beautiful in the eyes of the world but a disaster in the eyes of the Lord. Saul did not trust God. He rebelled against His form of sacrifice unto the Lord. Saul put himself above God. He was impatient. He refused to wait for Samuel because God's way was taking too long. Saul went ahead and performed the sacrifice himself, thus violating God's commandment (and, incidentally, also violating the God-ordained separation of duties of church and state!).

Thus was the kingdom lost to Saul. And, it was under him that the Philistines were able to defeat the Jews and put them into bondage. So great was the bondage exerted by the Philistines that, "Now there was no blacksmith to be found throughout all the land of Israel: for the Philistines said, 'Lest the Hebrews make them swords or spears.' But all the Israelites went down to the Philistines to sharpen each man's plowshare, his mattock, his ax, and his sickle....So it came about, on the day of battle, that there was neither sword nor spear found in the hand of any of the people who were with Saul and Jonathan..." (1 Samuel 13:19-20; 22-23).

Today, the same goals of the Philistines would be carried out by an oppressor who would ban gunsmiths from the land. The sword of today is the handgun, rifle, or shotgun. The sword control of the Philistines is today's gun control of those governments that do not trust their people with guns.

It is important to understand that what happened to the Jews at the time of Saul was not unexpected according to the sanctions spelled out by God in Leviticus 26 and Deuteronomy 28. In the first verses of those chapters, blessings are promised to a nation that keeps God's laws. In the latter parts of those chapters, the curses are spelled out for a nation that comes under judgment for its rebellion against God. Deuteronomy 28:47-48 helps us understand the reason for Israel's oppression by the Philistines during Saul's reign:

> Because you did not serve the Lord your God with joy and
> gladness of heart, for the abundance of all things, therefore

> you shall serve your enemies, whom the Lord will send
> against you, in hunger, in thirst, in nakedness, and in need
> of all things; and He will put a yoke of iron on your neck
> until He has destroyed you.

The Bible provides examples of God's blessing upon Israel for its faithfulness. These blessings included a strong national defense coupled with peace. A clear example occurred during the reign of Jehoshaphat. 2 Chronicles 17 tells of how Jehoshaphat led Israel back to faithfulness to God which included a strong national defense. The result: "And the fear of the Lord fell on all the kingdoms of the lands that were around Judah, so that they did not make war against Jehoshaphat" (2 Chronicles 17:10).

The Israelite army was a militia army (Numbers 1:3, ff.) which came to battle with each man bearing his own weapons—from the time of Moses, through the Judges, and beyond. When threatened by the Midianites, for example, "Moses spoke to the people, saying, 'Arm some of yourselves for the war, and let them go against the Midianites to take vengeance for the Lord on Midian'" (Numbers 31:3).

Again, to demonstrate the biblical heritage of individuals bearing and keeping arms, consider David's time in the wilderness avoiding capture by Saul. "David said to his men, 'Every man gird on his sword.' So every man girded on his sword, and David also girded on his sword" (1 Samuel 25:13).

Finally, consider Nehemiah and those who rebuilt the gates and walls of Jerusalem. They were both builders and defenders, each man—each servant —armed with his own weapon:

> Those who built on the wall, and those who carried burdens
> loaded themselves so that with one hand they worked at
> construction, and with the other held a weapon. Every one
> of the builders had his sword girded at his side as he built
> (Nehemiah 4:17-18).

Conclusion

The wisdom of the framers of the Constitution is consistent with the lessons of the Bible. Instruments of defense should be dispersed throughout the nation, not concentrated in the hands of the central government. In a godly country, righteousness governs each man through the Holy Spirit working within. The government has no cause to want a monopoly of force; the government that desires such a monopoly is a threat to the lives, liberty, and property of its citizens. The assumption that only danger can result from people carrying guns is used to justify the government's having a monopoly of force. The notion that the people cannot be trusted to keep and bear their own arms informs us that ours, like the time of Solomon, may be one of great riches but is also a time of peril to free people. If Christ is not our King, we shall have a dictator to rule over us, just as Samuel warned.

For those who think that God treated Israel differently from the way He will treat us today, please consider what God told the prophet Malachi: "For I am the Lord, I do not change..." (Malachi 3:6).

More Guns, Less Terrorism

The war against self-defense has opened the door to the tragedies produced by the terrorists who launched attacks against the United States on September 11, 2001. The anti-gun groups such as the Brady Center to Stop Gun Violence have been cheerleaders for the campaign to convince Americans that guns in private hands are bad.

Rep. Carolyn McCarthy (D-NY) got elected to Congress largely on a wave of sympathy for her husband who was tragically gunned down in a multiple killing on a Long Island commuter train. In a television debate I asked her if it would have been wrong for someone to have pulled a concealed firearm carried legally or illegally and shot the murderer. Rep. McCarthy had no response to that.

Neither did she respond when I asked her if it was wrong for the Mississippi high school assistant principal to get a gun and illegally carry it onto the school yard, where he stopped a student who was killing other kids.

When I challenged her by saying that her silence meant that she did not believe in self-defense, she still had no response.

The ability to defend one's self is the most basic right of all. It has been denigrated and circumscribed until many Americans are in an impossible situation. Where they live and work they are legally required to be unarmed as they face a well-armed criminal element.

The gun grabber crowd would have the police crack down on people who simply possess and carry guns. This is because their answer to crime is to criminalize self-defense and ignore the criminals. This very philosophy facilitated terrorists with knives being able to take over four airliners in which gun control had worked 100%. No armed passengers. No air marshals. No armed pilots. Just helpless victims.

Rep. Ron Paul of Texas has introduced a bill before Congress that could reverse this present insanity. His bill, H.R. 2896, would allow pilots to carry firearms.

How different would the hijacked airline tragedies been if the knife-wielding terrorists had been met by gun-firing pilots? Many of the Brady Center types cry out with alarm when shooting back is offered as the answer to crime: "Are you crazy? Innocent people could be shot!"

Let's be honest. Of course an innocent person could be shot. And the force of that concern has resulted in there having been no alternative to 266 passengers on four airliners being murdered not to mention the thousands of victims at Ground Zero in New York City.

Life can be risky. But the solution is not to surrender the responsibility for self-defense to the government. The government has proven it cannot protect us.

If we cede our most basic of rights to the government, what response do we have to the assertion by politicians and bureaucrats that we should also not be able to take care of our own retirement, health, education of our children, and the use of our property?

A wonderful offer has been made by Ignatius Piazza of the Front Site Firearms Training Institute of Las Vegas, Nevada. Front Sight is offering to train for free any pilot wishing to carry a concealed firearm in his cockpit. Hopefully Mr. Piazza will be meeting lots of pilots when Ron Paul's bill becomes law.

This is the time to tell the anti-self defense crowd that blood is on their hands, and we are taking back control of our own defense. Their deadly experiment in criminalizing self-defense must come to an end. Let's get behind Rep. Paul's first step in rolling back the disarmament crowd's anti-gun laws and get H.R. 2896 through Congress and signed by the President.

We already trust the lives of passengers to these pilots. We should also be eager to trust the pilots to protect their passengers with their guns.

Index

About the Author

Larry Pratt has been the executive director of Gun Owners of America for 25 years. GOA is a national membership organization of 300,000 Americans dedicated to promoting their Second Amendment freedom to keep and bear arms.

GOA lobbies for the pro-gun position in Washington and is involved in firearm issues in the states. GOA's work includes providing legal assistance to those involved in lawsuits with the Bureau of Alcohol, Tobacco and Firearms, the federal firearms law enforcement agency.

Pratt has appeared on numerous national radio and TV programs such as NBC's *Today Show,* CBS' *Good Morning America,* CNN's *Crossfire* and *Larry King Live,* Fox's *Hannity & Colmes,* and many others. He has debated Congressmen James Traficant, Jr. (D-OH), Charles Rangel (D-NY), Rep. Carolyn McCarthy (D-NY), Senator Frank Lautenberg (D-NJ), and former Vice President Al Gore, among others. His columns have appeared in newspapers across the country.

He published a book, *Armed People Victorious,* in 1990 and was editor of a book, *Safeguarding Liberty: The Constitution & Militias* (Legacy Publishing, 1995).

Pratt has held elective office in the state legislature of Virginia, serving in the House of Delegates. Pratt directs a number of other public interest organizations and serves as the Vice-Chairman of the American Institute for Cancer Research.

Publications and Resources
from the Gun Owners Foundation

afeguarding Liberty:
onstitutional Liberties and Citizen Militias
y Larry Pratt

This collection of essays edited by Larry Pratt of Gun Owners of America focuses on the real issues concerning the 2nd Amendment and the militia: first, that the Constitution guarantees individual citizens to join together to protect life and property apart from the government, and second, the fact that people – not guns – kill people. Social commentator Walter Williams stated that: "Among our God-given rights is e right of self-defense. The Founders knew this well and arged Congress, through the Second Amendment, to proct (not grant) that right. Safeguarding Liberty reminds us that; plus, if America is to remain free, we must not compmise with those who would strip us of our right to keep d bear arms." **$15.00**

tp://www.gunowners.com/books1001.htm

onfrontational Politics
′ Sen. H.L. Richardson, Ret.

nat's the matter with the Republicans? OA founder and chairman Richardson swers that question in Confrontational litics. During 22 years of legislative perience, Sen. Richardson found that e only thing that got things done was nfrontation. Democrats typically under- nd confrontation, like it and use it. nversely, Republicans do not under- nd confrontation, don't like it and flee from it. Many who ve already read the book have reported that "Now I derstand why Republicans keep losing." Readers of nfrontational Politics will also learn about the lobbying ilosophy that has earned GOA's reputation as the only -compromise gun lobby in Washington.
. . . . **$6.00**

tp://www.gunowners.com/books1002.htm

aco:
e Rules of Engagement

is is the shocking documentary (2 hours d 16 minutes) that has won rave reviews m even liberal newspapers such as the n Francisco Chronicle and The Washington st. Explosive film footage reveals BATF and l lies and their role in the tragic events of ril 19, 1993. This is a must see video.
. . . . **$24.95**

p://www.gunowners.com/videos1023.htm

aco:
Vew Revelation Waco

New Revelation is the film that triggered a w Congressional investigation of the Waco gedy, and caused the Justice Department d the FBI to reverse their long-held posi- ns on Waco. It has generated a firestorm of ents unprecedented in the history of docu- ntary filmmaking. After six years of

painstaking investigation, the complete story of the tragedy near Waco is finally coming to light. This compelling feature-length documentary presents new revelations about the events that led up to the deaths of 79 men, women and children at Mount Carmel on April 19, 1993. . . . .**$24.95**

http://www.gunowners.com/videos1022.htm

The F.L.I.R. Project

This new video by Michael McNulty continues the groundbreaking and award-winning documentary film work found in Waco: the Rules of Engagement and Waco: A New Revelation. Former Senator John Danforth's Special Counsel "investigation" of the events at Waco absolved the government of all wrongdoing. Crucial to this finding was a staged re-enactment of the debacle, which purported to discredit the Forward Looking Infrared (FLIR) evidence that was so convincingly documented in the two previous films. The crux of the investigation's "findings"– and the basis for the dismissal of a wrongful death lawsuit – was that the duration of muzzle flashes in the re-enactment was shorter than those seen on the FLIR tapes, and thus the FLIR evidence does not show gunfire. But the government investigators did not use the same type of camera. They did not use the same weapons – firing long-barreled M-16A2's with coated ammo designed to minimize flash, as opposed to the 14.5 inch CAR-16's and M-4's loaded with Federal ammo deployed at Waco.

They restricted the test to semi-auto fire only. The re-enactment was staged in weather 20 degrees colder. And, they had soaked the ground beforehand, which negated the dusty (and muzzle-blast extending) conditions encountered during the botched raid. Why? McNulty did his own re-enactment, under the proper conditions. The results cannot fail to convince a reasonable person that, once again, the government has lied and covered up. **$19.95**

http://www.gunowners.com/videos1045.htm

Citizens Rule Book
from Gun Owners Foundation

Pocket-sized but packing a big punch, this 62-page handbook is divided into three sections: A Handbook For Jurors, Give Me Liberty... and Original Documents. From a listing of jury rights, through the warnings of the Founders, and including the texts of the Declaration, Constitution, and the Bill of Rights, the Rule Book empowers every citizen in the never-ending struggle for liberty.
. . . . **$1.00**

http://www.gunowners.com/books1043.htm

For quantity discounts, call 1-703-321-8585.
Orders with check or money orders may be mailed to:
Gun Owners Foundation, 8001 Forbes Place, Suite 102,
Springfield, VA 22151. Please add $4.50 for shipping
and handling on all orders.

www.gunowners.com